Canyoneering

Canyoneering
The San Rafael Swell

Steve Allen
Foreword by Joseph M. Bauman, Jr.

University of Utah Press
Salt Lake City, Utah

∞ The paper in this book meets the standards for permanence and durability established by the Committee on Production Guidelines for Book Longevity of the Council on Library Resources

1999 1998
8 7 6 5 4

Library of Congress Cataloging-in-Publication Data

Allen, Steve, 1951–
    Canyoneering : the San Rafael Swell / Steve Allen ; foreword by
Joseph M. Bauman, Jr.
        p.   cm.
    Includes bibliographical references (p.) and index.
    ISBN 0-87480-372-1 (alk. paper)
    1. Hiking—Utah—San Rafael Swell—Guide-books. 2. San Rafael
Swell (Utah)—Description and travel—Guide-books. I. Title.
GV199.42.U82S263   1992
917.92′57—dc20   91-24599
                                                                              CIP

Contents

Foreword

Steve Allen has accomplished what I would have considered impossible: one man, living in the desert for something like eight months alone with his dog, half-ton van, and the spirit of adventure, hiked every significant canyon and side canyon and climbed practically every big knob in the million acres of the San Rafael Swell. Not only that, but he came out of it with a useful and interesting—at times wryly humorous—book. *Canyoneering: The San Rafael Swell* is the definitive hiking guide for the Swell.

In researching my own book, *Stone House Lands: The San Rafael Reef*, I was intimidated by the immensity, ruggedness, and danger of this remote desert. I confined my hiking to its eastern and southern edge, the Reef, which was rough enough. But through determination, skill, and nerve Steve conquered the whole Swell.

Not only that, but he kept careful notes and took scores of photos so he was able to reproduce hikes in great detail. He shows mileage on the road sections that lead to each hike, noting fence posts, canyon mouths, and intersections. Then in the hiking descriptions themselves, he points out the overhangs, potholes, gullies, pinions, or caves the hiker needs to know about to keep from getting lost. He states the relative ease or danger of each trip (which is rated according to standard scales), its important twists, directions, where to climb up or scramble down, and even how long it will take to get from this bowl formation to that ancient petroglyph panel.

Steve's purpose is to guide hikers of all skill levels, from novices to expert rock-climbers. It is a detailed compilation of sixty-three major hikes and numerous side excursions. In addition, it's like an old-fashioned pudding, with tasty nodules here and there: history, folklore, ancient Indians, guidance about walking gently on the land.

His elaboration about subtle landmarks might seem

like overkill to the uninitiated, but when you're working your way along some ledge that keeps narrowing while the canyon bottom is farther and farther down and rocks are flying off your sneakers and bouncing into space—at times like this you'll thank heaven for a guide who tells you it levels out in a few yards!

He walks you through with humor and a fanatic insistence on preserving the fragile desert environment. He is a rare breed, a throwback to the nineteenth-century explorers. Literate and intelligent, with an extensive library that he hauls through the desert in his van, he reminds me of John Wesley Powell reading Homer to his men as they floated the Colorado. And Steve's love of the desert shines through. Readers of this book, especially the hikers and climbers who use it, will wonder why the San Rafael Swell is not yet a national park.

What he did is remarkable; from personal experience of the terrors and joys of hiking the San Rafael, I know that it was more adventurous and scary than anyone might imagine. You have to know what it's like to be on a dangerous climb by yourself, at least fifty miles from help in a rugged landscape, to understand it in a visceral way.

I met Steve in April 1990, during a Sierra Club hike in the San Rafael Swell. He and I led the group through the Swell and San Rafael Reef. I had been asked by the club because I knew the Reef; Steve was a recent discovery, having shown up in the offices of the Southern Utah Wilderness Alliance in Cedar City. He impressed the SUWA people so much with his knowledge that they had him contact the Sierra officials who were planning the trip.

We gathered that first night, April 14, at the Wedge Overlook. I liked Steve immediately. He, club national director Bert Fingerhut, and I lounged in Steve's Ford Econoline van while he outlined plans for showing off the most spectacular country in the Swell. I recall that late afternoon vividly, the maps and talk, popping the tab on a soda, Steve's bronzed face with its stubble of beard. He was quite tall, muscular, athletic. Mostly I recall his jolly, driving energy.

I concentrated on guiding a few of the hikers in the easier and better-known canyons of the Reef—Spring, Nates, Bell, Little Wild Horse canyons—while Steve led the more adventurous and hardy through incredible climbs and hikes. They returned at the end of the day worn out but exhilarated. We camped the second night at Indian Bench. When we left, Steve didn't just police the site to make sure there was no trash left; he literally raked up our vehicles' tracks.

Then we headed for the center of the Swell, country that I had never explored. We drove to Hidden Splendor and camped on the runway of an abandoned uranium mine, close to a huge pile of what I presumed was uranium ore. Steve was such a fanatic about leaving no trace that he insisted on our camping in places that couldn't be harmed, like that runway. I remember that on one hike, some of us backtracked a little to climb out of a canyon and sure enough there was a cairn Steve had piled up for hikers. He led some of the strongest on a climb through Cistern Canyon and into a wild, barely accessible place that he called Ramp Canyon.

The next stop was Tomsich Butte on the western side, camping close to Hondoo Arch and some abandoned mining shacks. This was our jumping-off spot for a twenty-mile backpacking expedition, many of us carrying forty pounds apiece—basically, Hike #42 in the guidebook. We crossed and recrossed Muddy Creek so often that I lost count. I believe Steve had us hike about ten miles one day, mostly in Muddy Creek, heading through the stream's spectacular narrow chute.

We got out of the creek at Chimney Canyon and had to climb a couple of times to really explore the canyon. We camped for the night near some trickling potholes and by then we were nearly out of water. Steve used his two-micron filter for me, an efficient pump that cleaned the spring water; because I'm always worried about Giardia, I doused my water with iodine tablets too.

The trouble was, to quote from my journal, ''the water is so heavily mineralized in the Swell that we all got the runs soon afterward.'' (In retrospect, I admit I don't know for a fact that *everyone* was afflicted.)

Foreword author Joe Bauman in Muddy Creek.

To continue with my journal entry:

> Then on Friday we hiked all the way through Chimney,
> which turns out to be by far the most beautiful canyon
> in the San Rafael region. I parked near a great sheer cliff,
> with Swiss cheese in the foreground, a sheer varnished
> Wingate wall beyond. We also hiked through a side can-
> yon to Chimney, off to the left, before we went to the
> end of Chimney. It was while I was in that last part of
> Chimney that I came upon this most beautiful spot in
> the Swell. There were bighorn tracks and droppings and
> as I sat by myself I thought I heard one clattering and
> then tripping around. Also five dull thud sounds, that
> might have been head-butting. A delightful place.
>
> We hiked on then until we got around the Slaughter
> Slopes, I think, where we camped. We walked on narrow
> trails along sheer Moenkopi hills. Jon and Bert and I
> were walking together on the "Pasture Track." . . . Jon
> said, "Moenkopi blues." I then sang, "I got the sand in
> my face, loose shoes, sore feet, Moenkopi blues." I was
> bushed when we arrived at camp, a place with great
> views across the desert and about two or three buttes
> away from the trail we were going to. Plenty blowy that

night and a little rain. Like other rainstorms during the trip, it sounded fierce, with lightning, but in the morning there was no trace of moisture.

Next day we walked back to Tomsich Butte, picking up the river again and walking upriver to the original camp. I was last in, although I had been making good time, because I had an emergency and had to crawl off amid the tamarisk and willows. . . .

Back at the cars, we drank soft drinks and talked a little and [almost] everybody took off. . . . [Name omitted] decided she couldn't wait to get to civilization to shower, so she rigged up something right in camp and showered. . . . we were all walking around the camp right by her anyhow. I was walking around with Steve . . . I got a couple of shots of Steve, talked to him for a while, and we drove out of there.

That last day of the expedition, April 21, 1990, when we got back to the base camp at Tomsich Butte, I interviewed Steve. Admittedly, I had a little trouble concentrating because of the shower. He said he is a graduate of Colorado State University, had an auto repair shop in Fort Collins, and sold the shop so he could spend a couple of years hiking the deserts of the Colorado Plateau.

For eight months he had been hiking through the Swell with his notebook, camera, and Diz, his mixed-breed dog; she was stuck in Hanksville temporarily during our expedition. "She's an incredible animal. She climbs better than 99 percent of all humanoids. My climbing friends call her the metal mutt," he said.

He told about staying in the wilderness, making a run into Hanksville for supplies about every three weeks. He and Diz lived in the van. "It has a heater and a stove, a capacity for 25 gallons of water and 45 gallons of gas," he said. The interior was snug, with a shag carpet, table, and a library. A folding chair with a hole in the seat served either as an ordinary chair or a latrine. "Everything here is double-duty," he said.

Dozens of books were lined along the floor, held in place by a board. "Actually, I've got about 100 books—that's part of it, that's current reading," he said. I glanced at them: E. L. Doctorow, John Updike, James Joyce, Joyce Carol Oates, Saul Bellow.

"Thomas Hardy. That's something that I read," he said, noticing that I was scribbling authors' names.

"I have an on-board computer, lap-top, and that's what I do all my writing on." The computer was powered by twin batteries, which he recharged with the van's alternator.

Saying he spent about half his time on day hikes and half on backpacking trips, Steve insisted he never got lonely. I asked what the attraction was that could keep him occupied for eight months, and he said, "More canyons. New canyons." Along the way he was chased by wild horses on Sids Mountain. He saw many bighorn sheep but never any mountain lions. He was sorry he hadn't encountered any, he said.

He had wanted to explore the whole Swell. "I've done it all. That was my goal. I wanted to know it better than anybody."

Fishing for quotes, I asked whether he saw incredible views. "All the time," he said. "At least every day. The areas that I found to be the very most beautiful are the Moroni Slopes, which are not in any of the wilderness study areas, and you have just deep, beautiful canyons there that are essentially untouched. . . .

"This is as nice a piece of desert real estate as exists on the Colorado Plateau. It is not a second-rate area, and it deserves protection. This million acres probably has more variety in it than any other part of the canyon country."

I remember that at one point on the trip, while we sat in his van with the side door open, he was showing his hundreds of pages of manuscript. A gust of wind scattered them and we had to scramble to catch the papers— they were blowing toward the canyon of the Muddy Creek, landing in brush or flapping on the ground.

Now that I have read every one of those pages, I am certain nobody contributed as much to our knowledge about how to get around the San Rafael Swell. People like myself who always wondered how to reach certain canyons that show up temptingly on the topographic maps may now venture in, feeling we know something about what's ahead.

It may be useful to note that some of the hikes are in areas that were worked over by miners during the uranium boom of the 1950s and 1960s. Anyone with the kind of flesh-crawling phobia that haunts me about anything connected to uranium may wish to consult U.S. Geological Survey reports, or simply avoid places that have ore piles, mines, uranium shacks, or other workings. Another point to keep in mind is that Steve is an athletic young man; some of us may want to concentrate on the easier trails.

Steve Allen's work should help bring about greater appreciation of the San Rafael Swell, one of the largest, most beautiful, and least-known sections of the Colorado Plateau. The book will appeal to many who wish to explore the area, either for recreation or research, and it may be that this new generation of visitors will be the catalyst to prompt the preservation of the entire Swell as a national park. Without question, it deserves special care.

In a way, *Canyoneering: The San Rafael Swell* opens the region; places that seemed too remote to reach we know now can be hiked or climbed. Desert lovers should be grateful that it was written by a man with a fine sensitivity for the delicate natural environment. Steve sets the right tone here: awe, reverence for the land, adventure, taking care to protect nature. May that feeling carry on into the distant future.

Joseph M. Bauman, Jr.

Acknowledgments

When I started doing the field research for the guide, I knew no one in Southern Utah. After a year in the San Rafael Swell, I found I had made dozens of friends.

To the store owners in Price, Green River, and Hanksville who always had a word of encouragement and a moment to chat, thank you.

To the Bureau of Land Management personnel in Price and Hanksville, thank you for sharing your love of the San Rafael Swell with me, offering advice, and taking time out from a busy schedule to discuss routes and canyons.

To Wendy Chase, an extraordinary adventure partner, I have to thank you a hundred times over for hiking several of the routes, helping edit the manuscript, providing untiring support above and beyond the call of duty, and otherwise being instrumental in seeing this project to fruition.

To Ann Perius-Parker, thank you for providing several of the pictures, printing all the black-and-white photographs, and joining me for several weeks in the Swell.

To Trish Lindaman, thank you for your unflagging support and for drawing the maps for the guide.

To Jan Fenner, thank you for proofreading the manuscript.

To Lynn Jackson of the Moab Area BLM office, thank you for allowing me to include your geology cross-section chart.

To the many hikers who shared routes with me, thank you. My brother Ace was in on the project from the beginning and hiked several of the routes. Lou, my father, joined me on several occasions. It is due to him that many of the routes suitable for seniors are included in the guide. My young friends Jessica and Adrian Upham and Erin and Andy Sobick added a new dimension to the way I look at canyon country. They are responsible for the inclusion of many of the routes that youthful adventurers will enjoy. Mike Enos, Jonathan Rapp, Doug Sundling, Bill and Lynn Booker, and Bert Fingerhut joined me on backcountry excursions and offered criticism and advice.

Joe Bauman, author of *Stone House Lands*, added panache to the hikes we did together and introduced me to the University of Utah Press.

A cast of characters helped in essential ways. They include Ron and Sue Russel, Jim and Deborah Nickelson, Rick and Beverly Upham, Kris Patrick, Bob Wetzel, Tom Weinreich, and Wayne Ludington.

Special thanks goes to my mother, Ruth, a desert rat for fifty years, who encouraged me every step of the way.

Canyoneering

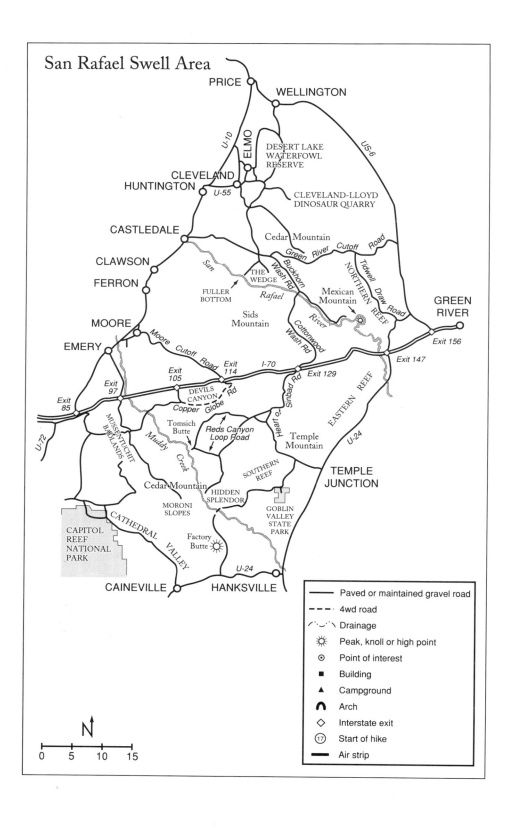

San Rafael Swell Area

PRICE
WELLINGTON

U-10
ELMO
DESERT LAKE
WATERFOWL
RESERVE
CLEVELAND
HUNTINGTON
U-55
CLEVELAND-LLOYD
DINOSAUR QUARRY
US-6

CASTLEDALE
Cedar Mountain
Green River Cutoff Road
CLAWSON
San
THE WEDGE
Buckhorn
Wash Rd
NORTHERN REEF
Tidwell Draw Road
FERRON
FULLER BOTTOM
Rafael
Mexican Mountain
GREEN RIVER
Sids Mountain
River
Cottonwood Wash Rd
Exit 156
MOORE
Moore Cutoff Road
Exit 147
EMERY
Exit 114
I-70
Exit 129
Exit 105
DEVILS CANYON Rd
Heart of Sinbad Rd
EASTERN REEF
Exit 97
Copper Globe
Exit 85
U-72
MUSSENTUCHIT BADLANDS
Tomsich Butte
Reds Canyon Loop Road
Temple Mountain
U-24
Muddy Creek
SOUTHERN REEF
TEMPLE JUNCTION
Cedar Mountain
HIDDEN SPLENDOR
MORONI SLOPES
GOBLIN VALLEY STATE PARK
CATHEDRAL VALLEY
CAPITOL REEF NATIONAL PARK
Factory Butte
U-24
CAINEVILLE
HANKSVILLE

N

0   5   10   15

Paved or maintained gravel road
4wd road
Drainage
Peak, knoll or high point
Point of interest
Building
Campground
Arch
Interstate exit
17 Start of hike
Air strip

Introduction

*I love wild canyons—dry, fragrant, stone-walled, with their
green-choked niches and gold-tipped ramparts.*

Zane Grey

The San Rafael Swell is located in the northern part of
what is commonly referred to as canyon country. Its
neighbors are Canyonlands National Park to the southeast and Capitol Reef National Park to the southwest. It
is a complex, million-acre area of seemingly endless expanses of slickrock, deep canyons, high walls, arches,
pinnacles, towers, mesas, and mountains. Several rivers
also run through the Swell.

Though equal in beauty to any of the more popular
canyon areas, it has only been in the last twenty years
that canyoneers have discovered the San Rafael Swell.
This was due, perhaps, to the overcrowding of other areas forcing canyon explorers to look beyond the national
parks for recreational opportunities. The construction of
Interstate 70 through the heart of the Swell in 1970
brought an influx of visitors who had previously not
known of its existence. A history of uranium mining and
exploring for oil may have given some the impression
that the San Rafael Swell was despoiled and not worthy
of attention. Though it is true that miners did leave evidence of their handiwork scattered throughout the
Swell, most of the area is still pristine. Many of the old
mining roads have fallen into disrepair and are now used
to access some of the most scenic lands in canyon
country.

During the first part of this century conservationists
recommended that three canyon areas in Utah be designated as national parks. The San Rafael Swell was one of
them. Economic pressures removed the Swell from the
list, but Arches and Natural Bridges national parks were
acquired. The San Rafael Swell was left open for mineral

development. The decades passed. Other areas in canyon country, Canyonlands and Capitol Reef national parks, Glen Canyon National Recreation Area, and Dead Horse Point State Park, came under federal or state protection. Again the San Rafael Swell was left open for development.

As the years passed the times changed. The public demand for more wilderness—areas suitable for recreation, relaxation, and solitude—have brought the canyon country of Utah and the San Rafael Swell into the limelight. The San Rafael Swell now contains five BLM wilderness study areas (WSAs). Another eight areas are being considered for inclusion as wilderness areas in Congressman Wayne Owens's Utah BLM Wilderness Bill. There is a group trying to have the Swell designated as a national park. The protection of the San Rafael Swell from further degradation has become a national issue. Environmental groups such as the Sierra Club, the Utah Wilderness Coalition, The Wilderness Society, and the Southern Utah Wilderness Alliance avidly support federal protection. Your support of these organizations will help protect the San Rafael Swell for all time.

The purpose of the guidebook is to provide accurate information for visitors to the San Rafael Swell. It is designed to be used by sightseers, picnickers, photographers, hikers, backpackers, rock-climbers, and mountain bike riders. People of all ages, from children to seniors, will find adventures that will fulfill their objectives.

In comparison to many hiking guides, the material presented in this guide may, to some, seem complex. The guide does not simply lead you from signpost to signpost along oft-trodden paths. There are few established trails in the San Rafael Swell. The advantage of this is that you will see few other hikers. Some of the terrain you will cover has never been thoroughly explored. There are still arches, bridges, pinnacles, and towers hidden in unknown canyons to be discovered and savored. This is the essence of adventure.

There are sixty-three major hikes delineated in the guide, with many short and side hikes detailed. There are hikes that will satisfy any canyoneer, from the novice to the expert. Day hikers can choose routes from an hour to a long day in length. Backpackers will find many multi-day hikes. With the use of the guide, longer routes, taking days or weeks, are easy to design.

The San Rafael Swell has been largely ignored by rock-climbers, though there are many pinnacles and towers up to 300 feet high that have never been touched or even described in the literature. Although this is not a climbing guide, there are several easy rock climbs in the guide. More valuable to the climber are the notes on the pinnacles and towers that have potential routes.

Mountain bikers, now common throughout canyon country, will find a joyful home in the San Rafael Swell. Though there are only two mountain bike routes in the guide, every Road Section mentions whether the road is suitable for bikes.

Thirty main roads and innumerable side roads are described in detail. These lead into every corner of the San Rafael Swell. With the maze of roads and tracks running through the Swell, the Road Sections eliminate the confusion often endured by hikers trying to find a trailhead.

An awareness of the physical world around you can greatly increase your appreciation for the land. Though it is not within the scope of the guide to provide comprehensive details, there are short chapters that will give you a general insight into the geology of the region and the Indians who lived there. The bibliography at the end of the guide provides a list of books for those wanting to learn more.

Like mountaineering, canyoneering often asks more of the traveler than hiking skills. Of foremost importance is a commitment to preserve the little wilderness we have left. Strict adherence to the skills presented in the chapter ''Protecting the Environment'' will increase your sensitivity to the environment and will help maintain its pristine condition.

In a land with few trails, route-finding and map-reading skills are important. On some routes, rock-climbing and rope-handling skills become paramount. For the more audacious, swimming skills may be needed while descending some of the canyons.

As with any outdoor activity done far from medical help, basic first aid skills, though rarely needed, become essential. Thinking and judgment become an integral part of the hikes.

Access

On the San Rafael Swell's north end, access is through Price, a large town with all the amenities. It is the home of the College of Eastern Utah. The Prehistoric Museum in the center of town is a worthwhile stop. The Price BLM office, located at 900 North 700 East (801–637–4584), is a valuable resource. The personnel there can provide information on road conditions, hiking, camping, and river-running opportunities.

Green River, several miles east of the Swell on Interstate 70, provides access to the heart of the Swell. Though not a large town, it does have motels, gas stations, two small markets, and a garage with towing services. The John Wesley Powell River History Museum, sitting on a hill overlooking the Green River, is a must for all canyoneers. Interstate 70 cuts through the middle of the San Rafael Swell making access to many areas convenient.

Hanksville, on Highway 24, provides access to the southern areas of the Swell. It has few services, but it does have a motel, a market, several cafes, two gas stations, and a garage with towing services. The personnel at the Hanksville BLM office, located at 406 South 100 West (801–542–3461), can offer advice on exploring the southern portions of the Swell.

Along the west side of the Swell, on Highway 10, are a number of small towns that have gas stations, cafes, and small markets. These include Huntington, Castle Dale, and Ferron.

The Environmental Imperative

". . . an area where the earth and its community of life are untrammeled by man, where man himself is a visitor who does not remain."
This definition of wilderness is from the Wilderness Act of 1964.

The desert from afar looks massive and solid. The towers, cliffs, mesas, and plateaus appear indestructible and unalterable. Up close though, the desert proves to be a fragile environment, one easily damaged. Wounds inflicted fester and rot. The scars remain.

By its beauty, the desert invites intrusion. The hiker, climber, biker, and river-runner are attracted, as are the photographer and picnicker.

By its potential for riches, the desert invites exploitation. The cattleman, the sheepherder, the horse packer, and the tour operator look to the desert to bring them wealth, as do the miner and the gem hunter.

By its lack of defenses, with no way to retaliate, the desert invites destruction. Holes gouged in its cloak, marks left on its skin, its bowels ripped asunder, the desert can only stand stoically.

The settlers and cowboys came and used the desert harshly. The hills that we see today look nothing like what the first pioneers saw. The plains of soil-holding grasses have been reduced to barren plains spotted with sage, pinyon, and juniper by the overgrazing of cattle. The scars remain.

The miners came with their bulldozers and graders, dynamite and drills. To explore Temple Mountain is to discover that it is a hollow shell, its innards removed to make atomic weapons. The Pasture Track above Muddy Creek, Tomsich Butte, Calf Mesa, and many other areas have been mutilated in the search for wealth. The scars remain.

Today it is the off-road vehicle (ORV) that is ravaging the San Rafael Swell. These two-, three-, and four-

ORV damage at the mouth of Ernie Canyon.

wheeled vehicles can, and do, go just about anywhere.
In the wilderness study areas, areas set aside until Congress can decide exactly how they should be used, it is illegal to take ORVs off of established roads. As with many sports, it is the few bad apples that are ruining it for the masses. The ORV riders who illegally enter wilderness study areas are the scourge of the San Rafael Swell.

In former years little notice was taken of the destruction. The times have changed. Though mining claims are kept current, it is unlikely that uranium will again be extracted from the Swell. The demand has ceased.

Though cattle still graze the canyon bottoms of the Swell, their days may be numbered. Many question whether the damage they do is worth the environmental cost. Many cattlemen realize this. They have full-time city jobs. Cattle are a sideline, a clinging to the past. As canyon country attracts more visitors, economic forces may dictate their removal.

It is time to let the San Rafael Swell recover. The rotted parts, over time, will heal. The grasses will reassert themselves. The mining tracks will wash away or be covered by rockfall. The tunnels will collapse. The convalescence will take a long time, certainly longer than our lives or the lives of our grandchildren. It will recover, though some scars will remain.

In 1976 Congress passed the Federal Land Policy and Management Act (FLPMA). That act required the BLM to inventory its holdings and to recommend areas worthy of wilderness designation. By 1980 they had done this. Of the 22 million acres the Utah BLM controls, 1.9 million acres were deemed suitable. These areas are called wilderness study areas.

In 1989 Representative Wayne Owens of Utah introduced a Utah BLM Wilderness Bill which would set aside 5.1 million acres in Utah as wilderness. These areas include the BLM wilderness study areas as well as many other deserving parts of canyon country.

To bring these numbers into perspective, the BLM has proposed only 265,000 acres of the San Rafael Swell as wilderness areas. Representative Owens's proposal would increase this to 674,000 acres, a dramatic increase. The BLM proposal does not include the following areas: Mussentuchit Badlands, Cedar and East Cedar Mountains, Moroni Slopes, Factory Butte, Black Dragon Wash, and the San Rafael Knob. This is a partial list that only includes familiar areas. They are all areas that are covered in the guide and are all worthy of wilderness designation.

There has been substantial politicking involved in all of this. To scare potential supporters of the Wilderness Bill, the opposition has often tried to give the impression that wilderness is just for the eastern rich. In reality, wilderness is based on a multiple-use concept. The FLPMA defines multiple use as a "combination of balanced and diverse resource uses that takes into account the long-term needs of future generations for renewable and non-renewable resources, including, but not limited to, recreational, range, timber, minerals, watershed, wildlife and fish, and natural scenic, scientific and historical values."

With wilderness designation the changes that occur would have almost no impact on the majority of people who now use and enjoy the San Rafael Swell. Current mining claims and cattle are allowed. Hunting would continue, as would the use of pack animals. As with other wilderness areas, there may be some restrictions placed on where camping is allowed, whether dogs need to be leashed on some trails, or whether camp fires are allowed in some areas. Some access roads would be closed. Most of them duplicate other roads, a common occurrence in the Swell. Other road closures would be those that are now used by ORVs. ORV use in designated wilderness areas would be eliminated, thus opening up many canyons to use by everybody—hikers, climbers, campers, picnickers, and horse packers. Such multiple use is desirable, and remember that ORVs would still have about 17 million acres of BLM land to ride on.

Protecting the Environment

To many of us, the wilderness truly unaltered by human inter-ference, the wilderness with its wealth of life rolling across it in great surges, ebbing and flowing with the seasons of the years, is inseparable from our innermost beings.

Ian McTaggert Cowan

There are a number of things we as individuals can do to protect the environment. None are difficult; none take much effort. The goal is to leave the desert as you found it, or better. There is nothing worse than reaching the end of a canyon and finding a fire pit with aluminum foil and beer cans in it.

Trash: The most obvious eyesore. Make it a practice to take out a little more than you brought in. This will make up for the sandwich bag that blew off the top of Pinnacle #1.

Bodily waste: Every group should carry a small spade. Dig a hole six to eight inches deep, preferably under trees or as close to vegetation as you can. The microorganisms they provide will speed the breakdown of the waste. Burn your toilet paper. Toilet paper flowers do not en-hance cliff roses. Always go well away from established campsites, trails, streams, and potholes. Three hundred feet is the minimum. In narrow canyons this can be diffi-cult. Scramble up a rubble heap or find a high ledge. Don't do it on a sandbar!

Campsite selection: There are three preferred campsites: (1.) Use an already established site. The damage has al-ready been done. (2.) Camp in a dry wash, weather per-mitting. The next rain will eradicate your sign. (3.) Camp on the slickrock. This is ideal. You can camp on the top of a dome or on a high ledge with fine views. Try not to camp next to streams or potholes. You may be keeping animals away from vital water sources if you do.

Fires: They are a thing of the past. The warmth is rarely needed in the Swell. The scars they leave remain for years. There is a new generation of lightweight backpack stoves—no muss, no fuss, no smell. If you must—stove broken or emergency—do not build a fire ring. This only blackens the rock. Build your fire in a wash and on the sand. Let it burn out completely. Don't leave a half-burned log.

Washing dishes: Do not dump leftovers in streams or potholes. They should go into a hole six to eight inches deep. Wash your dishes well away from water sources. Don't use soap to sterilize your dishes. Metal utensils can be held over the flame of a stove for several seconds. Carry rubbing alcohol and swab your dishes out with it. A tiny, two-ounce container of alcohol will last a week or more.

Bathing: Save your swimming for the creeks and rivers. Avoid swimming in potholes. Unless you are on a long hike there shouldn't be a great need to lather up. If you need to bathe, use pots and canteens to carry water well away from the water source. Try to stay near vegetation. Use only the pure soaps like Dr. Bronner's Castile soap or Ivory bar soap. They don't have the perfumes and additives that are damaging to the environment.

Cryptogamic soil: Made from a conglomeration of algae, fungi, moss, and lichen, cryptogamic soil is the black, castlelike soil that is spread throughout the desert. It is invaluable in holding the soil together and checking erosion. Try to stay off of it. This is often not possible. When you do walk on it, especially in groups, do not leave a trail where erosion can start.

Pictographs and petroglyphs: It was common to chalk these to make them stand out better for photographs. Don't. Often they look like a little brushing would help. Don't. Feel privileged to view rock art from a distance.

Indian artifacts: It is illegal to remove any Indian artifact or vandalize any archaeological feature. Look but don't touch.

Petrified wood: You can collect twenty-five pounds per day for noncommercial uses. Don't be greedy. Most petrified wood ends up in backyards where it is rarely seen or appreciated.

Dogs: At the present time there are no restrictions in the Swell. Be realistic about the quality of your animal. If it is loud, aggressive toward other hikers or wildlife, chases cattle, defecates on the trails, doesn't respond to your commands, or is in other ways obnoxious, leave it behind. In some areas water sources are infrequent and become very valuable. Don't let your dog muddy up an isolated water source.

Off-road vehicle use: Throughout most of the San Rafael Swell ORVs must stay on established roads that are not passable by regular vehicles, or in designated areas. There are several designated riding areas in the Swell. None are in wilderness study areas. Ask at the BLM or Forest Service offices for maps and details. Nonriders must realize that ORVs in some areas are legal. Report any illegal riding to the BLM office in Price.

The Geology of the San Rafael Swell

When speaking of these rocks, we must not conceive of piles of boulders, or heaps of fragments, but a whole land of naked rock, with giant forms carved on it; cathedral-shaped buttes, towering hundreds or thousands of feet; cliffs that cannot be scaled, and canyon walls that shrink the river into insignificance, with vast, hollow domes, and tall pinnacles, and shafts set on the verge overhead, and all highly colored—buff, gray, red, brown, and chocolate; never lichened; never moss-covered; but bare, and often polished.

John Wesley Powell

The geology of the Colorado Plateau and the San Rafael Swell, in particular, is complicated. For the canyoneer it is not necessary to know the technical details. A basic understanding of how the canyon country was created and a knowledge of the characteristics of the common formations will prove valuable. It will add insight and increase your sensitivity while hiking in the area.

The San Rafael Swell is part of a larger area, the Colorado Plateau, which comprises a vast area that contains most of what we now call canyon country. It is an area bounded by the Aquarius Plateau to the west, the San Juan and Colorado rivers to the south, the San Juan Mountains to the east, and the Book Cliffs to the north. The San Rafael Swell is in the northwest part of the Colorado Plateau in an area geologists call the Canyon Lands section.

The canyon country is composed primarily of sedimentary rock. The sedimentary rock is made of grains of minerals (geologists call these clastic particles), mainly silica, which were broken and weathered from igneous rock on the Uncompahgre Uplift, an area to the east of canyon country.

Several hundred million years ago the Uncompahgre Uplift and several lesser uplifts formed a partial ring around the eastern edge of the Colorado Plateau, much like the rim of a broken bowl. The area was the western boundary of the North American continent. Much of it was at times under the ocean. The sea level varied as forces under the earth's crust either pushed the area higher or let it sink back into the sea. The forces were induced by plate tectonics, the shifting of huge subsurface plates bumping into each other.

Also affecting the sea level were temperature variations which caused glaciers to advance and recede. With cooler temperatures large volumes of water were locked in the glaciers making the oceans shallower. Higher temperatures released the water from the glaciers making the oceans deeper, often inundating otherwise dry land.

From the uplifts a variety of forces brought the mineral grains down into the bottom of the bowl, separating them by size. Gravity, helped by the freeze-thaw cycle and the force of running water, brought down a mix of sizes from boulders to sand grains. The wind carried even smaller material, often just dust particles or volcanic ash from active volcanoes to the west and southwest.

As the material worked its way down from the high country other forces came into play. Not only were the mineral grains separated by size but the depositional environment, the bottom of the bowl, changed. The layers, or strata, that were formed by the accumulation of silica grains in the bottom of the bowl were deposited in two ways: parallel stratification (this is also called parallel-bedding and deposits of this type are referred to as a Formation) and cross stratification (this is also called cross-bedding and deposits of this type are referred to as a Sandstone).

Parallel-stratified formations were formed when the silica grains were deposited in layers. This indicates that deposition occurred in quiet water—the ocean bottom, tidal flats, or freshwater lakes. Layers of different thicknesses were formed. This was dependent on the nature of the forces bringing the material down from the heights, the amount of material, and the stability and length of the period of deposition. Thin, uniform layers are thought to have been deposited in concert with natural rhythms—the rise and fall of the tides or the change of the seasons. These thin layers are called varves.

The Moenkopi Formation is a classic example of a varved rock. This stratum was deposited in tidal pools and mud flats. Due to tidal variations different colored layers were formed. Lighter colored layers were deposited while under water and when there was little motion in the water. This allowed the buildup of salts and the accumulation of marine fossils. The darker layers were deposited while above water and do not contain salts and fossils. The Moenkopi, Chinle, and Summerville formations are examples of parallel-stratified deposition.

Cross-stratified sandstone is a deep, homogeneous layer that was deposited by the turbulent flow of wind or water. A large amount of material was deposited over a geologically short span of time. The climate and environment during the period of deposition was similar to that of the present-day Sahara Desert, hot and dry. Huge sand dunes drifted across the landscape. Once the material was deposited, either groundwater or the sea level rose, dampening the sand and holding it in place until it could harden. Coconino, Wingate, and Navajo sandstones are examples of cross-stratified deposition.

While the various layers were being laid down, external forces were at work. Individual layers in a plastic state were bent and folded. The forces acting on the layers came from the unequal weight of the material above, volcanic pressures, and movement in the crust of the earth. The bending of the strata is called folding.

There are three basic types of folds. Anticlines are arched or upfolded layers of rock. Synclines are downfolded or trough-shaped layers of rock. Monoclines are steplike bends in otherwise horizontal layers of rock. All of these folds can range from hundreds of miles long to just several yards across. The San Rafael Swell itself is an asymmetrical anticline. Smaller folds can be seen along the Southern Reef near Ding and Dang canyons and in lower Devils Canyon where they are particularly convoluted and spectacular.

The plastic rock, now formed into its final configuration, hardened. This was caused by two forces. First, the weight of the material above compressed and aligned the silica grains, increasing its density. Second, chemical reactions between the rock particles, water, and the atmosphere bonded the rock together.

Ten to 15 million years ago the deposition of the silica

Intense folding in Lower Devils Canyon.

particles stopped. The Colorado Plateau started to rise. Areas that had once been at sea level were lifted 10 to 15 thousand feet. Instead of being an area of deposition, the Colorado Plateau started to erode.

Softer layers and weaknesses in harder layers of sandstone were eroded by moving water. Sheet erosion acted on the rock when rain fell and the water moved over the rock in broad sheets. Stream erosion was the concentrated effect of the water while running in confined areas.

While the land lifted around it, the canyons became deeper. Slit canyons developed in layers of harder sandstone, those formed by cross-stratified deposition. They are uniform in width and height and typical of most of the canyons in the San Rafael Swell.

Stairstep canyons were formed when water cut through alternating soft and hard layers of sandstone. These are formed in canyons containing both parallel-stratified formations and cross-stratified sandstone. The Grand Canyon is a classic example of a stairstep canyon. V-shaped canyons were formed in uniformly softer rock. Many canyons are a combination of all three types: slit, stairstep, and V-shaped.

The San Rafael Swell started to form between 50 and 60 million years ago. Pressures from deep beneath the earth's crust pushed the strata upward like an expanding balloon, forming a dome-shaped anticline eighty miles long and forty miles wide. The strata on the periphery of the anticline were tilted back forming the near vertical walls that we see today along the Northern, Eastern, and Southern reefs. The area in the middle of the reef, the Swell (Sinbad Country), was higher than the reef itself. Higher elevations invited more rainfall making the area more susceptible to the forces of sheet and stream erosion. The rounded dome, or swell, slowly eroded forming the deep canyons that now cut through the area.

About a million years ago there was a period of volcanic activity to the south and west of the Swell. Two things happened during this time. First, molten rock forced its way into cracks in the sandstone forming dikes, sills, volcanic plugs, and more massive igneous intrusions. These can be seen throughout the Cathedral Valley, Mussentuchit Badlands, and Cedar Mountain areas.

Second, after the period of volcanic activity, a time of global cooling brought glaciers to Thousand Lakes Mountain, an area to the west of the Swell. The glaciers carried an immense amount of volcanic rock into Cathedral Valley and the Mussentuchit Badlands, leaving a layer of volcanic boulders sitting on top of the sandstone.

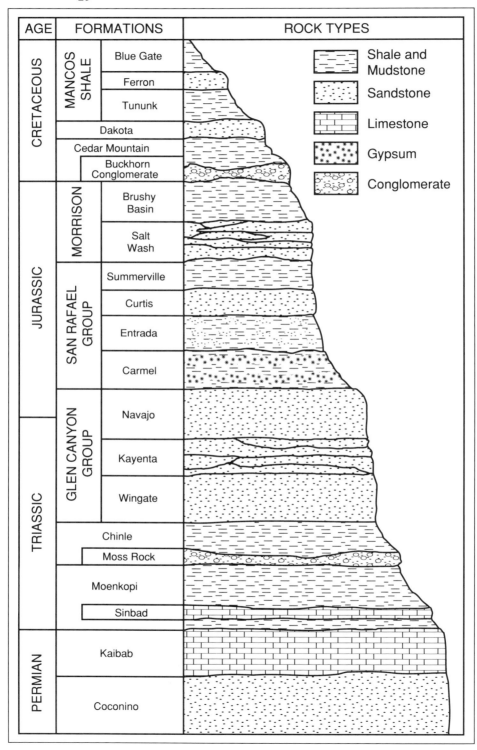

AGE	FORMATIONS			ROCK TYPES

AGE / FORMATIONS

CRETACEOUS
- MANCOS SHALE
  - Blue Gate
  - Ferron
  - Tununk
- Dakota
- Cedar Mountain
- Buckhorn Conglomerate

JURASSIC
- MORRISON
  - Brushy Basin
  - Salt Wash
- SAN RAFAEL GROUP
  - Summerville
  - Curtis
  - Entrada
  - Carmel

TRIASSIC
- GLEN CANYON GROUP
  - Navajo
  - Kayenta
  - Wingate
- Chinle
- Moss Rock
- Moenkopi
- Sinbad

PERMIAN
- Kaibab
- Coconino

ROCK TYPES

- Shale and Mudstone
- Sandstone
- Limestone
- Gypsum
- Conglomerate

The Strata

The sole actuality of nature resides in change.
Heraclitus

The sandstones and formations detailed below are listed in order of age, from the oldest or lowest stratum to the youngest or highest stratum. Only the dominant sandstones and formations found in the San Rafael Swell are described.

Coconino Sandstone is a part of the Cutler Formation. It is cross-stratified and is up to 400 feet thick. Coconino Sandstone is the petrified remains of huge sand dunes that once covered the area. Coconino Sandstone is fine grained, white to light brown in color, and its surface is soft. It forms vertical walls that are often coated with black varnish. One distinctive feature of Coconino Sandstone is that it is topped by a band of limestone that varies from ten to fifty feet in thickness. The band is called the Sinbad Member.

The *Moenkopi Formation* is one of the most common and easily recognized stratum in the Swell. It is parallel-stratified and is up to 400 feet thick. It was formed by stream-born silt and mud being deposited in tidal pools and mud flats. The layers vary considerably in color, ranging from near white to red, brown, and dark brown. The Moenkopi Formation has been characterized as looking like a chocolate torte cake. It forms either vertical walls or, at times, steep slopes.

The *Chinle Formation* is parallel-stratified and is up to 150 feet thick. It was formed by streams depositing mud, silt, and volcanic ash in alluvial plains. It contains a rainbow of colors—red, brown, purple, gray, and green—and forms steep and often shaley slopes. The gray to buff, finely grained layer in the Chinle Formation is ash from volcanoes that were active to the west and south. The Chinle Formation often contains petrified wood.

A substratum of the Chinle Formation, the Moss Back

Member, contains uranium. Uranium particles in solution were able to leach along the porous sandstone of the Moss Back Member, which for some unexplained reason were absorbed onto decomposed plant material. The plant material had been washed down streams and had collected in pockets and seams. Later, uranium miners looked for these pockets and seams. The presence of petrified wood was an indicator that uranium deposits were near.

Wingate Sandstone is a part of what is called the Glen Canyon group. It is cross-stratified and is up to 400 feet thick. It was formed during a period of high winds which carried an immense amount of material down from the highlands to the east and covered most of the Colorado Plateau in sand. Its usual colors range from a light red to a near brown. This varies considerably and it is not unusual to see near-white Wingate Sandstone. This can make it hard to differentiate from Navajo Sandstone. Often the context it is in, immediately above the Moenkopi and Chinle formations, is the clue to whether it is Wingate or Navajo. It forms vertical walls that have vertical cracks. It is the densest of the sandstones.

The *Kayenta Formation* is also a part of the Glen Canyon group. It is parallel-stratified and is up to 100 feet thick. It was formed by stream-deposited sand or the shuffling of the Wingate sands. It is red to brown in color and forms broken ledges and steep slopes. The Kayenta Formation is the friend of the backpacker as it can provide wide benches that are easy to negotiate. It often contains dinosaur bones and dinosaur footprints.

Navajo Sandstone, another member of the Glen Canyon group, is cross-stratified and is up to 500 feet thick. It was formed in the same environment as Wingate Sandstone. It is usually lighter in color than Wingate Sandstone, varying from dirty white to red. Navajo Sandstone forms vertical walls, but the tops of the cliffs tend to be more rounded than Wingate cliffs.

The *Carmel Formation* is parallel-stratified and is up to 100 feet thick, though it is commonly no more than twenty-five feet thick. It was formed by a combination of wind and stream deposition in a marine environment. Red to brown siltstone layers are intermixed with limestone layers that often contain marine fossils. It forms sloping ledges that are often unstable to walk on.

Entrada Sandstone is a bit of a puzzle. It is cross-stratified and is up to 500 feet thick, although it is more normal to see it in the 150-foot range. Though it usually presents itself as a homogeneous formation, it sometimes shows distinct parallel bedding. It was formed in two ways: by windblown silt and sand settling into quiet waters, and in other locations by the same forces that formed Wingate and Navajo sandstones. It is off-white to a rich red in color and usually forms steep, rounded walls and domes. The goblins in Goblin Valley State Park are formed from Entrada Sandstone.

The *Curtis Formation* is parallel-stratified and is up to 150 feet thick in the northern parts of the Swell. It was formed by silt deposition in a shallow marine environment. It has thin layers that contain microfossils and mollusks. It is brown to faded green in color and weathers into sandy benches or shaley walls.

The *Summerville Formation* is parallel-stratified and is up to 325 feet thick. It was formed as the sea retreated leaving tidal and mud flats into which deposition could occur. It is a fine-grained, chocolate-colored stratum that has thin layers that sometimes contain marine fossils. It forms either shaley walls or gradual slopes. The Summerville Formation often contains agates.

Note: Throughout the guide I have shortened the geologic descriptions of the various formations, e.g., Wingate-walled instead of a wall of Wingate Sandstone, and a Navajo dome instead of a dome of Navajo Sandstone, etc.

Man in the San Rafael Swell

If one is inclined to wonder at first how so many dwellers came to be in the loneliest land that ever came out of God's hands, what they do there and why stay, one does not wonder so much after having lived there. None other than this long brown land lays such a hold on affections. The rainbow hills, the tender bluish mists, the luminous radiance of the spring, have the lotus chosen.

Mary Austin

The story of man in the San Rafael Swell starts with the antecedents of the American Indians who came to the New World from Asia. They were a Stone Age people, possessing crude stone tools and living in caves and other natural shelters. They were the big game hunters, following the migration of the animals—mastodons, mammoths, long hair bison, sloths, and tapirs—as they slowly worked their way north into Siberia.

Twenty to fifty thousand years ago earth was locked in an ice age. As much of its water was tied up in glaciers, the level of the sea was lower. The area between Siberia and Alaska, called Beringia, was above water. Ocean currents, originating in equatorial waters near Japan, brought warm water up to Beringia and kept the temperatures reasonable. A small number of Stone Age men, called Paleo-Indians by archaeologists, crossed Beringia from Siberia to North America. It is doubtful they realized they were crossing onto a new continent. They were simply following sources of food and their instinct for survival.

Once in North America they slowly migrated south. Though tongues of glacial ice pushed southward, ice-free corridors were found. Two known corridors were along the McKenzie River and along the eastern edge of the Rocky Mountains. These led the Paleo-Indians into the Great Plains area. The archaeological evidence they left behind is scant.

The glaciers retreated allowing the level of the sea to

rise, burying Beringia under water and thwarting further migration. Some fifteen thousand years ago earth entered a new ice age. Once again Beringia was dry and again man crossed over to North America. Over a three-thousand-year period substantial numbers of Paleo-Indians made the journey. As with their predecessors, they followed the ice-free corridors into the Great Plains. From there they radiated throughout North and South America.

These early inhabitants were like the first migrants who had come before them. They, too, were still in the Stone Age, big game hunters who utilized crude stone tools and sharp sticks. There was some social organization as is demonstrated at a site in Wyoming where a mammoth was driven into a bog and killed with rocks. At other locations bison were stampeded off cliffs and the meat retrieved. Activities such as these could have only been perpetrated by groups working together toward a common goal.

From 13,000 B.C. to 5500 B.C Paleo-Indian Culture changed slowly. The most important advance was the invention of the projectile point, thin sharp slivers chipped from larger rocks. These points, tied to the end of a stick and used as a spear, were employed to kill game that had formerly been unobtainable. Man was better able to exploit the land. More food meant that the population could increase, and hunger became less of a worry.

Although there are a dozen recognized types of projectile points, two are common. The oldest of these, the Clovis point, has been found in association with mammoth, bison, horse, and camel kill sites. Folsom points, the most common of the Paleo-Indian period, were found only in bison kill sites.

On the Colorado Plateau there are few Paleo-Indian sites, remnants of the second wave of migration by Stone Age man. A Clovis point was found in Emery County, and a Plano point, slightly younger than a Clovis point, was discovered near Ferron. Both sites are on the western edge of the San Rafael Swell. Other signs of habitation were discovered south of Vernal, Utah, and many sites have been found along the Flaming Gorge in Wyoming.

Eight thousand years ago the larger mammals died

out. Two reasons are cited. First, the climate was getting warmer. The Great Plains were turning into the Great American Desert. Second, the Paleo-Indians may have precipitated the first man-made environmental crisis. Overhunting may have eradicated such large numbers of animals that there was no longer a sufficient breeding population. With the decline or decimation of the chief food source, man was again on the move looking for a hospitable environment. A new home was found in the Great Basin, the area to the west of the Colorado Plateau.

This leads up to the time of the Desert Culture which flourished from 5500 B.C. to A.D. 500. (The Desert Culture has also been called the Western or Desert Archaic Culture. To differentiate a general Desert Culture from the Indians living in the San Rafael Swell area, some researchers have called it the Barrier Canyon Culture.) They were the first to inhabit the Colorado Plateau and the Great Basin. The Desert Culture evolved from the Paleo-Indians with a big game hunting tradition to a people of cultural diversity. A hunter-gatherer tradition was born. Instead of meat being the main food staple, the gathering of nuts, roots, and berries predominated. A supply of these could be stored and saved for less prosperous times. Their diet diversified as new food sources were recognized and exploited. Manos and metates, or grinding stones, were used to grind the products of their foraging. Baskets, crudely woven at first, became more sophisticated, and pottery was soon introduced. Both were needed to store the new foods.

Atlatls, or spear throwers, increased the distance and velocity a spear could be thrown, multiplying its effectiveness. Later, the bow and arrow replaced the atlatl, another step up the cultural ladder. Antelope and bighorn sheep were added to the diet. Bone awls were used to pierce leather, making clothes easier to produce. Woven sandals and blankets also made life easier. The principal sources of shelter were caves, though simple lean-tos were also utilized.

The Desert Culture left behind ample evidence of its passing. Danger Cave and Hogup Cave near the Great Salt Lake in Utah and Lovelock Cave in Nevada, among many, provide definitive information about the Desert Culture. These caves show evidence of continual use from about 8000 B.C. to A.D. 1. The Cowboy Cave site in Horseshoe Canyon, part of Canyonlands National Park twenty-five miles east of the San Rafael Swell, was one of the few prolific sites on the Colorado Plateau. It was occupied from 6300 B.C. to the modern era.

Evidence of the Desert Culture is also apparent in the extensive pictograph panels the Indians left behind. Pictographs are paintings drawn on a rock surface. The Indians used colored minerals mixed with animal fat or vegetable oil which they brushed onto rock walls with twigs, branch ends, or bits of fur. Different colors were obtained from whatever was handy. Reds were produced from hematite, an iron oxide. Yellow was made from limonite, another type of iron oxide. Black was obtained from coal deposits. Other colors were procured from beds of clay.

In the San Rafael Swell the pictographs left behind by the Desert Culture are of the Barrier Canyon Style, dated from about 5000 B.C. to A.D. 500, though archaeologists have not been able to agree on either date. The pictographs are generally anthropomorphic (having a human form) figures, ghostlike and supernatural in appearance. The bodies are tapered and have elaborate headgear. Barrier Canyon Style pictographs are found throughout the San Rafael Swell: Cane Wash, Buckhorn Wash, Wild Horse Canyon, Old Woman Wash, and South Temple Wash, among others.

Barrier Canyon Style pictographs are also located outside the San Rafael Swell, the most famous panel being the Great Gallery in Horseshoe Canyon in Canyonlands National Park. There are other panels in Capitol Reef and Arches national parks, and in scattered locations across the Colorado Plateau.

To the south of the Colorado Plateau, in Mexico and Central America, the Indians developed a cultural identity of their own, one substantially more advanced than that of the Desert Culture. They developed a complex agricultural society. The significance of this was profound. No longer did primitive people have to constantly follow herds of animals. They could plant and harvest

Cliff dwelling behind the Sid and Charley Pinnacle.

corn, beans, and squash which could be stored and used at a later time.

A stratified society evolved. As with other developing societies there was a hierarchy. Those at the top controlled the society, telling others what to do. In this way larger and more sophisticated projects were possible. Complex irrigation systems were built, opening up more land to cultivation. Fewer people produced more food, leaving others time to devote to such diverse projects as building cities and temples. More time was available to develop religions. The arts flourished.

From A.D. 1 to A.D. 500 these developments were introduced into the Desert Cultures of the Colorado Plateau. Archaeologists call this period the Basketmaker Stage. By A.D. 500 the Basketmakers had divided into several distinct cultures. Among these were the Anasazi Indians, thought to have been descendants of a Basketmaker Culture that developed along the banks of the Colorado River and occupied the Four Corners Region in an area east of the Colorado River and south of the Escalante River. The Anasazi were quick to assimilate the new innovations that originated in the south, introducing horticulture, irrigation, and domesticated animals to the southwest.

Another group some archaeologists think were descendants of the Basketmakers were the Fremont Indians.

Other archaeologists think the Fremont Culture started with the remnants of a Desert Culture from the Great Basin, though there isn't conclusive proof. The Fremonts also may have been a group that broke away from the Anasazi, or the Mogollon, a group to the southwest of the Anasazi. Regardless of their origin, the Fremont Indians did become a distinct cultural group that occupied the territory to the north of the Anasazi. This area was west of the Colorado River and north of the Escalante River, an area that included the San Rafael Swell. Except for the Anasazi to the south, they dominated what is now the state of Utah.

The Fremont Culture developed somewhat differently from that of their Anasazi neighbors. The Fremonts had communities of up to several hundred people, though they did not build the walled cities so typical of the Anasazi. Instead, they built clusters of pit houses and utilized caves which were improved with crude masonry walls. Like the Anasazi, the Fremonts cultivated their food and built irrigation systems that stretched for miles. They became proficient fishermen. Feather and hide blankets, finely tailored leather clothes, leather moccasins, and jewelry were made. Simple, unpainted pots and finely woven baskets were used. Many small clay figurines have been found, as have round rock balls that were apparently used in games.

Evidence of the Fremont Culture is found throughout the region. There are Fremont sites in Nine-Mile Canyon near Price, in Arches, Canyonlands, and Capitol Reef national parks, and along the Escalante, Green, and Dirty Devil rivers. Small granaries are common. These, often found in small caves high above the floor of a canyon, were used to store corn and to keep it away from rodents. Pit-house towns, chipping beds, and grinding surfaces for corn have also been found.

Except for pictographs and petroglyphs, evidence of the Fremont Culture is relatively scarce in the San Rafael Swell. Caves in Black Dragon Wash and at the head of Cane Wash were certainly used. There is a cliff dwelling with masonry walls in a cave high on a cliff behind the Sid and Charley pinnacle near the Moore Cutoff road. The cultural detritus left by most Indians—chipping grounds, the remains of pit houses and areas of communal use, and burial sites—are nearly absent in the Swell.

In the San Rafael Swell the principal remnants left behind by the Fremont Indians are the many rock art panels we see today. Often extensive in nature, these are usually found associated with cultures that had enough free time to spend on activities not essential to their immediate existence.

Pictographs, so dominant in the Desert Culture, were secondary to petroglyphs in the Fremont Culture. Petroglyphs are shapes that were pecked onto rock walls. They are generally younger than the pictographs, ranging in age from A.D. 500 to historic times. In the San Rafael Swell petroglyphs are of the Southern San Rafael Style. The figures have an outline formed by solid pecking. Like the Barrier Canyon Style pictographs, human shapes tend to be tapered and have elaborate headgear. Facial features and jewelry are often shown. Fingers are splayed and the feet point out. The figures often hold shields. Later petroglyphs tended to be more realistic. Although there are petroglyphs scattered throughout the Swell, the two best panels are at Rochester Creek and in Three Finger Canyon.

By A.D. 1300 the Fremont Indians had left the canyon country. As with the Anasazi to the south, the reasons for this are not clear. Drought, disease, population pressures, or war-loving intruders are all possibilities.

The next inhabitants of the Swell were Ute and Piute Indians who migrated from the west and north. These Shoshoni-related peoples had not advanced culturally during the Basketmaker Stage as did the Fremont and Anasazi cultures. They retained the old Desert Culture tradition of hunting and gathering, and there is little evidence of their inhabitation of the Swell.

Spaniards and Mexicans entered the San Rafael Swell in the early 1800s. The Old Spanish Trail, a 1200-mile-long route going from Sante Fe to Los Angeles went along the east and north sides of the Swell bringing a large influx of newcomers. The trail took this northerly swing to avoid hostile Indians to the south. Used from 1829 to 1848, the Old Spanish Trail was utilized by traders taking goods from New Mexico to California and for taking cattle and horses from California to New Mexico.

The Mormons arrived en masse in the Great Salt Lake region in 1847 and 1848. It didn't take long for a few hardy Mormon pioneers to travel south and settle in the San Rafael Swell. They used the canyon bottoms in the winter and the top of the Swell (Sinbad Country) in the summer to graze their livestock. Though the Mormons did not build large settlements in the San Rafael Swell, they are responsible for the development of the towns surrounding the area: Ferron, Castle Dale, Grover, Hanksville, and Green River.

How to Use the Guide

> *One thing that appears clear to me now is that the moments of adventure—for the most adventurous—are widely separated by long periods of hard work. Perhaps it's best that way.*
>
> Kent Frost

The guide is set up in an orderly fashion. To get the most out of it and to help you understand some of the terminology, read this section carefully.

The guide is divided into eight chapters, each representing a cohesive and physically separate area. They are the Northern Reef and Mexican Mountain; Cedar Mountain and the Cleveland-Lloyd Dinosaur Quarry; Sids Mountain; Devils Canyon; the Mussentuchit Badlands, Cedar Mountain and the Moroni Slopes; Muddy Creek; Temple Mountain and the Southern Reef; and the Eastern Reef.

Each chapter is prefaced with a general overview of the area, its main features, and a short history. This is followed by a Road Section that describes the roads used to access the individual hikes. The Road Section is followed by a description of the hikes.

Road Sections

The San Rafael Swell is crisscrossed by a maze of roads. Most of these are unmarked, making it confusing for the first-time visitor. The Road Sections are designed to help alleviate the confusion.

The Road Sections direct you to the trailhead for each hike. They are placed in the guide immediately before the hikes to which they refer. The hikes accessed by a Road Section are noted at the top of each road description. In a few instances you will have to use two Road Sections to get to the start of a hike.

Each Road Section starts with a paragraph telling you how to get to the desired road from a major road, usually a highway or Interstate 70. The Road Section then informs you as to what type of vehicle is appropriate for that road. Vehicle type is broken down into four categories: any vehicle, light-duty vehicles, medium-duty vehicles, and four-wheel-drives (4WDs).

Any vehicle is just that: Winnebagos, Cadillacs, cars towing trailers, etc.

Light-duty vehicles include most small cars: Toyota Corollas, Subarus, Ford Tauruses, Nissans, etc.

Medium-duty vehicles include high-clearance vehicles: Volkswagen bugs and buses, short wheelbase vans, two-wheel-drive pickups, and mini-pickups.

Four-wheel-drive roads are rarely described in the guide. When they are mentioned, realize that these roads are for real 4WDs. The smaller four-wheel-drive cars—Audi, Subaru, and Toyota Tercels—do not have the ground clearance to make it over most of these roads.

With rain or snow any of the roads can be impassable even to 4WDs. On some roads short sections of deep sand can be encountered. Roads can change overnight. It is best to be wary. If in doubt walk through suspect sections of road first. Do not drive the roads at night. A black cow on a black road on a black night will not be seen. Roads that have washed out, sandy sections, deer, antelope, and jackasses (both types) will all conspire against you. Play it safe.

The introductory paragraph informs you whether there is camping in the area. This does not mean there is a campground. It simply means that there are short side roads, washes, or pullouts that can be used for camping. You can camp anywhere on the Swell as long as you do not damage the environment. Do not make your own track to a campsite. There are plenty enough already.

Next is the mileage list. It starts with a description of where the mileage starts. All mileage is cumulative. There are several features within the mileage lists. Often mileage is included so you can keep tabs on how things are going. This is meant to reassure. Though this may seem to be overkill at times, you will know whether you are at the right spot. Use these to add your own finds or to backtrack without having to go to the start of the road. When important side roads are reached, the mileage list for that road is included. At the trailhead, the number of the hike is printed in **bold type.**

There is a difference between a road and a track. A

road, though dirt or gravel, is one that is maintained by occasional grading. Tracks are not maintained. They tend to be rougher than roads.

If you don't have a trip odometer in your vehicle and you can't add and subtract in your head, bring a pocket calculator. I do. Maps can help, but they do not show many of the side roads.

Shorter hikes, those that don't warrant their own heading, are described in the Road Sections. They are all worthwhile.

Historical notes are added throughout the manuscript and often appear in the Road Sections.

Points of interest are noted in the Road Sections. These include exceptional overlooks, good campsites, and Indian art panels.

Some of the roads and tracks detailed in the guide may in the future be closed to vehicle traffic. Without definitive data it is impossible to provide accurate information on these possible closures. Most will be in wilderness areas.

The Road Sections may seem complicated at first, though they are infinitely less confusing than being lost in a maze of roads. Follow the Road Sections assiduously as you drive along.

Description of the Hikes

The description of each hike is prefaced by a concise section that will tell you at a glance the pertinent parameters for that hike. These include:

★   *Quality Star.* Hikes of exceptional quality are marked with a star.

Season. Any hike described can be done any time of year. I have picked the seasons I feel will be best for most people. I have also noted which seasons are considered the off-season, seasons when you will find little traffic and few people.

Early Spring and Spring—March to June—is usually an idyllic time on the Swell. Snowmelt ensures good water supplies. Occasional rain or snowstorms sweep the area.

Flowers start budding and blooming. This is the time to do hikes with potential water shortages in Cottonwood Wash and Devils Canyon. By the end of spring you will start seeing bugs in quantity.

Summer—June through July—has temperatures that occasionally go over 100 degrees and road temperatures that approach 140 degrees. This type of heat is unbearable to most hikers. Summer is the time to hike narrow canyons like Little Wild Horse, Quandary, or Cable. Hikes at higher elevations will be cooler. These include the San Rafael Knob and the Devils Racetrack. Bugs—gnats, mosquitoes, and deer flies—can be a real problem, especially along water courses. This is not the time to be on the San Rafael River or Muddy Creek.

Late Summer—August to mid-September—though still hot, has occasional rainstorms and fewer bugs. This is the time to do the Black Boxes.

Fall—September through November (off-season)—has the most settled weather, with warm days and cool nights. This is the ideal time to be on the Swell. All hikes are doable, though a lack of water can be a problem on some of the backpack trips.

Winter—December to March (off-season)—has temperatures that can drop to -10 degrees at night. Periods of cold weather are usually interspersed with periods of warm weather, with daytime temperatures getting up to 50 degrees. You should be prepared for the colder temperatures. There is rarely more than a couple of inches of snow on the ground except at the higher elevations and on north slopes. With snow on the ground, plan trips as you would for a winter mountaineering excursion. It is a rare day when there is enough snow to ski on. Winter is the time to do the nontechnical hikes in Eagle Canyon or to explore the Eastern and Northern reefs.

Roads have to be a consideration in winter. When snow covered they can be dangerous. When the days warm up, the roads turn into a slick clay, and even 4WDs will have problems.

Flash floods can occur in the narrower canyons. This becomes apparent when you see logs jammed well above the floor of a canyon. Stay out of narrow canyons when it is raining. They can flash flood even though it is not raining on you. An ominous rumble from up the canyon may signify a flood. Scramble to high ground.

Time. For the most part, the time listed is the time it will take the average, fit, and moderately experienced person to do the described hike. A hike that is for youngsters and seniors and takes three to four hours will take that long for them. A hike that takes ten to twelve hours for advanced canyoneers might take twenty hours for a beginner. The time does include a lunch break and short rest stops.

The mileage figures are to some extent guesswork. The mileage was measured on 7.5 series topographic maps and then compared to mileage guessed at in the field. None of the described hikes have been carefully measured on the ground. Time is a more accurate and more useful measurement than mileage.

Time is often mentioned in the body of the text, usually in terms of minutes, such as "it will take twelve minutes from the pinnacle to the next side canyon to the west." These time references are very important. Often you will have a choice to make among features that look similar. Time is often the element that ensures that you will make the right choice.

Elevation gain. This figure shows the most sustained single rise or fall on a hike. If there are multiple long ascents or descents they will be mentioned in the text.

Water. Water is invariably available through winter to early spring. After a good rain or snow, water can stay in potholes for days or weeks, even in the summer. Water is often the determining factor in deciding which hike to take. Many a desert agenda has changed due to a lack of or abundance of water. Springs marked on the maps are unreliable. Do not count on them to be where marked or to be full.

In hot weather water requirements go up. In midsummer, with temperatures near 100 degrees, two gallons over a twelve-hour period may be realistic. Alcohol promotes dehydration. Wait until the end of your hike to imbibe.

All water should be treated or filtered, without exception. Giardia is everywhere in the Swell. It is a protozoa that can cause you no end of bowel distress if you should happen to "get the bug." For some, hospitalization becomes necessary due to massive fluid loss leading to dehydration. Because Giardia protozoa is encased in a hard shell it is difficult to kill. Research has shown that there are several effective methods for eradicating the pest.

Heat your water. Giardia is killed at temperatures of about 170 degrees. You just need to bring the water to a boil. You don't have to keep boiling it.

Use iodine. The 2 percent tincture of iodine liquid available at the grocery store works well. Add two drops per quart if the water is clear. Add four drops per quart if the water is cloudy. If the water is over 68 degrees let it sit for thirty minutes before drinking it. If it is cooler than that, you will have to let it sit for a longer period. Iodine pills (Potable Aqua) work fine but are expensive. Always use fresh iodine liquid or pills. Iodine loses some of its effectiveness when exposed to air. Some people get a sore throat from using iodine for long periods of time.

Chlorine and halazone. These are ineffective against Giardia though they are effective against other bacteria.

Filters. Though some of the older, charcoal-based filters did not remove Giardia well, the new generation of filters will all do the trick. The ceramic Katydyn Filter works especially well and will last the average hiker a lifetime.

Some of the water in the Swell is either from sulphur springs or is highly mineralized. The taste can be masked with powdered drink mixes. Some of the water may act as a laxative, while water from other sources may cause constipation.

Maps. There are three types of maps listed in this guide. Those listed first are USGS 7.5 minute series topographic maps. The scale is 1:24,000. These are the most current maps available and have replaced the notoriously inaccurate and out-of-date 15 minute series topographic maps. They are listed in the order of overall importance to the hike. All map references contained in the text refer to the 7.5 minute maps.

The maps listed second, in parentheses ( ), are USGS 15 minute series topographic maps. The scale is 1:62,500. The 15 minute maps that are no longer available are not listed.

The maps listed third, in brackets [ ], are the USGS metric series topographic maps. These are at a scale of 1:100,000. They cover a lot of territory and are not detailed enough to use for hiking. They do show the roads well and are included for that purpose. Metric maps are noted at the top of each Road Section. Use the metric maps to get to the trailhead; then use the 7.5 minute maps on the hike itself.

All three map types are available from:

United States Geological Survey
Box 25286, Federal Center, Bldg. 25
Denver, Colorado 80225

Ask for the "Index to Topographic and Other Map Coverage for Utah" and an order form. These are free. The 7.5 and 15 minute maps are currently $2.50. The metric maps are $4.00. It takes the USGS about two months to process an order, so plan ahead. Most major university libraries have these maps. Look in the government documents section. They can be photocopied for half the price of new maps.

The metric maps are available at BLM and Forest Service offices throughout the state. These offices, however, do not have the 7.5 and 15 minute maps.

Circle trip. Most of the hikes are designed to be circle trips.

Skill level. Don't kid yourself here. Have an idea of your capabilities. Realize that if you are not prepared mentally and physically for some of the routes you could get yourself and your party into serious trouble. For those new to the canyon country, start with shorter, easier hikes. Get a feel for the terrain, your reaction to it, and the problems off-trail hiking present.

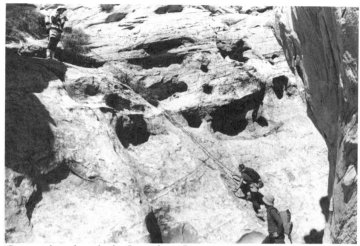

Overcoming obstacles in Quandary Canyon.

Many of the routes in the guide are technical, requir-
ing the use of climbing ropes and other specialized
equipment. Unless you have extensive experience using
this equipment, stay away from the technical routes.
Proper techniques can be learned by attending a climbing
school. Many universities offer such courses. At the
present time there are no commercial outfitters offering
backpacking and climbing trips into the San Rafael Swell.

Difficulties in route finding can take several forms. In-
terpreting the guide and matching it with what you see
admittedly can be confusing. Picking your way up or
down steep ledges or in and out of canyon systems can
be frustrating and time consuming. The 7.5 minute
maps have contour intervals of forty feet. A thirty-five-
foot cliff will not be shown on the map. After a 500-foot
hike up a steep, loose, and troublesome slope it is not
fun to find a twenty-foot cliff blocking progress. A hundred dead-end canyons were hiked in preparing this
guide so you wouldn't have to.

The Yosemite Decimal System is used to describe how
rough the terrain is. This system has been used for years
by hikers and climbers throughout the United States. It
describes only the hardest, most technical part of the
hike. The Yosemite Decimal System is broken down into
five classes:

1. Trail or flat walking. No objective dangers.

2. | Off-trail walking, some scrambling and boulder hopping. Steeper terrain.
3. | Definite scrambling. Hands may be needed for balance. Exposure to heights possible.
4. | Large hand and foot holds are used. A fall could have serious consequences. The use of a rope with beginners may be necessary. This is as hard as the average, experienced, and fit hiker can handle. If you get to a section that looks too hard, don't do it. A brave, dead canyoneer is remembered not as brave but as dead.
5. | The fifth class category, which is the start of roped climbing, is broken down into smaller segments: 5.0 to 5.14. In the guide no problems are over 5.6 in difficulty. If you are not familiar with roped climbing techniques you should stay away from the fifth class routes. Experienced rock-climbers may wish to forgo a rope on some routes. For them exposure levels are important. A 5.6 move on a ten-foot wall is not that dangerous while a 5.4 move thirty feet off the deck is a bit more serious. There should be at least one person in your party who can lead the hard parts of a route without protection. Belay anchors are usually nonexistent. Exposure heights are given in the description of the hike when applicable. Example: (5.4, 30') means there is a thirty-foot-high wall, slab, or chimney that has a 5.4 move at its hardest part. All ratings are assuming tennis shoes or hiking boots. Specialized rock boots could drastically lower the ratings.

There are other notes included under Skill level. Hikes that entail swimming are mentioned. Depending on the length of the swim, a life jacket or an inner tube may be needed. Hikes that involve wading will require the use of wading shoes. Overnight hikers *must* be skilled in low-impact camping techniques. (See the chapter "Protecting the Environment" for details.)

Although tennis shoes are adequate for wading, an old pair of lug-soled hiking shoes are preferred. Sandals and neoprene booties do not provide enough support or protection.

Hikes that have exposed sections of climbing or rappels may necessitate the use of a rope and other climbing paraphernalia. When ropes are mentioned, realize that old clothesline, ski ropes, or nylon parachute cord are not adequate. Suitable climbing equipment and a knowledge of how to use it properly is essential.

The use of mountain bikes continues to grow throughout the canyon country. They often work well in the Swell. Unlike ORVs, mountain bikes cannot go off road, with the rare exception of a hard-packed wash, and are, therefore, usually environmentally acceptable. Mountain bikes are not allowed in wilderness study areas. Abide by all posted signs. You will need a long cable or chain to lock your bike to trees.

Each route description starts with a brief summary of the hike. Within the body of the text are several things to note. *Digressions* describe short side trips or note points of interest. *Rock-climber's notes* describe short, difficult side trips or variations that will be of interest to rock-climbers. Pinnacles with potential routes are also mentioned. The *Historical notes* bring a sense of history to the hikes.

A compass is essential when using the guide. Compass readings are used extensively. Don't count on your innate sense of direction to get you through. A couple of sharp turns in a sinuous canyon and you will be confused. Inexpensive compasses work as well as expensive ones.

LDC means Looking Down Canyon. LUC means Looking Up Canyon.

Names for features are as historically accurate as possible. In several instances more than one name was found for a feature; e.g., Delicate Arch in Spring Canyon has at least three documented names. I picked the name I liked best. If no names were found, I took the liberty of putting a simple name on the feature. Those I named are followed with an (AN), Author's Name, after the first time the feature is mentioned in the text. Names may differ locally.

Nearly all of the mine sites in the San Rafael Swell are the remnants of the uranium mining that took place from the turn of the century to the mid-1960s. Though recent medical evidence has shown that there is little danger from short-term exposure to radon gas, which collects in the old mine shafts, the mine sites do contain other dangers. Stagnant, oxygenless air, caught in pockets in the mines, can cause asphyxiation. The old mine tunnels are also in imminent danger of collapsing and contain vertical shafts that are often difficult to see. Be safe. Stay out of the old mine shafts and tunnels.

1 | The Northern Reef and Mexican Mountain

The Northern Reef and the Mexican Mountain areas are in the northeastern part of the San Rafael Swell. They are bounded by the Cottonwood Wash road on the west, Interstate 70 on the south, the Tidwell Draw road on the east, and Cedar Mountain on the north.

The Northern Reef, located on the eastern edge of the Swell, is readily visible from Interstate 70. It is a compact area that has seen little use by canyoneers. Deep, unexplored canyons, seldom-visited arches, towers, pinnacles, and slickrock domes provide an opportunity for exceptional and usually solitary hiking.

The Mexican Mountain area is to the west of the Northern Reef. It is dominated by the San Rafael River as it sweeps through the Mexican Bend, around Mexican Mountain, and exits the reef to the north of Black Dragon Wash. The area is most well known for the Upper and Lower Black Boxes. These are sections of the San Rafael River where the river has cut deeply into the Coconino Sandstone, leaving a narrow, high-walled canyon behind. The boxes are beautiful and challenging to negotiate. A canyoneer's dream.

The Northern Reef and the Mexican Mountain areas are well suited for day hiking, though there are several backpacking trips described. With the use of the guide other multiday trips will be easy to design. Both areas are in the Mexican Mountain Wilderness Study Area.

The Buckhorn Wash, Mexican Mountain, and Black Dragon Wash roads are used by ORVs in the summer and on most holiday weekends. The track from the end of the Mexican Mountain road to Mexican Bend is closed to vehicles.

Historically the Northern Reef and Mexican Mountain areas are steeped in local lore. They were roamed by Butch Cassidy and his Hole-in-the-Wall gang in the 1880s. Spring Canyon, north of Mexican Bend, was the site of a shootout between one gang member, Joe Walker, and the local sheriff. The Horse Thief Trail, to

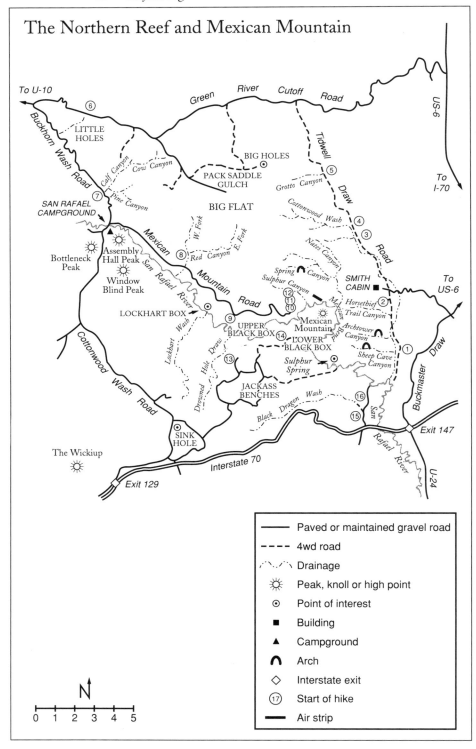

The Northern Reef and Mexican Mountain

To U-10

Green   River   Cutoff   Road

US-6

6

Buckhorn Wash Road

LITTLE
HOLES

To
I-70

Calf Canyon

Cow Canyon

BIG HOLES

Tidwell   Draw

Grotto Canyon

5

PACK SADDLE
GULCH

7

Pine Canyon

BIG FLAT

Cottonwood   Wash

4

3

SAN RAFAEL
CAMPGROUND

W. Fork

Nates Canyon

Road

To
US-6

Bottleneck
Peak

Assembly
Hall Peak

8

Red Canyon

E. Fork

Mexican

Spring   Canyon

SMITH
CABIN

2

Window
Blind Peak

San Rafael River

Mountain

Road

Sulphur Canyon

Horsethief

Mexican Trail Canyon

12
11
10

LOCKHART BOX

9

UPPER
BLACK BOX

Mexican
Mountain

Archtower
Canyon

Lockhart   Wash

14

LOWER
BLACK BOX

Sheep Cave
Canyon

1

Drowned   Hole   Draw

13

Sulphur
Spring

Buckmaster   Draw

Cottonwood   Wash   Road

JACKASS
BENCHES

Black   Dragon   Wash

16

San

15

SINK
HOLE

Rafael   River

Exit 147

The Wickiup

Interstate 70

U-24

Exit 129

——	Paved or maintained gravel road
- - - -	4wd road
⌒‿⌒	Drainage
☀	Peak, knoll or high point
⊙	Point of interest
■	Building
▲	Campground
⌒	Arch
◇	Interstate exit
⑰	Start of hike
▬	Air strip

N

0 1 2 3 4 5

the east of the bend, was used to bring stolen livestock from Tidwell Draw and the San Rafael Desert over the reef and into the bend.

The Old Spanish Trail followed the east side of the Northern Reef. It was a single track trail until 1849 when Mormon pioneers started using four-wheeled wagons. The main trail went along the east face of the Northern Reef, passing Trail Spring near Tidwell Draw. This was called Akanaquint Spring by the Ute Indians. It then went north to the Big Holes in Packsaddle Gulch and west, under Cedar Mountain, by the Little Holes, and finally to Red Seep. From there the trail dropped off the Swell into Castle Valley. Other versions went through Buckhorn Wash and Spotted Wolf Canyon, where Interstate 70 now cuts through the Reef.

Signs of Indian habitation are visible at the many pictograph and petroglyph panels scattered throughout the Mexican Mountain area. The most famous pictograph panel, at mile 5.6 on the Buckhorn Wash road, has been vandalized. The Cattle Guard panel at mile 2.3 on the Buckhorn Wash road, the pictograph panels in Black Dragon Wash, and the petroglyph panels at the mouth of Spring Canyon at Mexican Bend are now perhaps the best in the area.

Buckmaster Draw Road Section

Access to Hikes #1 through 5
Access is from Interstate 70.
Provides access to the Tidwell Draw tracks.
Metric map—San Rafael Desert. Huntington.

This road goes north from Interstate 70 and intersects the Tidwell Draw tracks. From Green River go west for eleven miles on Interstate 70 to Exit 147. This is also the exit for Highway 24, which goes south to Hanksville and Lake Powell. Though Highway 24 does not go north, the graded Buckmaster Draw road does. It is for light-duty vehicles. The road, though not particularly scenic, is suitable for mountain bikes. There is camping along the road.

0.0	Mileage starts at a cattle guard just north of Interstate 70 and goes north.
1.8	Corral on the left.
2.6	Mine works on the right.
3.4	Maintenance sheds on the left. For a short hike and spectacular views of the Northern and Eastern reefs hike up the hill to the west of the sheds. The Archtower is visible halfway up the face of the reef directly to the west. It is possible to get to Archtower Canyon from here by making your way down several cliff bands and crossing the strike valley to the west.
4.1	Derrick down and to the left.
4.6	Marked four-way junction. Sign to Highway 50–6 (now 191–6). Go left (N).
	The road to the right (S) goes to Buckmaster Reservoir. The road going straight ahead (E) intersects Highway 191–6 a mile north of I–70.
5.0	Metal buildings on the right.
6.9	Marked junction. Sign to Trail Spring and Tidwell. Go left (NW).
8.2	"Y." Go left.
10.2	Wire gate.
11.4	Junction with the Tidwell Draw tracks.
	If you go too far west you will run into the Smith Cabin. It was a well-known homestead in the 1920s. A spring watered the homestead until a seismograph crew did some test blasts nearby, which dried up the spring. The Smith Cabin was occupied by Tom Tidwell and his sons who ran cattle throughout the area. It is worth a look. On the Mexican Mountain map the cabin is shown but is unlabeled a quarter mile west of elevation 4548 at a marked spring.
	To find the junction with the Tidwell Draw tracks backtrack east from the Smith Cabin for 0.2 mile.

Tidwell Draw—South—Road Section

Access to Hikes #1 and 2
Access is from the Buckmaster Draw road.
Metric map—San Rafael Desert. Huntington.

This track starts east of the Smith Cabin on the Buckmaster Draw road and goes south along the foot of the Northern Reef to the San Rafael River. The area from the Smith Cabin south to mile 5.9 is considered Tidwell Draw. The area south of mile 5.9 to the San Rafael River is called Tidwell Bottoms. Light-duty vehicles may be able to get to mile 0.9. Medium-duty vehicles can get to mile 2.0. Mountain bikes can go about five miles down the track if the rider is willing to negotiate several sandy sections. There is camping in the area.

0.0	Mileage starts 0.2 mile east of the Smith Cabin on the Buckmaster Draw road at a multistemmed juniper. The track goes south up a small hill.
0.6	"Y." Go left (S) down the Tidwell Draw track.

The start of Acer's Arch and the Horse Thief Trail **Hike #2** is to the right. Go up the track for 0.2 mile (SW) to a flat area with a drill pipe standing at one end. Park at the pipe. (It is shown on the Mexican Mountain map as a Drill Hole southwest of elevation 4550.)

0.9	A bad gully crossing. It will stop some vehicles.
1.1	A break in the face of the reef to the west. This is the mouth of Horse Thief Trail Canyon and the exit point for Acer's Arch Hike #2.
1.6	At a watering trough. A track to the right (W) goes to a corral.
2.0	Start of a very rough section of road. Most vehicles will have to stop here. Since most will either walk or ride mountain bikes from this point, the track will be described in detail. Close attention should be paid to landmarks as the start to Hike #1 is hard to find.

From mile 2.0 the track goes down a bumpy, rocky section and enters a wash with fifteen-foot-high walls.

3.0	Start of a white sand trap. This will bog down 4WDs. Bicycles will have to be carried.
	To find the mouth of Archtower Canyon look for a wood trough to the right (W) just as the wash walls end. Archtower Canyon starts just past the trough and goes west.
3.1	End of the white sand trap.
	From here go up a red hill and across a flat area, then down a gentle hill to the start of a level plain. There are many cottonwoods to the left (E) as you enter a wash area. Continue on the track past one wash until a second wash is reached.
3.9	The wash is the start of Sheep Cave and Archtower Canyons **Hike #1.** To make sure you are in the right place, look to the southwest for a pyramid-shaped formation and to its right for a tower with a small pinnacle on its left side. The track exits the wash and goes up a red hill. Park or lock bikes at the wash. A line of cottonwoods and vegetation going west marks the start of Sheep Cave Canyon.

The track continues south for another two miles to a wire gate. It is a 20-minute walk from the gate to the San Rafael River. Many rarely explored canyons can be accessed from this section of the Tidwell Draw track.

Sheep Cave (AN) and Archtower Canyons (AN)—Hike #1

Season	Any. Spring and fall are best.
Time	5 to 7 hours. Add 1 to 1.5 hours if you start hiking at mile 2.0 on the Tidwell Draw track. A mountain bike can cut the road time considerably (8 miles).
Elevation gain	1100′
Water	Seasonal. There are springs extending halfway up Sheep Cave Canyon. There are small springs in lower Archtower Canyon. Bring your own water.

Maps	Spotted Wolf Canyon. Mexican Mountain. The canyons are shown but are not labeled on the maps. Archtower Canyon is south of elevation 4826 and Sheep Cave Canyon is between elevations 4343 and 4365 on the Spotted Wolf Canyon map. [San Rafael Desert. Huntington.]
Circle trip	Yes
Skill level	Moderate route finding. Class 3 scrambling. This can be a long day if you have to walk from mile 2.0 on the Tidwell Draw track.

Often the far view of an area does not reveal its hidden treasures. From a distance this part of the Northern Reef does not look like it has much to offer. The canyons that run into and through it are hidden in a tangle of Navajo slickrock faces and domes. Both Sheep Cave and Archtower canyons do not stand out. But once you have found your way into them, they are true gems.

The hike goes up Sheep Cave Canyon, under one of the few natural bridges in the San Rafael Swell, to the rim of an escarpment that overlooks the San Rafael River, with spectacular views of Mexican Mountain and Mexican Bend. To return, the route drops into Archtower Canyon and passes the Archtower before exiting back onto the Tidwell Draw track.

Hike up the wash to the west. Springs appear and grass lines the water course. After five minutes the shallow canyon divides. Stay left (W). A minute later, at the top of a grassy section, the canyon seems to end. Go left (SW) up a triangular slickrock ramp. It ends in fifty yards. Continue up the shallow wash. After passing an area of springs the canyon narrows. A series of large potholes is encountered. Above the potholes the canyon enters a park and divides. Continue straight (W). Pass a fall on either side. The Sheep Cave is high on the hillside to the right (LUC). As evidenced by the amount of scat in the cave, it is apparent that this is a favorite bighorn getaway. It is best not to hike up to the cave.

The next falls are terraced and can be passed on the right (LUC). At the top of the fall the canyon divides. Find your way into the canyon to the left (LUC)(S).

After a half hour of glorious walking, much of it on slickrock, pass under the undocumented Ednah Natural

Ednah Natural Bridge in Sheep Cave Canyon.

Bridge. This is a great lunch spot. It will take 2 to 2.5 hours to reach the bridge.

On up. Within ten minutes the now shallow canyon nearly ends in a parklike area. Continue northwest staying with the main channel. As the canyon tapers to nothing, a ridge straight ahead (W) comes into view. It is characterized by a pinnacle on its left side and two triangular-shaped domes on its right side. Pass the ridge on its north side. Hike up for several more minutes until an escarpment is reached. Below you is the San Rafael River as it makes the Mexican Bend around Mexican Mountain. Looking southwest one can see the start of the Lower Black Box and Swaseys Leap (Hike #14). To the north is the wide, barren mouth of Spring Canyon (Hikes #4 and 12).

> **Historical note:** Mexican Bend was named for a Mexican who ran horses along the river. It was also used by the Hole-in-the-Wall gang, and later the Tidwells, who brought their livestock over from Tidwell Draw on the Horse Thief Trail.

One-half mile to the northeast is a brown cliff band running northwest to southeast. This is the top of Archtower Canyon. It is the descent route. Hike northeast toward the brown cliff, crossing washes and gullies. Drop into the canyon just after passing the Archtower on its north side. The Archtower is a Northern Reef surprise. It is 200 feet tall, spectacular in itself, but it also contains a large arch. (The Archtower is a quarter mile northwest of elevation 5180 on the Spotted Wolf Canyon map.)

> **Rock-climber's note:** The Archtower, made of Navajo Sandstone, has several excellent route possibilities, especially for off-width specialists.

Below a beautiful set of slickrock potholes the canyon merges with several other canyons. The drop here can be passed on the right. The next fall can be descended to the right of center (Class 4) or up and around to the left (LDC). From here the hiking is easy. Springs appear as you approach Tidwell Draw.

Acer's Arch (AN) and the Horse Thief Trail—Hike #2

Season	Any. Summer can be hot.
Time	4 to 6 hours (7 miles)
Elevation gain	800'
Water	None. Bring your own water.
Maps	Mexican Mountain. Horse Thief Trail Canyon is shown but is not labeled on the map. It ends on the Tidwell Draw track at the prospect north of elevation 4475. (Tidwell Bottoms) [San Rafael Desert. Huntington.]
Circle trip	Yes
Skill level	Moderate route finding. Class 3 scrambling.

The hike to Acer's Arch is different, perhaps sublime. It goes nowhere exceptional, yet it winds its way up small canyons, around Navajo domes, in and out of sandy washes, and climaxes at the top of the Northern Reef with thrilling panoramas and a seldom-visited arch.

Though there is no exact route specified to take you to the top of the reef, there are two options detailed for returning to the start.

From the drill pipe simply ramble west as you make

your way up the face of the reef. There are many possibilities. Pick a route that suits your taste and abilities. It will take most people two to three hours to reach the top of the reef.

Once there you will be looking 900 feet down an escarpment at the San Rafael River as it makes the Mexican Bend around Mexican Mountain. You can see an abandoned airstrip paralleling the river. Coming into the bend from the right (N) is Spring Canyon (Hikes #4 and 12).

To return, there are two alternatives. Alternate 1 is technically harder, but it is shorter and goes past Acer's Arch and down the eastern section of the Horse Thief Trail. Alternate 2 is a couple of miles longer, but it is a must for the photographer as it follows the rim of Spring Canyon for a mile, always showing a new face to the camera enthusiast.

Alternate 1: Go south, following close to the rim of the escarpment. After a short hike you will intersect Horse Thief Trail Canyon as it comes in from the east. It is the first deep canyon you will run into. To descend into the canyon go downhill (E), again staying close to the rim. After several hundred yards an unlikely looking cleft appears to the right (LDC). A cairn is at its head. Scramble down the cleft (Class 3) until the small, double Acer's Arch is reached.

> **Digression:** From inside the arch look southwest toward a saddle at the top of Horse Thief Trail Canyon. On the rim is a large cairn. This marks the top of the route down to Mexican Bend via the western section of the Horse Thief Trail (Hike #11). (This is shown as elevation 5370 on the Mexican Mountain map.)

From Acer's Arch you can clearly see the route down Horse Thief Trail Canyon. The slope below the arch looks worse than it is. Pick your way down broken ledges until the canyon floor is reached; then hike east down the canyon to the Tidwell Draw track. Go north back to the start.

Alternate 2: Go right (N)—perhaps after a short excursion to Acer's Arch—and follow a bumpy course along the rim. There are varied views of Spring Canyon as the Mexican Bend is left behind. For the next fifty minutes try to stay as close to the rim as possible, veering away now and again to negotiate obstacles.

Approach a slickrock ridge that impedes progress. It is characterized by six domelike humps, with a seal-shaped pinnacle in the middle of them. (These are shown a quarter mile south of elevation 5642.) On the rim, several hundred yards before the domed ridge, there is a pipe-type bench mark in a cairn. It is a definitive landmark. Watch for it.

Deep in Spring Canyon you will see a freestanding, pinnacled fin. This fin is near the division of Spring and Nates canyons (Hikes #4 and 12). To the south of the fin on the far wall, visible only if the light is right, is Delicate Arch.

To the southeast of the cairn is the head of a southeast-running canyon. Descend this canyon. You will have to work your way past several boulder fields. As the canyon widens several plunge pools appear. Further along a large fall is encountered. Looking down the canyon you will recognize the Smith Cabin. Bypass the fall on either side and drop to the cabin, or cut diagonally right (SE) across several washes back to the start.

Tidwell Draw—North—Road Section

Access to Hikes #3 through 5
Access is from the Buckmaster Draw road.
Provides access to the Green River Cutoff road.
Metric map—San Rafael Desert. Huntington.

This track starts east of the Smith Cabin on the Buckmaster Draw road and goes north along the foot of the Northern Reef to the Green River Cutoff road. The Old Spanish Trail paralleled the track, though signs of it have been obliterated by time. The track is for medium-duty vehicles. This section of road is not suitable for mountain bikes. There is camping along the road.

0.0	Mileage starts 0.2 mile east of the Smith Cabin at a wire gate just north of the Buckmaster Draw road and goes north.
1.2	"Y." Go right.
1.3	Wire gate.
2.9	Cross Cottonwood Wash. The wash rarely has more than a couple of inches of water, so it is not hard to ford. The Old Spanish Trail went along Cottonwood Wash, though it did not enter the canyon itself. There are small pools along Cottonwood Wash in the mile above the crossing.
3.2	Start of Pinnacle Canyon **Hike #3**. Park next to power pole #1061.
	For the next several miles the track follows a line of power poles. Each pole has a number on a small silver tag. You will have to do a little exploring to find some of the numbered poles as they are often several hundred yards from the track.
4.5	Start of Cottonwood Wash **Hike #4.** You are on top of a rise. The mouth of Cottonwood Wash (a canyon) is to the west. Park just past power pole #1052.
	As you continue north the track winds under the power poles. Note numbers as this will help locate the start of Grotto Canyon Hike #5.
7.0	Start of Grotto Canyon **Hike #5.** The hike starts at power pole #1034, which is several hundred yards to the west of the track. You are in the middle of a flat plain. Unfortunately there are no landmarks here.
	You have been paralleling an old railroad bed. It was built in the 1880s, but track was never laid. Note the stonework culverts.
8.3	Wire gate.
10.2	Cross a slickrock wash. You can do a short, easy hike up the canyon to the west. Two-hour round trip.
10.4	Cattle troughs to the right.
12.5	El Rancho Not So Grande to the right.
12.6	Junction with the Green River Cutoff road.

Pinnacle Canyon (AN)—Hike #3

Season	Any. No snow.
Time	2 to 3 hours (3.5 miles)
Elevation gain	250'
Water	Seasonal potholes. Bring your own water.
Map	Mexican Mountain. Pinnacle Canyon is shown but is not labeled on the map. It starts at elevation 4770. [Huntington. San Rafael Desert.]
Circle trip	Yes
Skill level	Advanced route finding. Class 5.3 climbing. Rock-climbers only. Those less experienced will need a rope.

This short "after dinner" hike is designed for the adventurous rock-climber. Physical challenges combine with a beautiful backdrop to set the tone for the hike.

The route ascends the face of the Northern Reef while following a shallow canyon. After negotiating a steep slab, the route ends in a parklike area containing a 125-foot-tall pinnacle. A Navajo-walled canyon is followed back to the start.

From the power pole, go west across Cottonwood Wash. Hike up a shallow gully. Pass the first fall to the left. The second fall is three tiered. Pass it and the third fall on either side. Above the third fall enter a parklike area. Stay with the main, sand-floored wash. It enters another park, makes a backwards S-shaped turn, and straightens out. Near the end of the park the wash makes an abrupt right turn (NW). After six minutes the sandy wash divides. Stay with the main channel to the right. One minute later the wash divides again. Go right (NW).

The canyon deepens quickly and dead ends. The only outlet is a steep slickrock gully to the west. Scramble up this (Class 4). At its end climb a slickrock slab to the left (LUC)(5.3, 30'). Circle to the top of the fall. Continue up the main wash. After a couple of minutes it divides, the main course going left (S). Go right (W). In another minute the wash divides again. Go right (NW). Hike up an indistinct gully for several hundred yards. You are in a park with the pinnacle straight ahead.

The pinnacle in Pinnacle Canyon.

Digression: Several hundred yards west of the pinnacle is a small gully going through the north wall. It can provide some climbing fun. Chimney up the start of the gully, which invariably has water in it. Surmount a yellow-striped friction slab to the north (5.6, 35′). Continue west over a slickrock ridge to the rim of Nates Canyon (Hike #4). If you do not want to backclimb the route, you can follow the canyon to the north of Pinnacle Canyon back to the start.

To return go down the canyon that starts on the far side of the pinnacle (E). This canyon has many small arches hidden throughout its length. You will end up within a quarter mile of the start, between power poles #1156 and 1157.

★ | # Cottonwood Wash—Hike #4

Season | Any but summer. It is best in early spring, spring, or fall. Water can be a problem on the first two days, so try to do this hike after a rain.

Time	4 to 7 days. This will depend on which digressions you choose to do (29 miles without digressions).
Elevation gain	The most sustained vertical rise is 900 feet.
Water	Seasonal. There is always water in the first mile of Cottonwood Wash. There is seasonal water in its upper reaches. The area adjacent to the Thin Man Pinnacle in Sulphur Canyon has seasonal pothole water. It may be necessary to carry water for the first two days of the hike, from Cottonwood Wash to the San Rafael River. There is usually water in Spring Canyon just past the pinnacled fin. Lower Nates Canyon has seasonal potholes.
Maps	Mexican Mountain. Devils Hole. [Huntington. San Rafael Desert.]
Circle trip	Yes
Skill level	Moderate/advanced route finding. Class 4 climbing. Possibility of little water along the route. Familiarity with low-impact camping techniques is essential. A short rope will be useful for lowering packs.

This is a classic canyoneering trip. Variety, views, deep canyons, wide-open bench lands, arches, and pinnacles give character to these little-known and seldom-visited masterpieces. For the canyoneer there are falls to surmount, route-finding difficulties, a seasonal lack of water, and at several places a touch of the climbing challenge. Though a bit stiff, the rewards are exceptional. This trip could undoubtedly be hiked in three days, but four days allow for a more relaxed pace. With side adventures abounding, this could easily be extended to a week. Side-trip possibilities will be mentioned.

The route goes to the top of Cottonwood Wash (a canyon) and drops onto Big Flat. This is crossed to the top of Sulphur Canyon, which is descended to the San Rafael River. The river is followed to Mexican Bend. From there the route goes up Spring Canyon and into Nates Canyon, which you ascend to the top of the Northern Reef. You descend the reef back to the start.

Fifty yards past the power pole is a track going west. Walk down the track into the Navajo-walled canyon.

Digression: There is a petroglyph panel near the mouth of the canyon. It is a little tricky to find. Several minutes after entering the canyon it deepens. To the south are several down-sloping caves, one above the other, in the middle of the canyon wall. Up and to the right of the caves is a small pinnacle. Across the canyon, to the north, ascend a slope to the base of a red-and-black Navajo wall. The petroglyphs are on the wall fifty yards before the bench ends in a drop. Though well worn by time, they have not been vandalized.

For the first forty-five minutes the walking is easy, mostly along cattle trails. This first section would be an ideal, short day hike for those less active or with young children.

The canyon divides. Stay with the main course to the right (NW). Thirty minutes later the canyon divides again. Stay left this time (SW). The canyon gets a little narrower.

After another thirty minutes a large fall and pool are reached. Backtrack for several hundred yards. Go around the fall to the left (LUC). Stay high until the next fall is passed; then return to the canyon floor. A quarter mile above the second fall the canyon divides again. Stay to the right (NW). Thirty minutes later the canyon divides. Go right (N). (You will be below elevation 6105 on the Mexican Mountain map.) A short way up is a lovely seasonal pond and a hanging garden. The next split is in ten minutes. Make your way into the drainage to the right (LUC)(N).

Ten minutes later you reach the final split. Go right (N). Just past the split, pass a small fall to the left (Class 3). Before this fall, to the right (LUC), is a small seasonal spring and a pleasant overhang for camping. This may be the last water in the canyon. Camp here the first night. It will take four to five hours to reach this point.

The canyon enters a park. The walls are weatherworn and twisted. Hike straight ahead (W) up steep slickrock to a saddle. From the saddle pick your way down a steep slope to the west-northwest, heading toward a large flat area (Big Hole Wash). Note the small arch to the left. (You enter Big Hole Wash just south of elevation 6035 on the Devils Hole map.)

Once down to Big Hole Wash, follow it southwest for ten minutes until a large fall is reached. Pass this obstacle to the left (LUC). Three washes merge at the top of the fall. Go south, up the middle wash. After several minutes, pass a fall to the right (LUC). Continue up the wash for a short distance until you are on Big Flat. Go south-southwest down the middle of Big Flat until you intersect a track. Follow this south for thirty minutes until it takes you through a half-mile-long section of Navajo domes and buttresses. (You will be east of elevation 6460X on the Devils Hole map.)

> **Digression:** South of the domes, to the right (W), is a large canyon. This is the head of the East Fork of Red Canyon (Hike #8).

Past the buttresses, angle left (SE) for several minutes until on the top of a small rise. (The track ends at a fence, though ORVs have continued on.) Nates Ridge, with the Beaver's Tail Pinnacle (AN) on its left side, comes into view to the southeast. The Beaver's Tail is small and doesn't look like a beaver's tail yet, but it will shortly.

Hike cross-country to the west side of Nates Ridge; then head south.

> **Digression:** The first canyon head you pass to the east is Nates Canyon. You can follow it east down into Spring Canyon. There are several falls to negotiate, but all are easy. The fall at the east end of a long open area is the same fall mentioned at the end of this route description. You can follow those directions for exiting the canyon and returning to the start.

In a half hour you will intersect the North Fork of Spring Canyon. (See Hike #12 for details.) Go around the head of the canyon to the west, then continue south until you reach a grand overlook. (This overlook is shown halfway between elevations 6814 and 6832 on the Devils Hole map.) Below you is the San Rafael River. Far down the canyon to the east is the Mexican Bend sweeping around Mexican Mountain. You will see what looks like a perfectly straight section of road. This old landing strip is your destination.

From the overlook go northeast down a short hill and onto a white, flat area, then to the rim of an escarpment.

Follow the rim north for fifteen minutes until you reach a red, Wingate-walled canyon which drops steeply to the southeast toward the San Rafael River. This is Sulphur Canyon. (It is not named on either the Mexican Mountain or Devils Hole maps, but it is shown as the first major drainage to the south of Spring Canyon. The entrance to the canyon is a half mile to the east-southeast of elevation 6814 on the Devils Hole map.) If there are any doubts as to whether this is the correct canyon, continue along the rim of the escarpment for a couple of hundred yards; then look down into Sulphur Canyon. The Thin Man Pinnacle (AN) and its two smaller cousins should be visible.

> **Digression:** To go down the South Fork of Spring Canyon, go north-northeast from the top of Sulphur Canyon for a half mile. Once over a steep hill there are two Navajo domes to the right (E). (The dome to the south is elevation 6842 on the Devils Hole map.) (See Hike #12 for details on continuing from this point.)

To enter Sulphur Canyon go down to the right (LDC) toward a large detached flake. Descend a short wall behind the flake (Class 4, 20′); then scramble down 750 feet to a wonderful flat area, with the 175-foot-tall Thin Man Pinnacle to the right (S). If there is pothole water here, this is a delightful camping area. It is recommended for the second night out. It will take six to eight hours from the last recommended campsite to the Thin Man Pinnacle.

Drop another 950 feet down an arduous, boulder-choked gully; then hike down the canyon until the San Rafael River is reached.

> **Digression:** The Upper Black Box is a twenty-minute walk upriver (Hike #9). It would be impractical to hike the whole Black Box from here, as it would entail hiking along a motor road. It is feasible to hike and swim up its lower section. The start of the Mexican Mountain Traverse hike also starts near here (Hike #10).

The Mexican Mountain road runs parallel to the river on the left as you go east down the canyon. After several miles the canyon opens into a park with many cotton-

The Thin Man Pinnacle in Sulphur Canyon.

woods and the abandoned airstrip. If the cattle aren't out and there are no insects, Mexican Bend has good camping. It will take 6 hours from the Thin Man Pinnacle to the Mexican Bend.

> **Digression:** The Lower Black Box and Swaseys Leap are a ninety-minute hike down the river from Mexican Bend (Hike #14). They are worth a short day hike. Another good side trip from Mexican Bend is the Horse Thief Trail and Acer's Arch (Hike #11).

From the airstrip go north up Spring Canyon. (For more details on Spring Canyon see Hike #12.) After a couple of miles you will see Delicate Arch on the left-hand skyline. Continue past the arch, keeping to the right as several other canyons come in from the left. There are usually springs in the area. Past a freestanding, pinnacled fin the canyon divides. Stay to the right (NNE). You will enter Nates Canyon. After a short hike the canyon narrows at a seasonal pool, which also stops any cattle. This is the preferred place to camp for the third night if side trips from Mexican Bend are not planned. It will take two hours from Mexican Bend to the pool in Nates Canyon.

> **Digression:** This is an excellent base from which to hike the North and South forks of Spring Canyon (Hike #12).

Continue up Nates Canyon. The canyon ends in a fall with a long, thin, seasonal pool at its base. Backtrack one-quarter mile until a steep scramble up to the next higher bench becomes apparent on the right (LUC). Clamber up this (Class 3); then traverse along a wide ledge until the top of the fall is reached. As there is another fall one-half mile ahead, you will exit the canyon here.

> **Digression:** It is worth a quick side trip up the canyon to see the many gemlike, seasonal pools. If they are full, there is excellent camping in the area.

Scramble up a steep slope (S) to the top of one of several breaks going through the brown head wall (Class 3). Hike northwest along the rim until the top of the fall is reached.

From the top of the fall, Nates Canyon, now shallower, continues upward. Do not keep going up the canyon. There is a gully coming in from the north. Go up the gully for several hundred yards until you see an open area to the right (E). Cross this area and continue east until you see the Tidwell Draw track and the powerlines. There is a veritable maze of canyons going down. Try to hike a diagonal path to the northeast as you drop in and out of small canyons and gullies. That way you'll have less walking to do on the road, though even if you go straight down, you will end up within a mile of the start. It will take three to five hours from the pool in Nates Canyon to the start.

★ ## Grotto Canyon (AN)—Hike #5

Season	Early spring, spring, or fall
Time	Part 1—2 hours (2.5 miles)
	Part 2—5 to 7 hours (8 miles)
Elevation gain	Part 1—200′
	Part 2—600′

Water	Seasonal, though there is usually some water in the grotto. Bring your own water.
Maps	Mexican Mountain. The map is useless for this hike. [Huntington. San Rafael Desert.]
Circle trip	Part 1—No Part 2—Yes
Skill level	Moderate route finding. Class 3 scrambling. If you are not a rock climber, bring wading shoes. (For information on wading shoes, see ''How to Use the Guide.''

Sometimes a hike can surprise you. This one starts with nothing to recommend it. In fact the start, a flat plain and nondescript hills, is discouraging. With a little faith and perseverance, this changes quickly as you enter one of the finest short canyons in the Northern Reef.

The hike comes in two parts. Part 1 goes to the grotto, a large pothole nestled below a fall. The route is short, varied, and should be especially fun for youngsters. Part 2 goes out the top of Grotto Canyon, across a corner of Horse Heaven, by a special treat, and descends a charming canyon.

Part 1: Locate power pole #1034. It is several hundred yards to the west of the Tidwell Draw track. From the power pole walk west over a small rise into a gully, over another rise, and into a shallow wash. On the next rise is a four-by-four-inch post sticking straight up. Go up to it; then drop west into another shallow wash. This is not great through here. Have faith.

Follow the wash northwest. It narrows for a bit, then divides at a section of purple slickrock. Go left (LUC). A large pothole can be passed to the left. The canyon divides. Go right. The canyon becomes corridorlike and is easy walking for several hundred yards. Toward its end are several sections that may have to be waded. For climbers this section can be easily chimneyed (5.0). The grotto itself is exquisite—a special place. Return the way you came.

Part 2: Backtrack the narrows until you can exit the canyon on the left (LUC); then traverse to the top of the grotto and continue up the canyon. After five minutes the canyon is blocked at side-by-side drops. Scramble up steep slickrock into the right-hand drainage. After five minutes ascend a slickrock slab. Within minutes the canyon essentially dies at a half circle of low overhangs. Exit to the right (LUC).

Set a compass course northwest. Cross broken country (a section of Horse Heaven) for several minutes. Intersect a red-and-white, Navajo-walled canyon just as it pinches off and turns into a wash. Cross it and continue northwest. Within five minutes you will reach the top of another red-and-white-colored canyon that also pinches off and becomes a wash. Look up the wash. What a surprise! What a prize! An old cabin on a knoll. Although tumbled down, do note the old stove and the interesting chinking. The cabin has not been stripped of artifacts, probably because there is no longer a visible road to it. Please don't take anything so others can enjoy it.

After visiting the cabin, continue on your northwesterly course. Go up a rise and down into the apex of another shallow red-and-white-colored canyon. Cross it and continue northwest up a hillside. Note the cowboy cairn on top of a small knoll. Drop into yet another red-and-white-colored canyon. Hooray! Zip down this one. There are occasional obstacles, all easy to negotiate. There is a huge pool at the base of a big drop. Pass this to the right. The next half mile contains a succession of tantalizing pools. Magic.

As you exit the canyon continue east until you reach the flat plain where you started.

Green River Cutoff Road Section

Access to Hike #6
Access is from Highway 10 and Highway 191–6.
Provides access to the Fuller Bottom and Buckhorn Wash roads and the Tidwell Draw tracks.
Metric map—Huntington

This road runs west to east from Highway 10 north of Castle Dale, under Cedar Mountain, to Highway 191–6.

To find the west end of the road drive 1.6 miles north of Castle Dale on Highway 10. Turn east between mile markers 39 and 40. There is a sign to Buckhorn Wash, the Wedge Overlook, and US Highway 6.

To find the east end of the road go north from Interstate 70 on Highway 6–191. The unmarked Green River Cutoff road is 0.5 mile north of mile marker 284. There is a stop sign, but no road sign.

The Green River Cutoff road is well maintained. It is suitable for all vehicles. Although this is a scenic road, mountain bikers may find the dusty traffic intolerable. There are side roads that can be used for camping.

0.0	Mileage starts at the sign just off Highway 10 and goes east.
12.7	Marked junction. The buildings are the Buckhorn Flat Well. (This is not the Buckhorn Wash road.) Sign to the Wedge Overlook and Fuller Bottom.
	The road to Fuller Bottom, 6.5 miles long and for light-duty vehicles, is used as access to the San Rafael River by boaters. (See the Fuller Bottom Road Section in the Sids Mountain chapter for details.)
	The road to the Wedge Overlook, 6.1 miles long, is graded and is suitable for any vehicle. There are many side tracks leading to good camping. The views from the Wedge are terrific. This is a highly recommended excursion.
14.9	Marked junction. This is the north end of the Buckhorn Wash road. Sign to Castle Dale, Buckhorn Wash, and I–70. (See the Buckhorn Wash Road Section for details.)
15.1	Cattle guard.
17.3	Cattle guard.
17.4	Head of Furniture Draw. There is a washed-out bridge here.
19.4	The start of Little Holes Canyon **Hike #6**. A track comes in on the right (S) and goes over a small rise. Go down the track for 0.2 mile and park at the stock pond. The track is unmarked, but it goes by power pole #946.
20.0	Corral to the left (N).
21.1	Orsons Pond is to the right (S).
21.8	Track going right (S). This goes to a grand overlook above the junction of Calf and Cow canyons. Medium-duty vehicles or a short walk.

22.2	To the left (N) is Summit Pond. To the right (S) is the head of Calf Canyon, which is a wash at this point.
22.3	Cattle guard. Power pole #965. A track to the right (S) past the cattle guard goes to the rim of Calf Canyon.
23.2	"Tee." A road to the right (S) goes to Box Flat.

There is a short excursion accessed from this road.

Side road

0.0	Mileage starts at the "Tee" and goes south.
2.8	Wire gate. Just before this, to the left (E), is a track going to Pack Saddle Gulch.
5.7	To the right (W) is a wonderful Zane Grey-style box canyon. There is a poor track going into it. It is worth the one-half hour walk.
5.9	End of the road. Good views of Nates Ridge and the Beaver's Tail Pinnacle in the distance (Hikes #4 and 8).

End of side road

23.3	Under the powerlines.
27.1	"Tee." Track to the right (S) going to Lews Hole and the Big Holes in Pack Saddle Gulch.

There is a fun mountain bike ride to Pack Saddle Gulch and the Big Holes. Follow the track south, passing a huge metal watering trough. (Apparently these troughs used to hold jet engines.) Continue south for three miles. Pass under the powerlines. In a mile the track goes right, down a hill, and past a small watering trough. The shallow white canyon below is Pack Saddle Gulch. Walk down it (E) for a half mile to the Big Holes, which usually have water. This was a regular stop on the Old Spanish Trail.

If you are in need of more exercise, backtrack 0.1 mile from the last watering trough. Go left (NW) on a track. Follow it for four miles until it intersects a graded road. You are at a wire gate, which is the same gate mentioned on the Box Flat road at mile 2.8. Go right (N) back to the Green River Cutoff road.

27.5	"Tee." A track to the left (NE) goes to Chimney Rock. The track also goes to an old railroad grade and the ruins of a Chinese work camp.

Side road

0.0	Mileage starts at the "Tee" and goes northeast.
0.3	"Y." Stay right (NE) to the railroad grade and the remains of the work camp.
	Go left for a mile to Chimney Rock.
0.5	Cattle tank on the left.
0.7	A track comes in on the right. Stay to the left.
0.9	Go through a road cut. This is a part of the old railroad bed. Park after this and walk along the railroad bed for ten minutes. Cross two washes and go through three road cuts. The remains of the work camp are at the far side of the third one. The stone walls and chimneys of several houses are still standing. The rail bed was built in the early 1880s but was never used. Chinese laborers were imported to do the manual labor. Further signs of their work can be seen in the vicinity of mile 7.0 on the Tidwell Draw—North—track.

End of side road

28.3	Track coming in on the left (W).
31.2	Unmarked four-way junction. The Tidwell Draw track is to the right (S). It goes to the Smith Cabin and Hikes #1 through 5. (See the Tidwell Draw Road sections for details.)
32.4	Cattle guard.
38.1	Cattle guard.
40.9	Cattle guard.
41.6	Road divides. Follow the pavement under the railroad tracks.
42.1	"Tee." Go right, off the pavement onto the dirt road.
43.1	Cattle guard and Highway 191–6.

Little Holes Canyon—Hike #6

Season	Any
Time	2 to 3 hours (5 miles)
Elevation gain	250'

Water	Seasonal, though the canyon is rarely completely dry. Bring your own water.
Maps	Bob Hill Knoll. The hike starts at Little Holes. [Huntington]
Circle trip	No
Skill level	Easy route finding. Class 3 scrambling.

This is a short hike through an ever-deepening canyon. With easy access, high Wingate walls, two pinnacles, and a seasonal stream, it is surprising that this canyon is so rarely visited.

The route descends Little Holes Canyon, which runs between the Green River Cutoff and the Buckhorn Wash roads, and returns the same way.

From the stock pond you can drop south directly into the canyon. If you do this there can be wading involved, definitely some nasty tamarisk thrashing, and a little climbing (Class 5.0). A better alternative is to traverse along the north rim of the canyon, following a vague path west for a mile until the twin Conquistador Pinnacles (AN) are reached. The first mile is suitable for everyone and provides good views of the canyon and the pinnacles.

The Conquistador pinnacles in Little Holes Canyon.

Historical note: The Little Holes, below the stock pond at the head of the canyon, were a stopping spot on the Old Spanish Trail as there was usually water. It is fitting that the pinnacles have a name with a Spanish flair.

Once past the pinnacles scramble diagonally down to the canyon floor (Class 3). Hike to the end of the canyon at the Buckhorn Wash road. To return, retrace your steps, varying things by exiting to the right (LUC) at the pinnacles and following the south rim of the canyon back to the start.

Rock-climber's note: The lower part of the canyon may one day be a popular sandstone climbing area. A plethora of moderate routes on a variety of sandstone formations should prove irresistible to the rock explorer.

Buckhorn Wash Road Section

Access to Hike #7
Access is from the Green River Cutoff and the Cottonwood Wash roads.
Provides access to the Mexican Mountain road.
Metric map—Huntington

This road goes south from mile 14.9 on the Green River Cutoff road to the San Rafael River bridge and campground. The road is well maintained and suitable for all vehicles. This is an excellent mountain bike road, but only in the off-season. During the ORV season the road can be dusty, noisy, and distasteful. There is good off-season camping in Buckhorn Wash.

0.0   Mileage starts at the Buckhorn Wash signpost at the junction of the Buckhorn Wash and Green River Cutoff roads and goes south.

0.4   Bridge.

0.9   Barren plain to the left with a fence running across it. From the east end of the fence, against a slickrock wall, walk right (S) for 150 yards. There is a small petroglyph panel.

1.4   A track to the left (NE) goes to the mouth of Furniture Draw.

     An easy hike, suitable for everyone, goes up this short canyon. There is a section of narrows and several small obstacles to surmount (Class 2+). Round trip will take two hours. Some water is possible in the narrows.

1.6   There is a dinosaur footprint that can be mighty hard to find. Pass the Furniture Draw track at mile 1.4. The road makes a wide corner to the right and then straightens out a bit. There is a gray track angling off the main road to the right. Park here. Scramble up a twelve-foot-high cliff band to the east. The ledge on top is wider in one spot. The print is at the backside of the ledge under a one-by-two-foot slab of sandstone.

1.8   Dip.

2.1   The mouth of Triangle Canyon (AN). (It is just north of elevation 5889 on the Bob Hill Knoll map). There is a nice "after dinner" hike up the canyon. It will take thirty minutes round trip. A mutilated petroglyph panel can be found at the mouth of the canyon.

2.3   Cattle guard. Immediately past the cattle guard is a trail to the left (LDC)(N) going up a hill. It leads to a good set of pictographs and petroglyphs. These are called the Cattle Guard Glyphs.

2.8   The mouth of Little Holes Canyon (Hike #6).

3.2   Dip.

3.8   Bridge.

4.2   The Matt Warner inscription. You have rounded a jutting peninsula of rock and are going north. Several hundred yards from the point of the peninsula, to the left and fifty feet up on a cliff band, is the inscription. It is easy to spot from the road.

     Matt was one of the Hole-in-the-Wall gang who used to roam the San Rafael Swell and the Robbers Roost country in the 1880s. Warner's claim to fame was in helping Butch Cassidy rob the Telluride bank. He also led a gang called the "Invincible Three" in Oregon,

Washington, Wyoming, and Utah. Later, he became the marshall of Price.

5.6 | Buckhorn Indian Writings. At one time this was the best Barrier Canyon Style pictograph panel in the Swell. The panel has been extensively vandalized.

7.4 | The start of Calf, Cow, and Pine Canyons **Hike #7**. There is a dip at the mouth of Calf Canyon and a short rough track going up it to the east. Park along the track.

9.3 | Cattle guard. The road to Mexican Bend comes in on the left (S).

9.4 | San Rafael River bridge. A swinging (and it really does!) bridge built in 1928 by the CCC. Four-ton load limit.

9.5 | San Rafael River campground. No potable water. No trash disposal. It does have an outhouse, picnic tables, and tent sites.

Calf, Cow, and Pine Canyons—Hike #7

Season | Best in the fall, winter if there is little snow, or spring.

Time | 8 to 10 hours. With much exploring to do, this could be done as an overnight hike, though water would have to be carried (12 miles).

Elevation gain | 800'

Water | Seasonal springs in all three canyons. Bring your own water.

Map | Bob Hill Knoll. Bottleneck Peak. Chimney Rock. Devils Hole. [Huntington]

Circle trip | Yes

Skill level | Difficult route finding. Class 5.2 climbing. This is a long day hike. Advanced canyoneers only. The less experienced will find a rope useful.

This is one of the most demanding day hikes described. It is a classic canyoneering route that goes through two marvelous canyons and high along the rimrock on the edge of an escarpment. Technical and mental challenges await the dauntless day hiker.

The route goes up Calf Canyon, into Cow Canyon, and out its top. It then crosses a long sage, juniper, and pinyon plain to the head of Pine Canyon and down that canyon back to the start. The canyons are superb, the views from the top are unbeatable, and the route captivating.

From the Buckhorn Wash road go east up Calf Canyon on a track. The canyon divides in a quarter mile at the base of a large Wingate buttress. Calf Canyon is to the left (NE). Pine Canyon is to the right (E). Go left. After thirty minutes the canyon opens into a park. Toward the end of the park, past the double caves, the canyon divides. Calf Canyon continues to the left (N) and ends shortly, while Cow Canyon comes in on the right (E). The double caves are a worthy goal for those looking for a short day hike. They are accessible to all.

Go up Cow Canyon for an hour, usually hiking on a path. The canyon divides. Stay with the main canyon to the right (E). The canyon divides again. The canyon to the right is short and steep. Stay to the left. This canyon ends in a quarter mile, so after several hundred yards, watch for a likely series of ledges up and to the right (W). Scramble up these, at one point climbing a steep, high chute (Class 4, 50′). It leads to the rim of the canyon. Head south-southwest over a small rise. Drop immediately into a drainage. Follow this down until it ends at a large fall.

From the top of the fall continue south-southwest over another small rise. You are on the flats. Watch your compass carefully. Again bear south-southwest for fifteen to twenty minutes. Intersect a wide, shallow valley running north-south. Cross to the west side of the shallow valley and go south along the base of a low cliff band.

Toward the south end of the valley you will intersect a track. Go right (SW), following the track for several hundred yards until it divides in the middle of a pasture. Go right (W). Soon a canyon comes into view with a wall sculpted with inverted Vees. Continue following the track as it goes down a bumpy slickrock section into a valley. At the bottom of the bumpy section the track turns left and goes southeast up the valley.

Digression: At this point, if things aren't going as planned and you want to return to the start by the quickest route, turn right (NW) at the bottom of the bumpy slickrock section where the track goes left. This goes to the top of the inverted Vee canyon. (The top of this canyon is a quarter mile north of elevation 6570 on the Bottleneck Peak map.) At the apex of the canyon look to the left (LDC). Several hundred yards along the rim is a gully coming back toward you with several trees in it. Scramble down the gully. The rest of the canyon has several falls and seasonal pools that can all be passed on the right. After a mile of laborious boulder hopping intersect Pine Canyon. Go down this. The hike will take six hours.

From the bottom of the bumpy slickrock section, cross the valley (S) until you are below a Navajo cliff band. Follow the cliff band upvalley for several minutes until the first break (a slickrock-lined gully) is reached. The gully enters the valley above a short drop. Clamber up this to the southwest; then go south. The route goes to the left side of a small hill. Again go south, cross a shallow canyon, and scramble up a break (a slickrock depression) in a cliff band.

Set a compass course southwest. In five minutes you will be on a land bridge between two canyons, with stunning views of Window Blind Peak and the San Rafael River to the south. Continue southwest. If all else has failed, but you've been generally going south to southwest, you'll be at the rim of a large, white-walled canyon characterized by a white slickrock dome in its middle. (The dome is shown as elevation 6630, the one to the east, on the Bottleneck Peak map.) The land bridge narrows considerably as you traverse around the top of this canyon.

Follow the southwest rim of the white-walled canyon generally north until you are at the end of a peninsula. The large pinnacle to the southwest is Bottleneck Peak. From the end of the peninsula look west. Below is a three-humped, Navajo slickrock ridge heading away from you. Scramble down steep slabs to the saddle between the peninsula and the ridge. Go left down another slab

(5.1, 20′). Continue left on a bench until it starts to peter out; then pick your way carefully down another slab (5.2, 50′). You are at the top of Pine Canyon, which you will descend.

Hike along the south rim of the canyon for several hundred yards until you find a steep slot going into the canyon. (You will be descending just east of elevation 6630, the one on the west, on the Bottleneck Peak map.) Carefully climb down the slot/chimney (5.2, 60′). From its base go straight down. This looks improbable, but it avoids cliff bands on either side (Class 3+). At the first fall, look down the canyon. There is a large slide to the left. Traverse to the top of this; then scramble down into Pine Canyon. Follow the track back to the start.

Mexican Mountain Road Section

Access to Hikes #8 through 12
Access is from the Buckhorn Wash and Cottonwood Wash roads.
Metric map—Huntington. San Rafael Desert.

This road goes south from the San Rafael River bridge, along the east side of the San Rafael River, to Mexican Bend. It is suitable for light-duty vehicles. This is a popular mountain bike road, but ride it in the fall, or midweek, when there is little traffic. There are many short side roads that are good for camping.

0.0	Mileage starts on the Buckhorn Wash road 0.1 mile east of the San Rafael River bridge and goes south.
0.6	Assembly Hall Peak is to the right. Bottleneck Peak is the thin shaft in the background.
1.3	Stock corral to the left.
1.6	At the top of a hill. Window Blind Peak is to the south. It is the dominant landmark in the northern part of the Swell.
4.6	The start of Red Canyon—West Fork to East Fork **Hike**

#8. Drive north a mile up the wash until the canyon divides and park. This is a boundary for the Mexican Mountain Wilderness Study Area.

7.1 | Wire gate.

7.2 | White Horse Canyon is to the left (N). It doesn't look like a canyon.

7.4 | Lower White Horse Canyon to the southwest.

To go to the San Rafael River, walk down the canyon to a fall. Follow a ledge on the left of the fall (LDC) until it narrows; then go straight down (Class 3, some exposure). One hour round trip.

8.0 | Head of Lockhart Box. There is a BLM sign here. This is one way of starting Upper Black Box Hike #9. It adds two to three hours to an already long day.

A hike into Lockhart Box is worthwhile. Park by the roadside and walk down a track (SW). At a drop back-track fifty yards and ascend a steep white gully to the right (LDC)(W). Traverse 100 yards south on rocky terrain. Go down a long loose slope, then on to the river. There are several swim holes here. To return, hike up the San Rafael River for about a mile and exit at Lower White Horse Canyon (see mile 7.4 above). Total time 1.5 to 2 hours. You will have to wade the river several times.

9.6 | "Tee." The start of Upper Black Box **Hike #9.** Park at the intersection with a track coming in from the right (S). There are excellent places to camp and fine views of the San Rafael River gorge at the end of the track.

10.0 | Stock pond on the right.

11.4 | Wire gate. Unobstructed view of Lone Rock straight ahead. The Thin Man Pinnacle, near the head of Sulphur Canyon, can be seen dimly to the north-northwest.

13.5 | "Tee." A track to the right goes onto a peninsula of limestone. There is a campsite overlooking the lower part of the Upper Black Box. The limestone cliffs and boulders in this area can provide interesting and photogenic climbing and bouldering.

This is the location of the emergency exit from the drop in the Upper Black Box. To find the exit drive out to the end of the peninsula. Drop into a shallow canyon to the south. Walk down to its end. Read the warning in the Upper Black Box Hike #9 for more information on the exit route.

13.8	The start of **Hikes #10, 11, and 12.** The road is blocked by a berm and a fence. As the road is narrow at this point, it would be best to go back a little before parking. The area behind the berm is part of the Mexican Mountain Wilderness Study Area. There should be no vehicle traffic past the berm.
14.8	Approximate mileage. This is the first place the track comes close to the river. It is at the mouth of the Upper Black Box and is the place you cross the river on the Mexican Mountain Traverse Hike #10.
15.2	Approximate mileage. The mouth of Sulphur Canyon is a half-hour hike from the berm. The track has been following the river. Just past the mouth of Sulphur Canyon the track suddenly turns north, away from the river, and goes steeply up the side of a hill. The canyon mouth has a small mud pinnacle on the hill to the left.
16.3	Approximate mileage. The abandoned airstrip in the Mexican Bend. Spring Canyon comes in from the left (N). Mexican Mountain is to the right (S).

Red Canyon—West Fork to East Fork—Hike #8

Season	Any. Spring and fall are best.
Time	7–9 hours
Elevation gain	1500′
Water	Seasonal potholes. The East Fork has a seasonal spring in its upper reaches. Bring your own water.
Maps	Devils Hole. [Huntington]
Circle trip	Yes
Skill Level	Moderate route finding. Class 4 climbing. This is a long day hike.

This is a demanding hike that forces you to work for your just rewards . . . and the rewards are plentiful. The hike includes one nice canyon, one incredible canyon, a handful of pinnacles, far views, and great hiking along the rimrock.

The route goes to the end of the West Fork of Red

Canyon, up a wall, along the rimrock above Devils Hole to Box Flat, and then down the spectacular East Fork of Red Canyon. The upper reaches of both of these canyons are rarely explored.

From the parking area below the Wingate buttress that divides the West and East forks of Red Canyon go north up the West Fork, always staying in the main channel. The canyon ends after several miles. Zigzag up broken ledges and rubble to the left (LUC)(Class 4).

> **Rock-climber's note:** An alternate route goes up the steep slabs to the right. Ascend these (several twenty-foot steps of 5.0), then exit through a V-slot (5.5, 12').

Circle to the top of the slabs that the climbers ascend. The flat areas to the north and west could provide interesting side hikes, as well as having the potential for seasonal pools. From the top of the climber's route go east for several hundred yards. Locate a steep chute going through the wall to the left (NW). The chute is jumbled, with a tree near the top. Strain on up the chute. From the top of the chute continue to the rim. (You will be near elevation 6646.) To this point it will take two to three hours with an elevation gain of 1500 feet.

Go right, east then southeast, along the canyon rim. The area below the rim to the south is Devils Hole. After several miles you will see the Beaver's Tail Pinnacle on the left side of Nates Ridge. It is distinguishable but not conspicuous. To the left (N) of the Beaver's Tail is a balancing rock pinnacle that is more noticeable. Go across open, well-junipered country, aiming for the Beaver's Tail.

Soon you'll reach the edge of the East Fork of Red Canyon. Follow the rim up the canyon. At one point drop into and climb out of the head of a small intersecting canyon. Suddenly there is a wide, flat plain in front of you to the northeast. This is Box Flat. (It is the same flat mentioned, along with the Beaver's Tail Pinnacle, in Cottonwood Wash Hike #4.)

Drop onto Box Flat and hike east along the south end of the flat. About two-thirds of the way across there is a break in the domes to the right (S). Go south between the domes for several hundred yards to the apex of the

Pinnacles in Red Canyon.

East Fork of Red Canyon. (This is west of elevation 6460X.) To the left, past a fence, is a large cairn marking the entrance into the canyon. At this point you have two hours to go.

Descend a steep chute (S). At a big fall go left (LDC) on wide ledges past a small duckhead arch on the rim of the canyon. Intersect another canyon coming in from the left (SE). Look across the canyon. There is a steep chute on the far side. Circle around and go down the chute. Pass the next fall to the left before dropping into the main canyon. The ensuing several miles back to the start are a joy. There are many pinnacles.

★ | ## Upper Black Box—A Perilous Journey—Hike #9

Season | Best in late April to mid-May and August, September, or October. Spring can be cold. Water levels must be low.

Time | 9 to 12 hours. This time can be cut down substantially if you leave a car or mountain bike at the end of the Mexican Mountain road (10 miles if you have a car shuttle; 14.2 miles if you walk the whole way).

Elevation loss	600′
Water	San Rafael River. You will be in the water most of the time. Bring your own drinking water.
Maps	Mexican Mountain. Spotted Wolf Canyon. Devils Hole. Drowned Hole Draw. [Huntington. San Rafael Desert.]
Circle trip	Yes
Skill level	Easy route finding. Class 4 scrambling. This can be a very long day hike. Wading shoes are essential. Read the additional material below.

At the head of Lockhart Box, an alternate start for this hike, the BLM office in Price has posted a memorandum. To quote one sentence from it: ''Every year several parties underestimate the difficulty of this trip and have to be rescued, sometimes not until 24 long, wet and cold hours later.'' The quote accurately sets the tone for this hike. Danger, of course, can be invigorating if you are properly prepared, both physically and mentally. With a little forethought and preparation this trip is a blast.

Before describing the route you should have a better understanding of what you are getting into.

1. Water flow rates should be below 25 cfs. The water flow rates can be checked on the Daily River Recreational Recording at 801-539-1311.

2. There is nothing easy about any of the hike. You will be constantly boulder hopping, wading and probing, bush bashing, or swimming.

3. Be prepared for a vertical drop over a fifteen-foot-high boulder. You will need a rope. An old clothesline will not do. If a length of climbing rope is not available, buy fifty feet of one-inch tubular nylon webbing. It is inexpensive (25 cents per foot), strong, and will do the trick. Any climbing shop will have it. Tie knots in it for better hand holds. Wait until you are at the drop to see where they are needed. If there are old ropes dangling, be neat; cut them down and pack them out as trash. Never use an old rope; you don't know its history. A log has been used for years to tie ropes to. If it disappears a large boulder, though awkward, can be used. Weak-armed people should be lowered using a sitting belay. If you do not know how to belay find out before your trip. A weak-

armed person may not have the strength to go hand over hand down a slippery rope.

4. You need a walking stick for probing pools. Sticks can be found everywhere along the river. It is nice to know when you are going to have to swim. The first person in your group should not carry camera gear.

5. Every person needs an inner tube. These are used mainly for floating packs. Small, bicycle-type pumps are adequate for inflating them. If you are not a strong swimmer, bring a life vest.

6. If your dog hasn't been hiking and climbing regularly, leave him behind. He will slow you down. He should be accustomed to being lowered over a cliff on a rope. He will not be able to jump down the big drop.

7. Leave out the weak members. If they are still picking their way down the cattle trail an hour after everybody else, they will get your party into trouble when the going gets really rough. There is no egress from the canyon once started.

8. On a cold day hypothermia, which is life threatening, is a very real possibility. On an 80-degree day you will be chilled inside the box. Sunlight doesn't reach the bottom of the canyon very often. Wear a wet suit, or bring wool or polypropylene clothing. They insulate when wet.

9. No children. Very strong and experienced young teens may do OK at very low water levels.

10. Bring dry shoes and socks for the walk out.

11. It would be advisable to have a car or mountain bike at the end of the Mexican Mountain road (mile 13.8). There is a fence to lock bikes to. The walk back to your car from the end of the road will take two hours.

12. In the past this hike has been done by various youth groups. The larger the group, the slower it will move. Better alternatives are Lower Black Box Hike #14, Black Dragon Wash and the San Rafael River Hike #16, or The Chute of Muddy Creek Hike #42.

The hike starts on a flat plain, goes down an old cattle trail to the San Rafael River, and follows its course through a deep and spectacular Coconino-walled canyon. The canyon ends at the Mexican Bend. The Mexican Mountain road is followed back to the start.

From the parking area on the Mexican Mountain road look southeast across a sand and juniper plain. Several hundred yards out is a dead tree with many old limbs placed against it. Hike to the dead tree; then continue southeast across the barren plain. In a quarter mile you will reach some live junipers. Behind these the flat plain slowly turns into a shallow wash. There are cairns here and there along the wash. This is an old cattle trail. The wash turns into a shallow canyon that ends on the rim of the San Rafael River canyon. There are several cairns here to help you find the start of the drop to the river.

From the rim drop 600 feet to the river. It will take three hours to get to the start of the narrow section of the Black Box and another hour to get to the infamous big drop. Rappel or be lowered over the drop. The landing under the drop should be checked by the first person down. It is shallow here, which makes things considerably easier. The pool beyond the drop will, in all likelihood, need to be swum.

> **Warning:** There is an exit chute to the left just before the big drop (LDC)(N). It has been suggested by some that this is a quick solution for tired and cold hikers. *This chute should not be construed as an escape from the canyon.* It is 250 feet high, has a lot of loose rock, and several vertical sections. In rock-climber's jargon it is 5.3 to 5.4 and is three pitches in length. There are few places for placing protection. A rope and a skilled leader are essential for those attempting the route. If you fall when halfway up, you will not stop until you hit bottom. The people who need to escape the canyon—the tired, cold, and inexperienced—are the least likely candidates for attempting the climb.

Once over the drop it will take another 1.5 to 2.5 hours, with much swimming, to exit the canyon. Once out go left (N) up a slight rise to the Mexican Mountain road. Turn left again. It is a twenty-minute walk to the berm at the end of the road and, if some forethought has been used, a car or a mountain bike. It is 4.2 miles from the berm back to the start of the hike.

Mexican Mountain Traverse—Hike #10

Season	Any. No snow.
Time	5 to 6 hours if you return the way you came (6 miles)
	Alternate 1—7 to 8 hours (8 miles)
	Alternate 2—8 to 9 hours (11 miles)
Elevation gain	1800′
Water	San Rafael River. None on the mountain. Bring your own water.
Maps	Mexican Mountain. [Huntington. San Rafael Desert.]
Circle trip	Yes
Skill level	Moderate route finding. Much Class 3 scrambling. Some exposure. Climbing to Class 5.0. A forty-foot rope will be needed to belay beginners. Wading shoes (see ''How to Use the Guide'') are recommended for crossing the San Rafael River.

Views—Views—Views. Mexican Mountain is the king of the area. Its summit, rarely trodden, provides unparalleled vistas of the San Rafael Swell. The route itself is a stiff, long scramble that cuts through the Moenkopi, Chinle, Wingate, Kayenta, and Navajo formations. Though there are several sections of easy rock-climbing, the inexperienced should have no problems if there is competent leadership.

The route goes to the top of Mexican Mountain. Several alternatives are given for returning to the start. The longest alternative goes from the top of Mexican Mountain to Swaseys Leap at the head of the Lower Black Box and returns by going up the San Rafael River.

From the parking area at the end of the Mexican Mountain road hike one mile toward the Mexican Bend, to the first point the track comes close to the river. Look south toward Mexican Mountain. There is a triangular-shaped slope (Moenkopi) that appears to break through a red band of rock (Chinle). It is the only one that looks like it does. Cross the river and make your way up the arduous slope. At the red band climb a wall of fairly solid rock (5.0, 30′). Scramble up to the base of the Wingate wall above. Traverse under it to the left (E) until the formation comes to a point.

Continue following the Wingate wall as it turns west. Follow it (W) until a steep, U-shaped slickrock gully is reached. Ascend the gully to the next cliff band. Traverse left (S) until forced onto a large expanse of candy-striped slickrock. Drop a little to a red ledge that traverses the slickrock slab. There are several prevalent red bands. Pick the highest one that appears reasonable. Continue south on the ledge. Fun.

As you traverse the red ledge look for a cairn. If you go too far, the red ledge widens into a spectacular balcony with several large, white boulders sitting on it. The red ledge ends in a drop here. This is a perfect spot for a break. Backtrack on the red ledge for seventy-five yards or to the cairn. Ascend steep slickrock (W) until a white cliff band is reached. Ascend a sculpted wall of reasonable angle and zigzag up ledges to the top of the cliff band (Class 4). There are several cairns in this section. Note where you come out on top so you will be able to find it on your way back.

You are faced with the final challenge. Hike uphill (WNW) (Kayenta) until below the summit ridge (Navajo). Go to its north side. In the middle of the wall there is one low-angle area with a bush in it. Ascend this (Class 4, 40′). Zip to the summit (6393′). This section has cairns.

Descend the way you came, back to the red balcony. There are now three alternatives for returning to the start. You can retrace the route, or choose one of the two other alternatives.

Alternates 1 and 2—common descent section. To find the way down, walk to the end of the balcony. Below, to the southeast, is a steep canyon/gully. It will be the descent route. To get there, go north back to the cairn on the red ledge. Drop east to the gray slickrock plain below. You will be doing big zigs and zags, with some Class 4 climbing in between. From the slickrock plain traverse to the top of the canyon spotted from the balcony.

After dropping 500 feet, the canyon/gully levels out for 150 yards before ending in a sheer, yellow cliff. There are two alternatives. Alternate 1 is shorter and not too spectacular. Alternate 2 is quite a bit longer, has some hazards, but will take you by Smokestack Pinnacle and Swaseys Leap at the top of the Lower Black Box.

Alternate 1: Go north, staying at about your present elevation until the slope gently drops to the San Rafael River.

Alternate 2: Go south, following the canyon rim. Within five minutes you will be overlooking Smokestack Pinnacle. Past this there is an exceptional view of the river as it starts into the Lower Black Box.

Traverse along a sloping mud ledge above a 150-foot drop. It looks worse than it is (Class 3), but it has the exposure worthy of a Class 5 route.

> **Warning**: This section of traversing is not for the inexperienced, the faint of heart, or those with vertigo. One look may discourage many.

Continue south along the rim. Within several minutes there is a yellowish mud tower at the end of a mud ridge. Keeping to the rim, traverse until even with the tower. Drop onto the ridge and walk toward the tower. It looks improbable, but it is easy Class 4. Near the tower drop to the left (E). The track below leads to Swaseys Leap.

From the leap there is a trail going up the canyon for a short stretch on the left (LUC); then it disappears. You may have to wade the river a time or two depending on the water level. It takes 2 to 2.5 hours from the leap back to the end of the Mexican Mountain road.

Horse Thief Trail and Acer's Arch—Hike #11

Season	Any
Time	Alternate 1—5 to 6 hours (7.5 miles)
	Alternate 2—6 to 8 hours (10 miles)
Elevation gain	900'
Water	San Rafael River. Bring your own water.
Maps	Mexican Mountain. The Horse Thief Trail is not marked on the map. To locate it find the airstrip in Mexican Bend on the map. The trail goes east from the airstrip to

the Drill Hole at elevation **4485** and east again to elevation 5370. [Huntington. San Rafael Desert.]

Circle trip   Alternate 1—No
Alternate 2—Yes

Skill level   Alternate 1—Easy route finding. Steep Class 3 scrambling.
Alternate 2—Moderate route finding. Class 5.0 climbing.

Visions of dusty trails, the hoot of cowboys, and the bawling of cattle come alive when hiking the Horse Thief Trail. One can just imagine a herd of cattle winding their way down the steep trail.

There are two ways to do this hike. Alternate 1 follows an old horse and cattle trail through the west wall of the Northern Reef and returns the same way. Alternate 2 goes up Spring Canyon, climbs to the top of the reef, and descends the Horse Thief Trail.

> **Historical note:** The Horse Thief Trail was used to move cattle and horses, often stolen, from the Tidwell Draw area to Mexican Bend. Butch Cassidy and his Hole-in-the-Wall gang are known to have used the trail, as well as local ranchers. It has not been used for years. There are bits and pieces of the old trail still visible, though most of it has disappeared. It is most distinct just before topping out.

Alternate 1: From the end of the Mexican Mountain road, hike 2.5 miles to the airstrip. Continue east along the airstrip until it ends. Proceed east along a track until you come to a drill pipe sticking four feet out of the ground. The unmarked Horse Thief Trail is due east of the pipe. It goes up a steep slope to the left (N) of a pinnacle. Pick your way up the slope for 900 feet to a saddle. (This is shown as elevation 5370.)

From the saddle look up to the northeast. You will be able to see Acer's Arch. To get there go northeast and then up a steep gully to the northwest. The Horse Thief Trail itself goes east down the canyon to Tidwell Draw. (See Acer's Arch and the Horse Thief Trail Hike #2 for further possibilities.) Return the same way you came.

> **Digression:** For the more adventurous there are several other ways to go down. From the saddle go fifty feet

down the Horse Thief Trail (W); then edge south for
eight minutes to the next gully. Go down this narrow
gully (Class 3+). If this isn't hard enough, continue traversing for another five minutes to the next possible
gully. Partway down the gully there is a rotten chimney
(5.4, 30′). You will need a rope to get beginners, packs,
and dogs down safely.

Alternate 2: From the airstrip hike north up Spring
Canyon for an hour until even with Delicate Arch. To
the east is a steep, unlikely looking gully piercing the
Wingate wall. Ascend the gully for 800 feet. This is
mostly Class 3 and 4, but at the top there is a chimney
(5.0, 15′). A rope may be helpful for getting beginners
and packs up. The gully is exciting, but a little loose.

From the top, follow the rim south. Immediately you
will run into a long line of slickrock domes. (These are
shown a quarter mile south of elevation 5642.) Go
around these and return to the rim. Several hundred
yards past the domes is a pipe-type bench mark and
cairn. (This is mentioned in Acer's Arch and the Horse
Thief Trail Hike #2 description as part of Alternate 2.)
Continue south along the rim for forty minutes until you
intersect the rim of Horse Thief Trail Canyon. This is the
first canyon you meet.

Hike downhill (E), staying close to the rim of Horse
Thief Trail Canyon. After several hundred yards an unlikely looking cleft appears. A cairn is at its head.
Scramble down the cleft until the small, double, Acer's
Arch is reached. From inside the arch look toward the
head of Horse Thief Trail Canyon. On the rim, in a saddle,
is a large cairn. It marks the start of the Horse Thief Trail.

★ **North and South Forks of Spring Canyon—
Hike #12**

Season Any. Spring and fall are best.
Time 2 to 3 days. From the end of the Mexican Mountain

road, this hike will take a strenuous 9 to 12 hours (18 miles). It is recommended that you take at least 2 days. From the junction of Spring and Nates canyons the hike will take 6 to 9 hours (9 miles).

Elevation gain	1200′
Water	San Rafael River. Seasonal water in both forks of Spring Canyon.
Maps	Mexican Mountain. Devils Hole. [Huntington. San Rafael Desert.]
Circle trip	Yes
Skill level	Advanced route finding. Class 3 scrambling. Familiarity with low-impact camping techniques is essential.

Rabid dogs can be out of control. Downhill skiers can be out of control. Can the North and South forks of Spring Canyon be out of control? To find out, treat yourself to this fabulous route as it wends its way through deep, Wingate-walled canyons, by Navajo domes, and beneath or above two large arches.

The route goes up the North Fork of Spring Canyon, crosses a broken plain past the head of Sulphur Canyon, and descends the South Fork of Spring Canyon.

From the end of the Mexican Mountain road, hike 2.5 miles to the landing strip at the Mexican Bend. Go north into Spring Canyon. At the northwest corner of the junction of the Mexican Bend and Spring Canyon circle carefully through an area of large boulders. There are at least a half dozen South San Rafael Style petroglyph panels on the boulders. Walk north up Spring Canyon. After an hour Delicate Arch comes into view on the skyline to the left. (It is marked but unnamed on the Mexican Mountain map.) It has also been called Bumpy Road Arch and Leaning Arch. Past the arch is a spectacular, freestanding, pinnacled fin that divides Spring and Nates canyons. (This is mentioned in Hike #2, Alternate 2.) The North Fork of Spring Canyon comes in on the left (W), past the pinnacled fin.

For those who are going to camp, there are several choices. If there are cattle and their associated insects about, hike north into Nates Canyon for a short way. Above a small fall and pool, where the canyon narrows, there is adequate camping. The fall will stop the cattle. If cattle are not a concern, there is better camping along the North Fork of Spring Canyon.

From the pinnacled fin hike west up the North Fork of Spring Canyon for several miles. The inner canyon within the bigger canyon opens up. The canyon divides at a prow, with the South Fork coming in from the left (WSW). Continue north up the North Fork. As you walk by the prow look at it carefully. The prow will be an important landmark later on.

Proceed up the canyon, passing a Beware Blasting sign whitewashed on a boulder. The canyon continues for several miles and ends in a fall. One-half mile from the fall you will see a large alcove with a pinnacle in it on the right side of the canyon. When you first see the pinnacle, exit the canyon to the left (LUC)(S) by hiking up a steep slope; then traverse west to the top of the fall at the end of the canyon.

> **Rock-climber's note:** Go past the alcove that has the pinnacle in it. Scramble up a steep slope to the left (LUC). Near the top are some short climbing challenges (5.0 to 5.2). After surmounting these go to the top of the fall.

From the junction of Spring and Nates canyons to the top of the fall will take two hours.

From the top of the fall hike west up the much shallower canyon, passing several small falls. After forty-five minutes the canyon widens into a park and divides. Go left (SSW), past a twin-tiered fall. The canyon opens up even more. The canyon wall to the left tapers down. There is a small dome to the left on a ridge, with a larger dome further along on the same ridge. Scramble south up between the domes. (You will be in a saddle to the east of elevation 6814 on the Devils Hole map.) To the southeast is the top of Sulphur Canyon. (See Hike #4 for details.)

To find the top of the South Fork of Spring Canyon, go up a steep hill to the north-northeast for a half mile. From the top of the hill go east toward two Navajo towers. Aim for the middle of them; then drop between the towers. (The tower to the south is elevation 6842 on the Devils Hole map.) As there are several choices here make

Undocumented arch in the South Fork of Spring Canyon.

sure there are two ten-to-fifteen-foot-high pinnacles in the bowl at the head of the canyon.

Hike down between the towers until a large fall is reached. Skirt left (LDC); then go down a steep gully or cleft to the right (Class 3+). At the next big fall go left. Go down on ledges (Kayenta Formation), sometimes having to ascend to better ledges, then dropping again. Keep your eyes to the right (LDC) as you make a long drop to a wide, white bench. There is a pinnacled ridge on the other side of the canyon. In the middle of the ridge is an undocumented arch. It is the largest arch in the San Rafael Swell—quite amazing and rarely seen.

Go down the white ledges on easier terrain until the prow that divides the North and South forks of Spring Canyon is reached. Recognize it? Walk out the ridge for a short way. To the left, near a small cairn, zigzag down a steep slope into the North Fork of Spring Canyon (Class 3+).

It is also possible to do this hike from the end of the Mexican Mountain road by going up Sulphur Canyon, then dropping into the South Fork of Spring Canyon and out via Mexican Bend. Plan on nine to twelve hours.

Cottonwood Wash Road Section

Access to Hikes #13, 14, and 19 through 21
Access is from the Buckhorn Wash road and Exit 129
on Interstate 70.
Provides access to the Sink Hole Flat/Jackass Bench,
the Oil Well Flat/Saddle Horse Canyon, and the
Buckhorn Wash roads.
Metric map—Huntington. San Rafael Desert.

This road goes south from the San Rafael River bridge to Interstate 70. The Cottonwood Wash road divides the Mexican Mountain area from the Sids Mountain area. It is for light-duty vehicles. Though not particularly scenic, it is suitable for mountain bikes in the off-season. There are many side roads that can be used for camping.

0.0	Mileage starts at the San Rafael River bridge and goes south.
0.1	The San Rafael River campground is to the left.
0.4	There is a track to the right (W). It goes to the start of San Rafael River and Cane Wash **Hike #19** and Virgin Springs Canyon **Hike #20**. (These hikes are described in the Sids Mountain chapter.) Go through several wire gates to a corral. Park near the corral.
0.8	Bottleneck Peak is to the right (W).
1.6	Window Blind Peak is to the left (E). It is an important landmark.
2.7	Cross a small wash. Pinnacle #1 is straight ahead. It is the larger tower to the left of the smaller, pointed tower.
3.8	Track to the Dexter Mine and Cane Wash to the right (W).
4.7	A fence starts on the right.
6.0	Oil Well Flat/Saddle Horse Canyon road is to the right (S). (See that road section in the Sids Mountain chapter for details.) This road provides access to the Pinnacle #1 Hike/Climb #21.
7.3	Track to a corral on the right. Good camping.
7.5	Across a big wash.

7.7	Track to the left.
9.0	Track to the right.
9.1	Track to the right. Good camping.
11.7	"Tee." Track on the left (NE). It goes to Lockhart Box. Mountain bikers can follow the track to the San Rafael River. In a mile the track divides at a stock pond. Go north. After seven miles a fence with sandstone sheets tied to it (the only one on the route) marks a boundary for the Mexican Mountain Wilderness Study Area. Bikes shouldn't go further. Instead, lock your bike to the fence and find a route east, down a steep slope into Lockhart Box Canyon. Follow the canyon down for fifteen minutes, passing several easy obstacles, to the San Rafael River. There are several swim holes here.
13.3	Marked junction. The Sinkhole Flat/Jackass Bench road is to the left (E). (See that road section for details.) This road goes to the start of Drowned Hole Draw Hike #13 and to Lower Black Box Hike #14.
13.5	The Sinkhole, surrounded by a fence.
14.2	Cow tank on the left.
15.5	Marked junction. The road turns west.
	A track to Hyde Draw is to the left (SSE). Hyde Draw is south of I–70 through an underpass. The track provides access to Cliff Dweller Flat, and the Eardley Canyon, Straight Wash, and Greasewood Draw Hike #57. (See the Cliff Dweller Flat Road Section in the Eastern Reef chapter for details.)
16.8	Sagebrush test area to the right. Worth a look.
17.0	Cattle guard.
17.5	Former staging area for construction on I-70 to the left (S).
18.9	I–70 sign.
18.9 + 100 yards.	Vague track to the right (N). This is the start of a good mountain bike ride. Follow the track (N) as it goes by the south side of the Wickiup. Past it the track enters a wash for a hundred yards, then exits the wash to the left (LDC). As the track cuts across a plain it becomes vague. Persevere. The track joins the Oil Well Flat road near the base of Pinnacle #1. Go right (E). It will take you back to the Cottonwood Wash road at mile 6.0. Follow it south back to the start. This is a twenty-five-mile ride.

19.0	Cattle guard.
19.1	Ranch Exit 129 on I-70. To the south, under the interstate, is the Heart of Sinbad road. (See that road section in the Muddy Creek chapter for details.)

Sink Hole Flat/Jackass Bench Road Section

Access to Hikes #13 and 14
Access is from the Cottonwood Wash road.
Metric map—San Rafael Desert. Huntington.

This track goes east from the Cottonwood Wash road to the top of the Lower Black Box and Swaseys Leap on the San Rafael River. It starts 13.3 miles south of the San Rafael River bridge, or 5.8 miles north of Interstate 70, on the Cottonwood Wash road. There is a sign at the junction. The track is good for light-duty vehicles until mile 8.9. It is a 4WD road after mile 10.2. This track is fine for mountain bikes. There is camping throughout the area.

0.0	Mileage starts at the Sink Hole Flat/Jackass Bench sign and goes east.
0.2	Sinkhole Reservoir on the right.
1.3	Cattle guard.
1.8	"Tee." Go left (NE).
3.1	Rattlesnake Reservoir on the right.
4.5	"Tee." Go left (W). Believe me.
	To reach the *bottom* of the Lower Black Box, go right (E).

Side road

0.0	Mileage starts at the junction and goes east. The track is for medium-duty vehicles and mountain bikes.
0.5	Black Dragon Reservoir on the right.

2.2	"Y." Follow the main road north.
3.5	"Tee." Go right (E).
3.7	Track gets rough. 4WDs and mountain bikes only.
6.2	Track divides. Go left.
8.4	Track divides. Go right.
8.8	Track enters a wash. This is the bottom of the same wash as described in Hike #16—Part 3.
9.1	Track ends at the San Rafael River. The sulphur springs are a short walk upriver. The bottom of the Lower Black Box is a half-hour walk upriver, with wading. **End of side road**
5.5	In the middle of Jackass Bench. There will be much evidence on the roadway. The donkeys are often visible.
6.4	Top of a hill. Mexican Mountain is straight ahead.
6.8	Middle of more Jackass Bench.
7.2	A short track to the right ends at a cow tank.
7.3	"Tee." The start of Drowned Hole Draw **Hike #13.** There is a vague track to the left (NNW). Park at the junction. To continue to Swaseys Leap follow the main road to the right (NNE).
8.9	"Y." Go left (N) to go to the Lower Black Box and Swaseys Leap. Have faith. The track gets noticeably rougher. Medium-duty vehicles only.
10.2	At a small, flat area. The track starts going downhill just past this. It is the end of the two-wheel-drive track. 4WDs and mountain bikes only. There is camping here.
13.3	Locally famous big hill. It will stop all but "real" 4WDs. This is a Mexican Mountain Wilderness Study Area boundary line.
13.4	Wreck of a car that did not believe 13.3.
15.2	The start of Lower Black Box **Hike #14.** The Swaseys Leap overlook.

For those without 4WDs, camp near mile 10.2. The walk to the leap will take 2 to 2.5 hours one way. On a mountain bike it will take forty-five minutes to ride down and seventy minutes to ride back up. Though a little rocky in places, the track is generally smooth. There are several short pushes on the way up. The road may be closed here in the future. Contact the local BLM office (801-637-4584) for up-to-date information.

Drowned Hole Draw—Hike #13

Season	Any. No recent rain or snow.
Time	2 to 3 hours (3 miles)
Elevation gain	400'
Water	Seasonal pools. Bring your own water.
Map	Drowned Hole Draw. (The Wickiup) [San Rafael Desert. Huntington.]
Circle trip	Yes
Skill level	Easy route finding. Class 5.1 climbing, with exposure. Rock-climbers only on this hike. A rope may be helpful.

Drowned Hole Draw is the type of canyon no one in their right mind would think of hiking. Even the map shows it as barely being a wash. Rock climbers, though, will find a pristine and pretty little canyon that presents several vertical challenges.

The route goes down Drowned Hole Draw, past several obstacles, to a pothole on the edge of an impassable drop overlooking the San Rafael River as it winds its way through the upper section of the Upper Black Box.

From the Sinkhole Flat/Jackass Bench road drive (medium-duty vehicles), walk, or mountain bike north-northwest for 1.3 miles on the track. There are two buttes ahead of you. The first is flat topped with a large cowboy cairn at its west end. (This is elevation 5962.) The second has a castellated top and is yellow. (This also has an elevation of 5962.) Several hundred yards before the first butte a canyon head comes close to the track, to the left (W). There are trees to lock bikes to. Go down the canyon into Drowned Hole Draw.

Hike north down Drowned Hole Draw. The first big obstacle is a fall that is passed on the right (LDC), down a striped friction slab (5.0, 30'). At some large boulders there are several ways down. The easiest is to cross a log onto a large boulder and climb down a chimney/chute to the left (5.0, 30'). At the double drop, traverse a ledge that is up ten feet and to the right (LDC). There is one tricky move (5.1, 40'). A rope is advisable for the less skilled.

Either return the way you came, or at almost any point exit the canyon to the east, up steep slopes or gullies. This will take you to the track on which you came in.

This short route is an ''after dinner'' delight.

★ | ## Lower Black Box—Hike #14

Season	Best in late April to mid-May and August, September, or October. Spring can be cold. Water levels must be low.
Time	If you can drive to Swaseys Leap at the head of the canyon on the Sink Hole Flat/Jackass Bench road, the hike will take 4 to 6 hours (5 miles). If you have a light- or medium-duty vehicle you can only get to mile 10.2. This is 5 miles from the leap. Add an extra 4 hours, round trip, to walk this. On a mountain bike the time can be cut in half. (See the Sink Hole Flat/Jackass Bench Road Section for further information.)
	From the end of the Mexican Mountain road, the hike will take 9 to 12 hours (14 miles). From Mexican Bend the hike will take 8 to 10 hours (9 miles).
Elevation gain	400′
Water	You are in the river most of the time. Bring your own drinking water.
Map	Mexican Mountain. Spotted Wolf Canyon. (Tidwell Bottoms) [San Rafael Desert. Huntington.]
Circle trip	Yes
Skill level	No route-finding difficulties. You must be willing to spend a day hiking and swimming in the river. Class 3 scrambling. Wading shoes are essential. Read below.

The Lower Black Box is a little brother to the Upper Black Box. But like all little brothers, it should be taken seriously. The Lower Black Box is a real treasure. The Coconino walls are up to 400 feet high and in places only ten yards apart. Unlike the Upper Black Box, you do not have three hours of boulder hopping and bush bashing before getting to the good stuff. You start swimming almost immediately and, at times, for long stretches.

Before reading about the hike, realize that, though shorter and less committing than the Upper Black Box, it is nonetheless a hike for which you must be properly prepared. Read the following section carefully.

1. Water flow rates must be below 25 cfs.
2. You will be swimming and wading almost continuously.
3. A short rope may be handy for lowering packs over boulders.
4. A walking stick for probing pools will prove invaluable.
5. Every person needs an inner tube for floating packs. If you are not a strong swimmer, wear a life vest.
6. Dogs will have problems on some boulder-hopping sections.
7. On a cold day hypothermia, which is life threatening, is a very real possibility. On an 80-degree day you will be chilled inside the box. Wear a wet suit, or bring wool or polypropylene clothing. They insulate when wet.
8. With cold water and large boulders to negotiate, leave children behind. A well-prepared group of youngsters, with competent leadership, could have a lot of fun doing the hike.
9. Bring dry shoes for the hike back to Swaseys Leap.

The hike goes down the San Rafael River through the Black Box to its end. You return by hiking back upriver along the rim of the box, with good viewpoints along the way.

There are two access points to the Lower Black Box. The first is through Mexican Bend. If you are doing other hikes in the bend area, this access will work fine. The hike from the bend to Swaseys Leap, at the head of the box, entails wading the river several times. The length of this hike indicates an overnight trip. There is camping above the mouth of the box near Swaseys Leap.

The second and most popular access is from the Sink Hole Flat/Jackass Bench road. (See that road section for details.) As most cars cannot drive all the way to the leap, an overnight hike is indicated. Walking five miles down

Diz enjoying the Lower Black Box from Swaseys Leap.

the jeep road is easy but can be hot. There is no water along the way. It has become de rigueur to drive down the track as far as possible, then to ride mountain bikes the rest of the way. This makes for a moderate day.

> **Historical note:** Swaseys Leap (also called Sids Leap) is named after Sid Swasey. Sid bet his brother Joe that he could jump the gap on his saddle horse. According to the legend he did. Later, sheepherder Paul Hansen built the "bridge" over the leap with cottonwood logs and an old wagon box. The bridge has taken on a cancerous appearance. Do not use it.

Start into the box. You will immediately go under Swaseys Leap. For the next 1.5 to 2 hours there is much swimming at any water level. After this the swimming becomes sporadic. There are quite a few escape routes out of the canyon. Most are Class 3, but should be checked carefully before bringing up tired or cold swimmers. Plan on three to four hours of actual hiking and swimming time. With picture taking and other diversions, this could take substantially longer.

Once out of the box simply go left (LDC)(NE) up a hill.

> **Digression:** Go down the canyon for another fifteen minutes to a series of sulphur springs. Continue down for yet another fifteen minutes to reach the side canyon mentioned in Hike #16 that joins Black Dragon Wash and the San Rafael River.

The return trail is below the yellow cliff band and is quite good. It will take 1 to 1.5 hours to get back to Swaseys Leap.

Black Dragon Wash Road Section

Access to Hikes #15 and 16
Access is from Interstate 70.
Metric map—San Rafael Desert

This short road goes north from Interstate 70 to the San Rafael River. From Green River go west on Interstate 70 for 13.2 miles until 0.2 mile past mile marker 145. The Black Dragon Wash road starts in a little basin to the right (N). There is a wire gate across the road, but no sign. The road is suitable for light-duty vehicles. It is seasonally popular with the ORV crowd. There is camping along the road.

0.0	Mileage starts at the wire gate just north of Interstate 70 and goes north.
0.7	Start of Box Spring, Double Arch, and Petroglyph Canyons **Hike #15**. A track comes in on the left (W) and goes several hundred yards toward a canyon mouth. There is parking and camping at the end of the track.
1.0	Start of Black Dragon Wash and the San Rafael River **Hike #16**. There is a track coming in on the left (W). It goes to the mouth of Black Dragon Wash. Go up the road for several hundred yards and park at a clearing.
	There are tentative plans to use Black Dragon Wash as part of a mountain bike/ORV trail that will eventually join the Great Western Trail and the Kokopelli Trail.
1.8	The San Rafael River and the end of the road. There is seasonal camping here. The bugs can be bad in the spring and summer.

Box Spring (AN), Double Arch (AN), and Petroglyph Canyons (AN)—Hike #15

Season	Any. Spring or fall are best.
Time	2 to 4 hours (3.5 miles)
Elevation gain	100'
Water	Potholes. Seasonal springs. Box Spring Canyon has a reasonably reliable spring. Bring your own water.
Maps	Spotted Wolf Canyon. These canyons are shown but are not labeled on the map. Box Spring Canyon is the first canyon south of Black Dragon Wash. (Tidwell Bottoms) [San Rafael Desert]

Circle trip	Yes
Skill level	Easy/moderate route finding. Class 2 walking. This is an easy hike. It is especially suited for youngsters and seniors.

Exceptional and rare, this short hike exemplifies variety. The route goes along the face of the Northern Reef, with side trips into three unique box canyons. Box Spring Canyon is noteworthy for its springs and lush riparian habitat. Double Arch Canyon has two sets of double arches, one large and one small. Petroglyph Canyon has two petroglyph panels, one faded and violated, the other as crisp and detailed as any on the Swell.

From the end of the track, go west into Box Spring Canyon. The canyon can be muddy after rains. There is a little bush bashing and some stream hopping. Usually, though, you follow cattle trails. There are several seasonal springs and a large pool at the head of the canyon. This is a perfect place for lunch. Return to the face of the reef.

Go southwest for ten minutes until the next canyon is reached. Go west up the canyon to its end. There is a seasonal pool and a small hanging garden below the arches. Return to the face of the reef.

Continue south for fifteen minutes along the face of the reef to the next canyon. Go southwest up the canyon. Keep a sharp eye on a well-varnished wall to the right (N) until you see the petroglyph panel. This is a short canyon, so there shouldn't be a problem finding it. The faded panel is down and to the right. It has been lightly vandalized. Return to the face of the reef. Go east for several hundred yards before going north to get varied views of the Reef.

★ Black Dragon Wash and the San Rafael River—Hike #16

Season	Parts 1 and 2—Any Part 3—Spring through fall, except during spring runoff (mid-May to July)

Time	Part 1—1 hour (0.5 mile)
	Part 2—4 to 5 hours (8 miles)
	Part 3—10 to 12 hours or 2 days (14 miles)
Elevation gain	Part 1—negligible
	Parts 2 and 3—850'
Water	Parts 1 and 2—None. Bring your own water.
	Part 3—San Rafael River. It is often silt laden. Cattle are run throughout the upper river. Treat with extra care or carry your own water.
Maps	Spotted Wolf Canyon. (Tidwell Bottoms) [San Rafael Desert]
Circle trip	Parts 1 and 2—No
	Part 3—Yes
Skill level	Part 1—This is a hike all can do.
	Part 2—Easy route finding. Class 2+ scrambling.
	Part 3—Moderate route finding. This is a long day hike. For those doing the hike in two days, low-impact camping skills are essential. Bring a pair of wading shoes.

Black Dragon Wash is one of the most frequently visited canyons in the San Rafael Swell. It contains several large panels of Barrier Canyon Style pictographs. It is not unusual to find large groups of people at the panels, though they rarely continue up the canyon. It is pleasant to hike, with easy walking along an old roadbed.

The hike is divided into three parts. Part 1 goes to the famous Black Dragon rock art panels. Part 2 proceeds up Black Dragon Wash and ascends a steep hillside to a marvelous overlook. Part 3 continues past the overlook, intersects the San Rafael River, and follows it as it cuts through the Northern Reef.

Part 1: Follow the track west into the deepening canyon.

> **Historical note:** The road was built in 1918 to service mining activity that never paid off. Before Interstate 70 was forced through Spotted Wolf Canyon, this was the only road through the northern part of the Swell.

After a ten-minute walk the main pictograph panel can be seen high on a wall to the right (N), above a steep slope.

Part 2: Continue up the canyon. The scenery is splendid. The track and the wash tend to intermingle. Always stay to the right, especially the two times the track goes left and uphill. After ninety minutes the track exits the canyon to the right (LUC) up a hill and then follows its rim. The red Wingate wall that has been on your right (N) starts to taper down. The goal is to get to the shoulder below the Wingate wall.

The track turns hard left, away from the wall. Leave the track. Go right, up a wash; then exit the wash to the left before getting to a sixty-foot-high mud pinnacle. Make your way north up small gullies and hills to the shoulder of the Wingate wall where it joins the Chinle Formation. (This is just west of elevation 5309.) From the shoulder the view is expansive. It will take two hours to get to the overlook. Return the way you came.

Part 3: From the overlook drop into a canyon that goes north. As you descend there are several drops to negotiate. The first is passed to the right (LDC). The second drop is large. Traverse left (NW) along the rim for a quarter mile until a break in the cliff band is reached. There is a cairn on the rim. Go down a steep slope and back into the main canyon.

This canyon intersects another canyon that runs southwest-northeast. Go down the canyon (NE) for an hour. The canyon is wide, the walking is easy. Before reaching the San Rafael River a spectacular pinnacle comes into view to the right. There is good camping at the junction of the canyon and the San Rafael River. It will take four to five hours to reach this spot.

> **Digression:** Hike upstream for a half hour. You will pass a string of sulphur springs and get to the mouth of the Lower Black Box (Hike #14).

Follow the river down the canyon. It is possible to avoid wading in the river for many miles by thrashing through tamarisk forests and traversing along ledges. Eventually though, unless the water is very low, you will have to wade. It is easier to wade the whole thing. The water rarely gets above knee deep and the bottom of the river is smooth and sandy. Campsites can be found all along the river, generally behind the walls of tamarisks.

There is one short side canyon that comes in on the right (LDC). Several pinnacles are encountered.

As soon as you break through the reef exit the river to the right (SE). You will run into a maze of tracks. Using your best judgment, follow the tracks south. You will be between the river and the reef. After several miles the tracks funnel into the main road going back to the mouth of Black Dragon Wash.

Cedar Mountain and the Cleveland-Lloyd Dinosaur Quarry

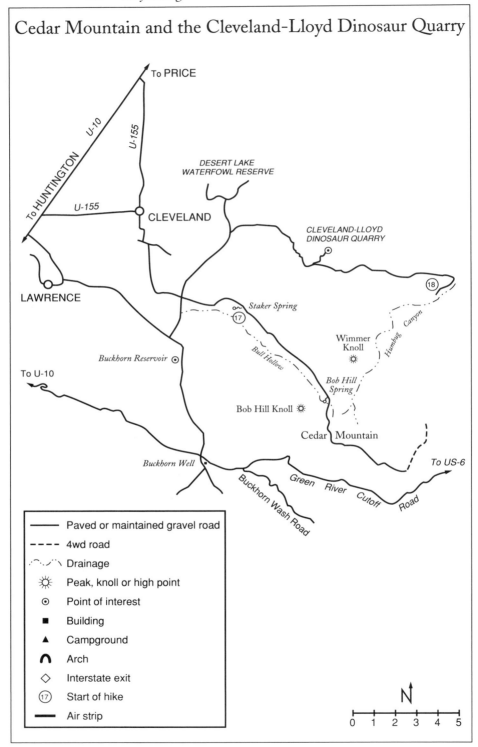

2 | Cedar Mountain and the Cleveland-Lloyd Dinosaur Quarry

Cedar Mountain and the Cleveland Lloyd Dinosaur Quarry are at the northern terminus of the San Rafael Swell. Unlike the other areas in the guide, the Cedar Mountain area does not have many routes for the canyoneer, though it does offer two day hikes, excellent views, and good camping. The picnic/view area at the top of the mountain has grates for BBQs, a short nature trail, and plenty for children to do.

For rock climbers the conglomerate cap that sits atop Cedar Mountain offers good bouldering and top rope problems up to fifty feet in length. The rock consists of smooth river pebbles embedded in a tough matrix. Pinch holds on near vertical walls predominate. These walls are rarely ascended, so loose rock will be encountered.

The Canyonlands Natural History Association has published an excellent pamphlet titled the ''Cedar Mountain Driving Tour.'' This is available at many area restaurants and motels, as well as the Price BLM office.

The Cleveland-Lloyd Dinosaur Quarry is part of what is known as the Colorado/Utah Dinosaur Triangle. The other corners of the triangle are Vernal, Utah, and Grand Junction, Colorado. All three areas are known for their fossilized dinosaur bones. At the dinosaur quarry there is a visitor's center which has interpretive exhibits, sells books and souvenirs, and has picnic tables and water. In the dinosaur quarry you will see dinosaur bones still embedded in the sandstone.

At the present time the dinosaur quarry has limited hours. It is open from 10:00 A.M. to 5:00 P.M. on weekends from Easter to Memorial Day and is open seven days a week from Memorial Day through Labor Day.

Cedar Mountain Road Section

Access to Hike #17
Access is from Highway 10.
Metric map—Huntington

This packed dirt road goes from the town of Cleveland to the top of Cedar Mountain. To get to Cleveland go south from Price on Highway 10 for twelve miles. Turn east on Highway 155. From Cleveland go south on a well-marked road going toward the Cleveland-Lloyd Dinosaur Quarry and Cedar Mountain until you come to an intersection that has several signs. A sign to the east directs you to Cedar Mountain. (A sign to the north directs you to the dinosaur quarry and a sign to the south directs you to the San Rafael Campground, Highway 50–6, and I-70.) The road is for any vehicle. There is good mountain bike riding during the off-season. There are side tracks that can be used for camping.

0.0	Mileage starts at the intersection with the signs. Go east toward Cedar Mountain.
0.2	Cattle guard.
4.8	The start of Staker Spring, Bull Hollow, and Bob Hill Spring **Hike/Bike #17**. There is a track on the right (S). This is the Staker Spring Trail access road. There is no sign. Go right (S) on the track for 0.2 mile until at the edge of a canyon. There is a trail sign on the edge of the cliff.
7.4	Cattle guard. There is a stock tank to the right.
8.1	Fenced sagebrush test plot to the right. It was fenced in 1936. This is worth a look to see the difference between natural vegetation and that grazed by cattle.
9.8	Marked Bob Hill Spring access road to the right (SW). Drive down the track for 0.2 mile. A canyon starts to the right (NW). This is the exit point for those doing Hike #17. If you are riding a mountain bike back to Staker Spring, cache your bike in this area.

The Bob Hill Spring trail goes down the left side of the canyon (LDC). There is a sign once you start down the

	trail. Go down the trail for several hundred yards to Bob Hill Spring. Behind the spring there is a small overhang that was used by Fremont Indians.
10.3	Cattle guard. Much of the land to the west has been chained.
12.2	Cattle guard.
12.8	To the left there is an area that was chained in 1984.
13.2	Cattle guard.
14.8	Marked overlook. Stop here. There is a relief map showing the important features of the San Rafael Swell. It will help orient you to the area.
15.4	Designated picnic area to the right, with an outhouse, garbage cans, picnic tables, and fire grates (bring your own wood). There is no water. A short nature trail goes to a piece of petrified wood embedded in a conglomerate cliff. It is behind a fence. Youngsters may enjoy narrow slots, caves, and rock formations. Bouldering is available throughout the area.
15.7	Area of radio and telephone towers. The road deteriorates beyond this point.

Staker Spring, Bull Hollow, and Bob Hill Spring—Hike/Bike #17

Season	Any. There is much boulder hopping, so no snow.
Time	3.5 to 5 hours if you bike back or 4.5 to 6 hours if you hike back (5 miles one-way; 10 miles round trip)
Elevation gain	1100′
Water	Perennial springs throughout Bull Hollow. Bring your own water.
Maps	Bob Hill Knoll. Cow Flats. Bob Hill Spring is labeled on the Bob Hill Knoll map. Staker Spring is labeled on the Cow Flats map. [Huntington]
Circle trip	Yes
Skill level	Easy/moderate route finding. Class 3 scrambling. Easy mountain bike riding. This is a moderate hike/bike.

Often routes are appreciated for the grandeur of their

surroundings. The far view is what catches the eye. In Bull Hollow the far view is fair to middling. The view up close, especially while going by a series of springs and pools surrounded by huge boulders, is captivating.

The route goes down a cattle trail, by Staker Spring, and into Bull Hollow. It is a shallow canyon that has broken through the conglomerate crust that overlays all of Cedar Mountain. The route then goes up Bull Hollow and exits at Bob Hill Spring. The return journey is either by hiking along the southwest side of Bull Hollow, or preferably, by mountain biking back to Staker Spring along the main road.

Before starting, if you are going to ride a mountain bike on the final leg, cache it at Bob Hill Spring. You can lock your bike to a tree.

Start at the marked Staker Spring Trail. Descend this still-used cattle trail. Once in Bull Hollow go up the canyon (SE), following cattle trails or a shallow wash. In fifteen minutes the wash becomes choked with boulders. Past the boulders the canyon divides. Go left (SE). The canyon becomes intermittently choked with boulders from here up. Often these are thirty to forty feet high and can be a challenge to ascend, though there is always an easy way, usually by hiking well around them. Climbers may wish to confront obstacles more directly.

In the several-mile-long boulder section there are small springs that sometimes run like a stream and form small pools. This is the best section of the canyon. Always follow the main canyon. If in doubt go left, or east to southeast. At one spot, below several huge boulders, the canyon seems to turn right (SW) into a narrow grassy area. This dies in several hundred yards. The route you want is above the boulders to the east.

As the canyon ends you will reach a stock pond. Go straight (E). There is a track on the right side of the canyon. Follow the track. Do not go up the canyon to the south.

> **Digression:** The side canyon to the south goes to Bob Hill Knoll. Go up the canyon, following a track on its left side. Toward the top of the canyon, past a developed spring, the track ends. Continue south for several min-

utes. This goes to a track on the flats. Bob Hill Knoll is to the right (W). Follow the track until directly below it and ascend easy slopes to the top. Walk to its south end for terrific views.

In minutes you will reach Bob Hill Spring. It is well developed and even has a faucet. The canyon ends in several more minutes. If you left a mountain bike, it will take thirty minutes to ride back to Staker Spring. If you are walking back, look to the west. Bob Hill Knoll is the highest point. Hike to it on a track. From here you are on your own. There are tracks paralleling Bull Hollow, though it is more scenic to stay close to the rim. It is easy walking either way. It will take two hours to walk back.

Cleveland-Lloyd Dinosaur Quarry Road Section

Access to Hike #18
Access is from Highway 10.
Metric map—Huntington

This road goes from Highway 10 to the Cleveland-Lloyd Dinosaur Quarry and continues to Humbug Canyon. Go south from Price on Highway 10 for twelve miles. Turn east on Highway 155 toward Cleveland and Elmo. Simply follow signs to the dinosaur quarry.

There is a group of petroglyph panels just off the road to the dinosaur quarry. To find them, follow the signs to the Dinosaur Quarry. Once at the 6-mile sign start your mileage. Go 1.3 miles down a steep hill and across a cattle guard. Take the first possible right after the cattle guard onto a track. Follow this for 0.3 mile until you intersect the first wash. The track is rough. You may want to walk it. At the wash go left. After a five-minute walk there is a fifteen-foot-high, weathered, overhanging boulder with vertical black stripes on its face. There are at least eight small panels within 100 yards of the boulder. Some are across the wash.

Continue along the main road. It divides once at a sign saying Dinosaur Quarry 1 mile. Go left to the quarry. Go right to get to Humbug Canyon Hike #18. Stay on the main road, ignoring side roads. The road turns right (SSW) near the rim of Humbug Canyon. Continue for 200 yards. There is a sign at the head of the Jump Trail, the start of Humbug Canyon **Hike #18.**

The road is good for any vehicle. There is good mountain bike riding during the off-season. Side tracks can be used for camping.

Humbug Canyon—Hike #18

Season	Any. There is much boulder hopping, so no snow.
Time	Part 1—1 hour (1.5 miles)
	Part 2—6 to 7 hours (9 miles)
Elevation gain	Part 1—250'
	Part 2—1200'
Water	There is always some water in Humbug Canyon. Bring your own water.
Maps	Cow Flats. Flattop Mountain. Bob Hill Knoll. [Huntington]
Circle trip	Part 1—No
	Part 2—Yes
Skill level	Part 1—Easy route finding. Class 1 walking.
	Part 2—Easy/moderate route finding. Class 3+ scrambling.

Humbug Canyon is a pleasant surprise. Its walls are composed of a variety of sandstone layers that are not normally seen in the San Rafael Swell: the Summerville, Morrison, Cedar Mountain, and Dakota formations. The canyon contains a medley of sparkling spring-fed pools and is often choked with huge conglomerate boulders, some containing petrified logs.

The route comes in two parts. Part 1 starts at the

Jump Trail, a constructed cattle trail going down a 200-foot cliff into Humbug Canyon. It then goes up Humbug Canyon until the going gets rough. Part 2 continues up the canyon, exits near its top, and follows the rim back to the start.

Part 1: Descend the marked Jump Trail. (The Jump Trail starts a half mile to the southeast of elevation 6183 on the Flattop Mountain map.) It cuts through a half dozen different sandstone layers as it diagonals down the cliff face. At the bottom of the Jump Trail go south to a wash; then go west up the wash into Humbug Canyon. After twenty-five minutes the going gets rougher. The sand-floored wash becomes boulder choked. Go as far as you feel comfortable. There are several seasonal pools up a short distance. Return the way you came.

The Jump Trail descending into Humbug Canyon.

Part 2: Continue up the canyon. It is occasionally blocked by large conglomerate boulders. Pick your way through or around them. Climbers can have a blast here. A seasonal stream runs in and around the boulders, forming pools and small waterfalls. Watch for petrified logs embedded in the boulders.

After two hours the canyon reaches a parklike area and divides. A vague track crosses the canyon. You can see it down the canyon to the left (LDC) going diagonally along a hill. The track comes in at the tongue of land that divides the canyon. It is hard to see, but follow it up. After 100 yards the track has washed away. Continue uphill and rejoin the track. Follow the track for a half hour. Pass through a small stand of birches. The track disappears in sagebrush as it enters a wide valley. Exit the canyon here. Go right (LUC)(NW) up a hill to the rim of the canyon. Crest the hill in an area that has been chained.

As you follow the rim to the north the terrain gets prettier. There are occasional tracks paralleling the rim. Use these, or stay on the rim itself. The walking is easy either way. Toward the end of the hike you will go down several steep hillsides. There are no difficult obstacles to negotiate.

3 | Sids Mountain

The Sids Mountain area is located in the northwestern part of the San Rafael Swell. It is bounded by the Cottonwood Wash road on the east, the Green River Cutoff road on the north, Highway 10 on the west, and Interstate 70 on the south. It is an area of wide, deep canyons that all eventually run into the San Rafael River as it slices through an area called the Little Grand Canyon. The dominant feature is Sids Mountain, a mesa in the center of the area. Without roads or tracks, it is accessible only to hikers and horse packers.

Sids Mountain is an area rich in history, starting with the Desert Culture Indians. They left their indelible mark of Barrier Canyon Style pictograph panels in Cane Wash, Virgin Springs Canyon, along the San Rafael River, and in other scattered locations. The Fremont Indians left a remarkable set of petroglyph panels at Rochester Creek. The early Mormon pioneers used the canyon bottoms for grazing cattle and horses. Their signs, too, are scattered about. There was little mining in the area, though there was extensive exploration. Many glory holes and access roads were left behind. The San Rafael River, between Fuller Bottom and the San Rafael River bridge, is a favorite area for river runners when there is enough water. Sids Mountain is in the Sids Mountain Wilderness Study Area.

The next two hikes, #19 and 20, are accessed by the Cottonwood Wash road. Please see that road section in the Northern Reef and Mexican Mountain chapter for details.

San Rafael River and Cane Wash—Hike #19

Season | Any. After rains or during high water the old mining road you follow along the San Rafael River to Cane Wash could be muddy.

Sids Mountain

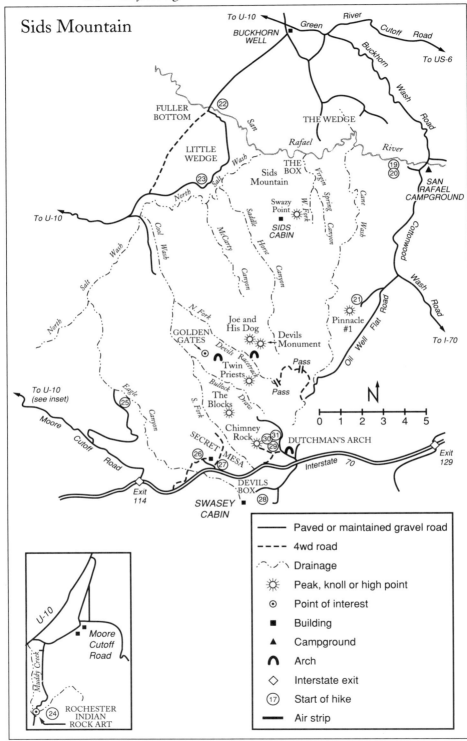

To U-10
BUCKHORN WELL
River
Green
Cutoff   Road
Buckhorn
To US-6
Wash
Road

FULLER BOTTOM
San
THE WEDGE
Rafael
River
22

LITTLE WEDGE
Salt
Wash
THE BOX
Sids Mountain
19
20
SAN RAFAEL CAMPGROUND
23

North
Virgin
Swazy Point
W. Fork
Spring
Canyon
Cane
Wash
SIDS CABIN

To U-10
Cool
Wash
Salt
Wash
McCarty
Canyon
Saddle
Horse
Canyon

Cottonwood
Wash
Road

North
N. Fork
Joe and His Dog
Devils Monument
21
Pinnacle #1

GOLDEN GATES
Devils
Racetrack
Twin Priests
Pass
Pass
Oil
Well
Flat
Road
To I-70

Eagle
Canyon
Bullock
Draw
S. Fork
The Blocks

To U-10 (see inset)
Moore
Cutoff
Road
25

N

Chimney Rock
SECRET MESA
30 31
29
DUTCHMAN'S ARCH
26
27
Interstate   70
Exit 129

Exit 114
DEVILS BOX
28
SWASEY CABIN

0	1	2	3	4	5

Legend

— Paved or maintained gravel road

--- 4wd road

⌇⌇ Drainage

☀ Peak, knoll or high point

⊙ Point of interest

■ Building

▲ Campground

∩ Arch

◇ Interstate exit

⑰ Start of hike

▬ Air strip

Inset

U-10
Moore Cutoff Road
Muddy Creek
24
ROCHESTER INDIAN ROCK ART

Time	Part 1—3 to 4 hours to Cane Wash and back (6 miles); 4 to 6 hours if you go to the second set of pictographs (8 miles). Part 2—8 to 10 hours. This can be done as an overnight hike, but water will have to be carried if you don't camp next to the river (14 miles).
Elevation gain	Part 1—Negligible to Cane Wash; 100′ to the second pictograph panel Part 2—400′
Water	San Rafael River. Seasonal in Cane Wash and Moore Canyon. Bring your own water.
Maps	Bottleneck Peak. Moore Canyon is shown but is not named on the map. It is the first canyon to the west of Bottleneck Peak. It runs generally north to south and tops out on Calf Mesa. [Huntington]
Circle trip	Part 1—No Part 2—Yes
Skill level	Part 1—Easy route finding. Class 2+ walking. This is a good hike for everyone. Part 2—Moderate route finding. Class 3 scrambling. This is a long day hike. If you do this as an overnight hike, low-impact camping skills are essential.

See the Cottonwood Wash Road Section in the Northern Reef and Mexican Mountain chapter for details on finding the trailhead to this hike.

This is the premier short hike in the Sids Mountain area. Its enjoyment is three-way. You enjoy the San Rafael River, which you follow for most of the hike. You hike in the Little Grand Canyon, an area that many look into from the Wedge Overlook, but few enjoy from a river-level perspective. You gain a sense of history by seeing pioneer cabins and viewing Barrier Canyon Style pictograph panels.

The hike comes in two parts. Part 1 goes along the San Rafael River on a mining track to the confluence with Cane Wash and its pictograph panel. A digression takes you to another fabulous pictograph panel an hour away. Part 2 goes up Cane Wash with its towers, spires, and pinnacles. The route exits Cane Wash and crosses Calf

Mesa to Moore Canyon, which is descended back to the start.

Part 1: From the Johansen cabin (red) take a track going northwest then west along the river. After ten minutes watch for several old, collapsed cabins made from hand-hewn logs to the right (N). The track continues for forty-five minutes. It ends after a steep downhill section that leads into a wash.

It takes another forty-five minutes on a footpath/cow trail to reach Cane Wash. The pictograph panel is up the wash 100 yards on the left (E).

> **Digression:** The round trip to the next pictograph panel takes two hours. From the Cane Wash pictograph panel look west. The canyon, going west until it gets to Cane Wash, turns north under a large Wingate wall. Visually follow the wall south for a quarter mile. The wall drops and forms a notch. It is visible from the pictographs. Hike through the notch. Go down steep but easy slopes to the river; then go downriver for several hundred yards. You will be between the river and the Wingate wall to the east. Negotiate a pile of large boulders by using a cattle trail that goes through them. From the boulders look up to the right (LDC)(E) at the yellowish Wingate wall. If you cannot see the pictographs, look for an irregular hole, or window, in the wall. The panel is to the right of the window. (The pictographs are on the west side of elevation 5723.)
>
> Return to Cane Wash the way you came. You can also follow the river back instead of going through the notch, but this is a longer route and entails a high, steep traverse above the river.

Part 2: Go up Cane Wash (S). After 3 to 3.5 hours you start to exit the canyon part of Cane Wash. Watch for a seven-strand barbed-wire fence coming down to the wash from the right. Ten minutes past the fence, to the left (LUC), is an old mining track going diagonally northwest up a yellow hill. (This road starts a half mile southwest of elevation 6025.)

Ascend the track. At the top of the hill follow a track to the right (SE) for a short way. To the north is a Wingate ridge. Hike east parallel to the ridge until it ends; then follow one of several small washes or gullies northeast into the shallow head of Moore Canyon. Hike down the canyon. There is a section of boulder hopping before reaching the canyon floor. From there the walking is easy in a hard-packed wash. Toward the bottom of the canyon look for a large boulder to the left that has been hollowed out and used as a line camp. It will take 2.5 to 3.5 hours to hike from Cane Wash to the Johansen cabin.

Virgin Springs Canyon Hike #20 is an overnight extension of this hike. Read on!

★ Virgin Springs Canyon—Hike #20

Season	Any. Spring and fall are best.
Time	2 days (18 miles with the Moore Canyon end; 20 miles with the San Rafael River end); 3 days if you do the Swazy digression (add 7 miles)
Elevation gain	900′
Water	San Rafael River. There is always spring water in the box of Virgin Springs Canyon. There are seasonal springs further up the canyon. Cane Wash also has seasonal springs, but they are not reliable.
Maps	Bottleneck Peak. Sids Mountain. [Huntington]
Circle trip	Yes
Skill level	Moderate route finding. Class 3 scrambling. A long last day. Familiarity with low-impact camping techniques is essential.

See the Cottonwood Wash Road Section in the Northern Reef and Mexican Mountain chapter for details on finding the trailhead to this hike.

No humorous riposte, no pedantic diatribe, no scintillating verse. I'll be blunt—Virgin Springs Canyon is the best darn canyon in the Sids Mountain area. It is one of the few canyons that cannot be entered and trashed by cattle. It is truly virgin.

This hike is a continuation of Hike #19. From Cane

Wash it continues up the San Rafael River to Virgin
Springs Canyon, with its box, a perennial spring, and a
Barrier Canyon Style pictograph panel. After camping
near the box the route goes up Virgin Springs Canyon. It
exits the canyon by crossing a steep ridge and dropping
back into Cane Wash. You can finish the hike by either
going down Cane Wash to the San Rafael River or across
Calf Mesa to Moore Canyon.

From the pictograph panel at the mouth of Cane
Wash go through the notch. After a quick diversion
downriver to the second pictograph panel, go upriver.
The path deteriorates quickly. There is much bush bashing and long pants are recommended.

It takes 2.5 to 3 hours to reach Virgin Springs Canyon
from Cane Wash. There are several side canyons coming
in from the south. Don't worry. You will not miss Virgin
Springs Canyon. The river sweeps across the mouth of
the box and blocks the way at a black-and-white wall.
Climbers can carefully traverse around and into the Box.
Others can wade. The river bottom here is mud and
sand.

> **Digression:** There is another way to enter the canyon
> and avoid wading. Backtrack several hundred yards from
> the black-and-white wall. Look for the first break in the
> cliff band to the south. It is marked with a cairn. There is
> an old cattle trail going up the cliff. Toward the top you
> can see the engineering involved. Once up, walk to the
> edge of the box. Go uphill along the rim. After several
> hundred yards you will be hiking parallel to a yellowish,
> submarine-shaped dome that is across the canyon (W).
> You can drop into the canyon on ledges when you are
> even with the upcanyon end of the dome formation
> (Class 3).

The box is about a half mile long. The pictograph panels are about halfway up, on the right (LUC), and are fifteen feet above the ground. The exit ledges are 150 yards
above the pictographs to the left (LUC)(E). The spring is
150 yards past the pictographs at the head of the box.
Though there is camping in the box, the area is becoming impacted by backpackers and river runners. Try not
to camp in the box itself.

From the top of the box go up the canyon. It is difficult to describe the exit point you will use to cross from Virgin Springs Canyon to Cane Wash. Pay close attention to the times and landmarks mentioned. The time is cumulative. In thirty-five minutes you will reach a spring area. In forty minutes the streambed is partially blocked by a jumble of yellow boulders from a recent rockfall. From the top of the boulder pile look up and to the right (SW). Note the pothole arch in a cliff band. After forty-five minutes a major canyon comes in on the right (SSW). There are good springs in this area and, if running, there is camping here.

> **Digression:** This is the West Fork of Virgin Springs Canyon. It leads to Swazy, the highest point on Sids Mountain, and to a unique line cabin that is worth seeing. Start up the canyon (SSW). After ten minutes the canyon divides. Stay with the main course to the left (S). After fifty minutes the canyon divides at the base of a buttress. Do not follow the main canyon to the left (SE). Instead go right (SW). Pass a large fall to the left (LUC). Once on the canyon rim look west. The elongated dome is Swazy (6610). Climb it on the north side. From the summit you will see many large Navajo domes around you. It is especially gratifying not to see roads or tracks anywhere!
>
> To find the line cabin look to the west-southwest. There is a large, steep-sided, flat-topped dome sitting by itself in a sizable meadow. The cabin is between the dome and a slickrock ridge to the north.–Plan on four to six hours round trip, 1100-foot elevation gain, easy route finding, and Class 3 scrambling.

After sixty minutes a tower comes into view high on the rimrock to the southeast. After sixty-three minutes a nice-looking canyon comes in on the left (LUC)(E). After sixty-eight minutes you will be due west of the tower. After seventy-three minutes a short side drainage comes in on the left (LUC)(E). This drainage will be your exit route. (This is shown as an indent in the cliff band between elevations 5952 and 6419 on the Sids Mountain map.) However, don't enter the drainage yet because it is blocked after 150 yards by a fall that has two vertical black streaks. There are several cairns in the vicinity. It is important to be in the right place here, not because it is hard to get out of Virgin Springs Canyon, but because there is only one way to drop into Cane Wash.

To pass the fall with the two black streaks, go up Virgin Springs Canyon for another minute. Exit the canyon by hiking up easy slopes to the left (LUC)(E); then go northeast back into the side drainage. Once there, go up the canyon for several hundred yards; then plod up a rubbly hill to the left (LUC). Go up as high as you can on the slope until it ends on a ledge below the last cliff band. Circle right, under an overhang. After several hundred yards go up an easy break in the cliff. Go back into the main watercourse. Continue up a quarter mile until it ends, then up a steep slope to a saddle.

From the saddle look far down to the northeast. You can see Cane Wash. You could go straight down, but there are several difficult cliff bands to negotiate. Instead, drop 100 feet onto a white, discontinuous ledge system. Traverse right (SE), around a point. Continue following the ledge for five minutes. There are occasional cairns along the way. Go down a broken area (N). For the first several hundred feet go diagonally left toward a wide, yellow ledge system. Once there, go right (S). Follow the ledge system for a quarter mile until a slide/gully is reached. Descend this to a slickrock plain. (You will be going down the cliff band to the northwest of elevation 6105 on the Bottleneck Peak map.)

From the plain go north, staying between the main cliff and a red, 100-foot-high mud dome. Catch a wide wash that is going your way and follow it for twenty minutes. The wash descends into a pleasant canyon before dropping you into Cane Wash. It will take four to six hours from the box in Virgin Springs Canyon to this point. There are now two choices. If you continue down Cane Wash and out the San Rafael River it will take four to six hours. Going over Calf Mesa and down Moore Canyon, as described in Hike #19, will take three to four hours.

To go over Calf Mesa and down Moore Canyon, go up Cane Wash (S) for several minutes until an old mining track is reached that diagonals up a yellow hill to the left (LUC)(NW). Follow the directions given in Part 2 of Hike #19 to return to the Johansen cabin.

Either way, this is a long day. Slower groups should camp near the West Fork of Virgin Springs Canyon. This will save some time and let you do the big uphill section while it is still cool. Cane Wash is definitely prettier than Moore Canyon, but Moore Canyon is certainly quicker.

Oil Well Flat/Saddle Horse Canyon Road Section

Access to Hike #21
Access is from the Cottonwood Wash road.
Metric map—San Rafael Desert. Huntington.

This road goes south from mile 6.0 on the Cottonwood Wash road to the head of Cane Wash, and then through a pass to Saddle Horse Canyon. (The Cottonwood Wash road is detailed in the Northern Reef and Mexican Mountain chapter.) The Oil Well Flat road is for medium-duty vehicles and mountain bikes. The Saddle Horse Canyon track is for 4WDs. It is a fine mountain bike track, but there are several long pushes. There is good camping throughout the area.

0.0	Mileage starts at the junction of the Cottonwood Wash and the Oil Well Flat/Saddle Horse Canyon road and goes south.
0.1	Cattle guard.
0.6	Old sign to Mexican Seeps on the left.
1.1	"Tee." Track to the right (W). It goes to Cane Wash in the vicinity of the Mexican Seeps.
1.6	Track to the left goes to a stock reservoir.
2.9	Pinnacle #1 is to the right (W).
3.8	The start of the Pinnacle #1 **Hike/Climb #21.** You are in the middle of a plain. There is no established parking area.
4.0	Gully crossing. A track comes in on the left.
6.1	Up a big hill.

7.1	Junction with Cane Wash. This is the start of the Saddle Horse Canyon track. Restart mileage here.
0.0	Junction of Cane Wash and the Oil Well Flat/Saddle Horse Canyon road. Go generally south up Cane Wash.
1.6	Indian Caves on the right. These are several caves in a cliff at wash level. You will not miss them.
1.6 + 100 yards.	Just past the Indian Caves the track divides. Go right (N), out of the wash. The track is hard to see. Hike #31 comes in at this point.
1.7	"Y." Go right.
4.2	At a pass. Fine views of Joe and His Dog, Devils Monument, and the Wickiup.
5.7	The track divides before reaching the bottom of Saddle Horse Canyon. Go left (S). It is 1.1 miles up the canyon, still on a track, to a pass going into the North Fork of Coal Canyon. The track to the pass is good for mountain bikes. Go right to go down Saddle Horse Canyon. This track may be closed to vehicles in the future.

Side road

0.0	Mileage starts at the "Y." Go right (N).
0.1	Once in Saddle Horse Canyon go north. The canyon is too sandy for mountain bikes.
1.0	A large canyon comes in on the left (W), below Devils Monument and Joe and His Dog.
1.8	Developed sulphur spring and an oil seep.
4.1	A canyon to the right (E). At the top of the canyon there is a pinnacled fin. You can hike up to the pinnacled fin and drop into Cane Wash. This shortcut was often used by cattlemen.
4.2	Partially developed spring to the right.
5.9	Even with an arch on the right. It cannot be seen from here but will become visible if you look back as you continue down the canyon. This arch is mentioned in Hike #22.
8.8	End of the 4WD track. The canyon starts to close in. You will be at a gnarled cottonwood in the middle of the wash in front of a red, swiss cheese wall. The canyon continues to Salt Wash. (See Hike #22 for details.)

★ | # Pinnacle #1—Hike/Climb #21

Season	Any, but no rain or snow.
Time	3 to 4 hours (4 miles)
Elevation gain	1100'
Water	None. Bring your own water.
Maps	The Wickiup. Bottleneck Peak. Pinnacle #1 is shown as Pinnacle at elevation 7010 on the Wickiup map. [San Rafael Desert. Huntington.]
Circle trip	No
Skill level	Easy/moderate route finding. Class 4+ climbing. Much uphill scrambling. A rope may be useful for beginners.

This hike/climb has it all. It is for the person who has seen the great desert spires—the Totem Pole, Castleton Tower, the Fisher Towers—and has wanted to climb one of them. Unfortunately they take an immense amount of skill, training, and equipment to surmount. A hike up Pinnacle #1 will give you a similar thrill, but you can scramble up it! There is never an exposure problem if you follow the route. You are always safe, secure, and well away from big drops.

Look west from the Oil Well Flat road. The monolith to the right is Pinnacle #1; the one to the left is unnamed. At the base of Pinnacle #1 there is a brown, triangular-shaped rubble heap. Hike across the plain and ascend the rubble heap until under the summit tower. Traverse east along the base of the wall. Follow it as it turns north, then south until a series of steep but not vertical ledges and slabs are reached. There are several ponderosa pines here. Zigzag east up the ledges and slabs for 400 feet. There is one moderate (Class 4, 12') section at the start, behind a boulder. The other hard section is halfway up (Class 4, 15'). The summit is to the left (N). It is labeled Pinnacle #1 (7010) on a USGS bench mark from 1937! Hats off to those men. Plan on spending a little time on the marvelous summit platform. Return the way you came.

This is an adventure any fit person, with competent leadership, can handle. It is worth the effort.

Surmounting a short wall on the way to the summit of Pinnacle #1.

Fuller Bottom Road Section

Access to Hikes #22 and 23
Access is from the Green River Cutoff road.
Metric map—Huntington

This road goes south from mile 12.7 on the Green River Cutoff road to Fuller Bottom on the San Rafael River and continues to the rim of Salt Wash above the confluence with Saddle Horse Canyon. (The Green River Cutoff road is detailed in the Northern Reef and Mexican Mountain chapter.) The track is for light-duty vehicles to the river. After that it is for medium-duty vehicles. This is an excellent mountain bike track. There are several tracks branching off from the road that can be used for camping. The area near the river has campsites, but it is often buggy. From the river excess detail is given so you can find the track going to the intersection of Saddle Horse Canyon and Salt Wash, whether in a car or on a mountain bike.

0.0	Mileage starts on the Green River Cutoff road at a sign to Fuller Bottom and goes south.
6.5	The start of Fuller Bottom, Virgin Springs Canyon, Sids Mountain, Saddle Horse Canyon, and Salt Wash **Hike #22.** You are at the river, which can only be crossed during low water. The bottom is gravel, so even medium-duty vehicles can usually cross it. If in doubt, wade the river first. This could save much aggravation.
6.5 + 100 yards.	Once across the river go left (E). The track now goes through an area called the Little Wedge.
	There is a track going to the right (W). It parallels the river and ends in 1.7 miles. To get to Horn Silver Gulch take this 4WD track. The track ''Tees'' a wire gate. Go south through the gate. Stay on the track for about ten miles until you reach Horn Silver Gulch.
7.1	Wire gate and a corral.
7.5	Fence to the left.
7.7	Track to the left, past the fence. There is camping here. A cattle trail starts at the camping spot and goes to the river. This is an alternate start to **Hike #22.**
8.2	The track goes up a gently winding hill and turns from east to south. A track comes diagonally in on the left (S).
8.9	Track divides. Stay with the main track to the right.
9.7	Track comes in on the left. It goes immediately down a hill to the east and continues to Salt Wash.
10.6	Track to the left. In 100 yards it goes to the top of a barren gray area.
11.2	There is a vague track to the left (E). It leads to the confluence of Saddle Horse Canyon and Salt Wash. This is the alternate start for **Hike #23.** After 100 yards this track improves greatly and veers south down a steep hill, drops through a ravine, and ends at the edge of Salt Wash. There is a pack trail into the canyon. Look for a cairn on the rim of the canyon to the east. If this cannot be found, simply drop through cliff bands on ledges. There are many options here. You should run into the pack trail.
11.7	Track divides. To the left the track goes northeast down a steep hill. It is possible to get into Salt Wash from here.
	To the right, the track goes away from Salt Wash toward Horn Silver Gulch.

Mountain biker's note: The track from Fuller Bottom south is great. The side tracks at miles 10.1, 10.6, 11.2, and 11.7 all go to the rim of Salt Wash and provide challenging riding and good views. If this isn't enough, go right at mile 11.7. After three miles the track divides. Go right (N). The track goes back to the San Rafael River. This makes a nice twenty-mile circuit.

★ | ## Fuller Bottom, Virgin Springs Canyon, Sids Mountain, Saddle Horse Canyon, and Salt Wash—Hike #22

Season	Early spring or fall
Time	2 to 3 days. Two days is difficult and leaves no time for exploring. Three days should be taken if possible. This could take longer if a day hike is added (See Hike #23.) (30 miles).
Elevation gain	1200'
Water	San Rafael River. There is an excellent spring in the box of Virgin Springs Canyon that is always flowing. Upper Virgin Springs Canyon has seasonal springs. There is no reliable water on Sids Mountain. Saddle Horse Canyon and Salt Wash have small perennial springs. You can depend on them.
Maps	Sids Mountain. [Huntington]
Circle trip	Yes
Skill level	Moderate route finding. Class 3 scrambling. There is one long uphill section at the top of Virgin Springs Canyon that is jading with a pack. Low-impact camping techniques are essential. Wading shoes are needed for the San Rafael River portion.

Backpacking trips are generally swell. Camping high on a slickrock wall or deep in a sand-floored canyon are unforgettable experiences. This hike provides the opportunity to do both. The route not only goes through several outstanding canyons, but it also goes to the top of Sids Mountain, a mesa dotted with Navajo domes.

The route goes down the San Rafael River, past Salt Wash to Virgin Springs Canyon, up the canyon, and out its head onto Sids Mountain. After crossing the mountain, the route drops into Saddle Horse Canyon. This is followed to Salt Wash, which is descended back to the San Rafael River.

Enough information is given in this section to allow you to tie into Hikes #19, 20, and 23. The steadfast adventurer could easily spend a week hiking the maze of canyons in and around Sids Mountain.

From Fuller Bottom follow a trail on the south side of the river as you go down. Depending on the river flow, you will have to wade four to eight times between Fuller Bottom and Salt Wash. Plan on 1.5 to 2 hours to Salt Wash.

> **Digression:** After an hour keep your eyes to the right (LDC). Look for a narrow side canyon. Past the canyon you will see the light-colored slag from a mine high on a hill. This is the Sorrel Mule Mine, a copper mine excavated in 1898. It goes 2000 feet into the mountain. The narrow canyon next to the mine is worth a short side trip. There are miner's glyphs etched on a wall.

Immediately after the first river crossing past Salt Wash, note the Barrier Canyon Style pictograph on the left (NW). The path deteriorates. There are several more river crossings. You will have to wade to get into the box of Virgin Springs Canyon. It takes 2 to 2.5 hours from Salt Wash to Virgin Springs Canyon.

Once in the box the pictograph panel is a quarter mile up the canyon on the right (W). It is fifteen feet above the ground. To exit the box find a break in the wall to the left (LUC), 150 yards above the pictographs. A perennial spring pool is 150 yards further up, at the head of the box. If you are planning to do the hike in three days, camp near here. Though there is camping in the box, the area is becoming impacted by backpackers and river runners. Try not to camp in the box itself. There are seasonal springs forty-five minutes up the canyon at the junction with the West Fork of Virgin Springs Canyon. They are usually running well in the spring and fall. There is camping in the area.

Digression: Instead of going all the way up Virgin Springs Canyon, you can go up its West Fork to Swazy on Sids Mountain; then find the line cabins and follow the horse trail down to the junction of Saddle Horse Canyon and Salt Wash. (See the second digression in Hike #20, and Hike #23 for details.) This will save four to six hours of hiking, at the expense of bypassing much beautiful scenery.

After the junction with the West Fork, continue up the main canyon (ESE), always going right when the canyon divides. As the canyon narrows and steepens a high, red mud fall is reached. Pass the fall to the left (LUC). Go up steep slopes, working up and along ledges and at one point going through an arch. There are many variations here. Pick a safe, suitable route. At the last cliff band the main canyon goes left (S). Go right (W) into a short canyon and then immediately go up a steep, rocky slope. This section is tiring with a pack on. At the top go up onto terrific slickrock. You will be north of a Navajo-walled buttress. (This is shown as elevation 6714.)

Digression: You can do a short day hike to Swazy and the line cabins from here. Go northwest across the slickrock back to the rim of Virgin Springs Canyon. Hike between the rim and a cliff band on the left. The ledge system looks thinner than it is. As you exit, come around a corner (W) into a meadow. To the right (N) there is a cliff band. Follow below this to the west, then northwest until it peters out. Swazy is to the north. It doesn't look like much from here. It is a rounded oblong dome with a red horizontal stripe halfway up it. (For details on climbing Swazy and finding the cabins see the second digression in Hike #20.)

To the west is a saddle between a wall to the north and a dome to the south. The dome has three blocks on its right side. (The dome is at elevation 6605.) For those on a two-day hike, camp in this area. To the west of the saddle is a ridge that has a small tower at its south end. The tower looks froggish once you get closer to it. Cross a meadow and go to the south end of the froggish tower.

From the froggish tower go southwest to the rim of a side canyon going into Saddle Horse Canyon. Looking across it, you will see a boulder slope going top to bot-

Springs and pinnacle in Lower Saddle Horse Canyon.

tom. Skirt the rim of the side canyon and descend the 800-foot slope into Saddle Horse Canyon. (This is just north of elevation 6466.) Look up the canyon. There is an arch, which is mentioned in the Oil Well Flat/Saddle Horse Canyon Road Section at mile 5.9. From the box of Virgin Springs Canyon it will take a strenuous four to five hours to Sids Mountain and another two hours to the floor of Saddle Horse Canyon.

Go north down Saddle Horse Canyon. In forty-five minutes you will reach a gnarled and broken cottonwood sitting in the middle of the wash just before a red, swiss cheese wall that marks the end of the 4WD track. (See the Oil Well Flat/Saddle Horse Canyon Road Section, mile 8.8, for details.) Within an hour pass a 100-foot-high, freestanding pinnacle. It is ten minutes before you reach Salt Wash. The springs you have been seeing disappear near the pinnacle. Those on a three-day hike should try to camp near the pinnacle. The Saddle Horse Canyon section takes two hours.

From the confluence go down Salt Wash. Salt Wash is a great, Wingate-walled canyon. At one point, fifteen minutes below the Saddle Horse Canyon junction, the wash passes through a narrow gap.

Digression: The gap marks the start of a horse trail going up to Sids Mountain (Hike #23). This is a fine day hike.

If the springs in Salt Wash are running well, there could be a little ankle-deep wading. Keep your eyes peeled for occasional pictograph panels. It will take two to three hours from Saddle Horse Canyon, down Salt Wash, to the San Rafael River.

House Hunting on Sids Mountain—Hike #23

Season	Any. Spring and fall are best. It would be hard to see the horse trail with snow on the ground.
Time	From the junction of Salt Wash and Saddle Horse Canyon: Part 1—5 to 7 hours (10 miles) Part 2—8 to 10 hours. The length of this hike would indicate an overnight hike (14 miles).
Elevation gain	1150′
Water	Salt Wash always has water. There is no dependable source of water on Sids Mountain. Bring your own water.
Maps	Sids Mountain. [Huntington]
Circle trip	Part 1—No Part 2—Partial
Skill level	Part 1—Moderate route finding. Class 2 walking, mostly on a horse trail. Part 2—Moderate route finding. Class 2+ walking. If you do this as an overnight hike, low-impact camping techniques are essential.

Fantasyland is an apt description of Sids Mountain. It is a flat-topped mesa strewn with large Navajo domes. There is much to see and do. The goal of the hike is to get atop Sids Mountain and among its many domes. On the way you will encounter a unique line cabin tucked between two of the domes.

The hike comes in two parts. Part 2 is an extension of Part 1. Both parts start at the confluence of Saddle Horse

Canyon and Salt Wash and follow a horse trail to the top of Sids Mountain. Part 1 returns the same way. Part 2 follows a side canyon to the rim of Salt Wash and then rejoins the horse trail.

This hike is meant to be an adjunct to Hike #22, or it can be used as a separate day hike by starting from the Fuller Bottom road. (See that road section, at mile 11.2, for details.)

Part 1: From the junction of Saddle Horse Canyon and Salt Wash go down Salt Wash for fifteen minutes. After two corners the wash, going northeast, turns sharply northwest at a narrow gap. (This is just south of elevation 5723.) Before reaching the gap you may notice the horse trail to the right (LDC), five feet above the wash. If you don't, just before reaching the gap go east up a shallow dirt gully that is partially blocked by tamarisks. You will find the horse trail behind the tamarisks. The trail, going east up the side of Sids Mountain, is generally easy to follow, though it tends to disappear from time to time. Persevere. It only disappears for short stretches.

From the rim of Sids Mountain the trail goes generally southeast. In places it is a foot deep, in others it is hard to see. Past a log fence that goes across a narrow neck, the trail drops south onto a large meadow. Follow the trail as it turns east and goes between two domes. This is where the cabins are located. There is camping throughout the area.

> **Historical note:** Sids Mountain is named after Sid Swasey who, according to legend, followed a bighorn up its steep flanks and so discovered the mesa. The line cabins were apparently built at different times. The unique cabin on stilts was built in the 1940s by Rex Koffard and was later sold to the Swaseys. Do not disturb the cabin. There are the remains of an older cabin, but the construction date is unknown.

> **Digression:** The highest point on Sids Mountain is a slickrock dome simply called Swazy (6610). From the cabins go east across a meadow. Swazy is at the far side of the meadow. From this angle it looks like a slickrock bump with a rounded dirt top (Carmel Formation on top of Navajo Sandstone). Ascend steep slickrock on the

A unique line cabin on Sids Mountain.

southwest side, or go up slightly easier ground on the north side. It will take one hour to complete the trip.

For those doing Part 1, return the way you came.

Part 2: From the cabins go northeast for several hundred yards on a trail. Follow it as it turns north-northeast into the head of a shallow canyon. Follow the trail as it goes along the left side (LDC) of the bottom of the canyon. In three hours you will reach a fall overlooking Salt Wash.

Exit the canyon to the left (SW), past a cave/arch. Follow the rim of Salt Wash for an hour, skirting one large side canyon and several smaller ones until you intersect the horse trail. Follow the trail down to Salt Wash.

Moore Cutoff Road Section

Access to Hikes #24 and 25
Access is from Interstate 70 and Highway 10.
Metric map—San Rafael Desert. Salina.

This gravel road goes from Interstate 70 to the small

town of Moore. A paved road then goes to Highway 10 south of Ferron. It saves many miles of travel if you are going from Interstate 70 to the upper Castle Valley area (Price and Castle Dale). From Green River go west on Interstate 70 for forty-four miles to Ranch Exit 114. The road is good for all vehicles, but is not suitable for mountain bikes. There is limited camping along the road.

0.0	Mileage starts at the cattle guard just north of Interstate 70 and goes northwest.
0.6	Great views of Eagle Canyon and beyond to the right.
1.6	Track on the right. It goes through a wire gate.
2.5	Small water tank on the left.
3.1	Wire gate and track to the right (NW), twenty feet from the road. It is easy to miss. This track goes to the start of Eagle Canyon—North—and Forgotten Canyon Hike #25. It is a medium-duty vehicle/4WD road. Extra detail is given for those riding mountain bikes to the trailhead. It will take bikers sixty to seventy-five minutes going up and fifty to sixty minutes going down.

Side road

0.0	Mileage starts at the wire gate and goes northwest.
0.1	"Y." Stay left.
0.9	In and out of a wash. The track turns and goes east.
3.4	The track goes up a rocky gray hill.
3.6	The track flattens out. Though the ground is barren, there are many trees. There is good camping in the area. The track turns north.
4.2	Top of a small rise. There is a road cut through gray shale.
4.5	Track divides. Go right.
4.6	In and out of a small gully. This may be the end for medium-duty vehicles.
5.1	In and out of a gully. 4WDs only.
6.1	Vague track to the right, which you should take. It gets better as you go along.
6.8	Start of Eagle Canyon—North—and Forgotten Canyon **Hike #25.** End of the track. (This is southwest of elevation 6396 on the Sid and Charley map.) Eagle Canyon is a short distance to the north. **End of side road**

5.0	Small water tank on the left.
6.5	Track to the left that goes south along the Red Cliffs.
6.6	Track to the right going north along the base of the Red Cliffs. It passes the Sid and Charley pinnacle in three miles. This is a freestanding pinnacle formed from Entrada Sandstone that sits in the middle of a barren plain. Behind the pinnacle, to the northwest high on a cliff, are several Fremont Culture pictograph panels and the remnants of a cliff dwelling. Though you cannot get up to them, they are easy to see and photograph. This is the upper end of North Salt Wash. Mountain bikes work well on this 4WD road.
7.3	Top of a hill. The Red Cliffs and a pinnacle/arch are to the left. This is called Lookout Point.
12.0	Dip, marked.
12.3	Corral on the right.
13.9	There are several petroglyphs on scattered boulders as you make a sweeping right-hand turn around a bluff. They are visible from the road.
18.1	Town of Moore. Go right (N). The road will take you to Highway 10 in 3.5 miles.

To get to Rochester Indian Rock Art Hike #24 go left (S). This is a light-duty road until mile 3.7.

Side road

0.0	Mileage starts at the town of Moore and the Moore Cutoff road intersection and goes south.
2.0	A gravel road intersects on the left (S). Take this.
3.6	"Y." Go left toward a radio tower. The road to the right goes to a gravel pit.
3.7	Road divides before the radio tower. Go right. The road deteriorates into a medium-duty track. The track from here to the trailhead is good for mountain bikes.
3.9	Go through a wire gate and along a barbed-wire fence.
4.6	Under powerlines.
4.8	Track divides. Go right, away from the fence and up a small rise.
5.6	The start of Rochester Indian Rock Art **Hike #24** is at the edge of a shallow canyon. There is a sign at the trailhead.

End of side road

If you are coming from Highway 10, turn off the highway at the well-marked Moore exit south of Ferron. After 1.8 miles the road divides. Go right. In another 1.7 miles you will reach the town of Moore. If you are going to Rochester Indian Rock Art Hike #24 continue straight ahead (S).

The Moore Cutoff road starts immediately before the first building in the town of Moore is reached and goes east. In one-half mile the road divides. Go right, off the pavement onto the gravel Moore Cutoff road.

★ | ## Rochester Indian Rock Art—Hike #24

Season	Any
Time	1 to 2 hours. Actual hiking time is 20 minutes (0.5 mile).
Elevation gain	75′
Water	None. Bring your own water.
Maps	Emery East. The petroglyph panels are a quarter mile to the south of elevation 6198, which is south of the radio facility. [Salina]
Circle trip	No
Skill level	Easy route finding. Class 1 walking. This is a good hike for all, from kids to seniors.

It is out of character to have such a short hike in the guide, but the quality of this excursion deserves more than a sidebar in a road section. The route follows a short trail to an extraordinary set of Southern San Rafael Style petroglyph panels located on a peninsula of rock overlooking Muddy Creek as it enters the San Rafael Swell.

From the sign, the trail goes northeast for fifty yards then switches back and heads south. It goes along the hillside above the canyon floor. At the first panel, which has four characters on it, the trail, now less distinct, goes along the top of a ridge to the end of a peninsula. This is

Petroglyph detail at Rochester Creek.

where the bulk of the petroglyphs are. Look carefully as there are panels all around the end of the ridge.

There has been little vandalism here. These panels share honors with the Three Finger Canyon petroglyphs for the best on the Swell.

> **Rock-climber's note:** There is a cliff band of exceptionally solid rock running through the area. It is from fifteen to sixty feet high and provides many crack climbs—on-width to chimneys. These are within a minute of the trailhead to the south.

★ ## Eagle Canyon—North—and Forgotten Canyon (AN)—Hike #25

Season	Any. Spring and fall are best. There is the potential for flash floods in both canyons.
Time	4 to 5 hours (8 miles)
Elevation gain	300'
Water	There is always water at the fall in Eagle Canyon. Forgotten Canyon has seasonal potholes. Bring your own water.

Maps | Sid and Charley. Forgotten Canyon is shown but is not labeled on the map. It is the east-west-running drainage north of elevation 7022. The natural arch is marked on the map. (San Rafael Knob) [San Rafael Desert]

Circle trip | No

Skill level | Easy route finding. Class 2 walking.

Eagle Canyon, as it drops from south to north, from the Swasey Cabin area at the Head of Sinbad to North Salt Wash, is divided at its northern end by an impassable fall. The Eagle Canyon—Midsection—and an Overland Excursion Hike #26 goes north down the canyon to the fall. Because of its easy access, that hike is popular. Unbeknownst to most, though, is that the north part of Eagle Canyon, the section beyond the fall, contains one of the premier canyons on the Swell (Forgotten Canyon).

The hike starts at the western edge of the San Rafael Swell and goes up Eagle Canyon to the impassable fall. It returns the same way. Forgotten Canyon is presented as a digression.

From the parking area go northeast down steep slopes into the canyon. There are many options here. Pick a route that is safe. Go up the canyon. In ninety minutes there is a narrow section which is fun to negotiate but, if wet, can be passed on ledges to the right (LUC). The canyon ends at a perennial pool, and a Douglas-fir tree at the bottom of a fall. Return the way you came.

> **Digression:** From the mouth (downstream portion) of the narrow section mentioned above hike down the canyon for twenty-two minutes. A flat, sand-floored canyon comes in on the right (LDC)(NE). It is hard to miss. This is Forgotten Canyon. (Author's note: For some inexplicable reason this fantastic canyon has been left out of the literature. With its long, tight narrows and a great arch, it deserves notice.)
>
> Go up the canyon. There are several Class 4 obstacles. At a large drop ascend a friction slab to the right (LUC); then traverse over the head of the fall to the left (Class 4, 30′). Beginners may want a rope. Once through the narrow section the canyon enters a parklike area. Follow the main streambed through here; then keep a watch to the

left. The arch is at the top of a small side canyon near the skyline. It is easy to miss. Return the way you came. This digression will take two hours.

Eagle Canyon Road Section

Access to Hikes #26 and 27
Access is from Interstate 70.
Metric map—San Rafael Desert

This short road goes north from Interstate 70 to a highway maintenance building. From Green River go west on Interstate 70 for thirty-nine miles until 0.7 mile past milepost 119. Turn right (N) onto a gravel road. The road is suitable for any vehicle. There is camping along the road. This road may be closed in the future. You will still be able to use the direction and mileage to find the trailheads.

0.0   Mileage starts at the cattle guard just north of Interstate 70 and goes north.

0.1   Road divides. Stay left (W).

The start of South Fork of Coal Wash **Hike #27**. There is a road to the right (E). It immediately goes through a road cut. Go down the road for 0.1 mile. There is a track going across a dike to the left (N). Drive down the track for several hundred yards and park.

0.6   The start of Eagle Canyon—Midsection—and an Overland Excursion **Hike #26**. There is a track going west. Park here. The track drops into Eagle Canyon, then continues west up the other side of the canyon to I–70. It can be ridden on mountain bikes. It is long and steep, with a little sand.

| 0.7 | Continue through the U-turn on the gravel road and reach a highway maintenance building. |

Eagle Canyon—Midsection—and an Overland Excursion—Hike #26

Season	Part 1—Any. There is the potential for ORV traffic in this part of Eagle Canyon. Off-season or midweek would be best.
	Part 2—Any, but no snow or recent rains.
Time	Part 1—4 to 5 hours (8 miles)
	Part 2—5 to 6 hours (10 miles)
Elevation gain	Part 1—500'
	Part 2—800'
Water	Seasonal potholes. Bring your own water.
Map	San Rafael Knob. Copper Globe. Sid and Charley. (San Rafael Knob) [San Rafael Desert]
Circle trip	Part 1—No
	Part 2—Yes
Skill level	Part 1—Easy route finding. Class 1 walking. This is a good hike for all.
	Part 2—Advanced route finding. Class 4 climbing. Steep uphill scrambling. Some exposure. Experienced canyoneers only.

The midsection of Eagle Canyon is wide, deep, Navajo-walled, easy to walk, and has several short side canyons to explore. Because of its easy access it is a popular canyon.

The hike comes in two parts. Part 1 goes down a track into the bottom of Eagle Canyon. It then goes down to an impassable fall. Return the way you came. Part 2 goes from the impassable fall, over a high ridge, and back to the start.

Part 1: Hike down the track (W) into the bottom of the canyon. Turn right (W). After forty-five minutes there is a set of "Indian" caves to the right. In front of these there is an ORV-mutilated hill. It is a prominent landmark. Continue around a corner. The canyon goes northeast and straightens out for a quarter mile. As the canyon makes a sharp corner west, a small side canyon comes in on the right (E). This is the exit point for those doing Part 2. Remember this place.

You will reach the end of the canyon in another fifteen minutes. There is no easy way around the fall. (Hike #25 describes the lower portion of Eagle Canyon.) For those doing Part 1, return the way you came, perhaps taking the time to explore some of the side canyons.

Part 2: Return to the aforementioned side canyon and go up it to the east. After two minutes the canyon enters a narrow section which is bypassed to the right (LUC). Immediately after the narrow section the canyon divides. Go right. At a fall go left following the same, but now shallower, drainage south across a parklike area. At its end go left (LUC)(E) up an easy slope; then go south, traversing between cliff bands. After several minutes, as you turn a corner and go east, things ease up. What views!

Continue traversing at the same level, first east, then south again. Traverse until you see the bridges on I–70 to the southeast. If you continue traversing there is a dead end in several hundred yards. Instead, ascend a steep slope to the left (N). The slope is shaley and loose near the top. From the top of the small mesa go east to its end. Looking northeast beyond an area of slickrock is a large open area. This is Secret Mesa, which is a mis-nomer; it is not a mesa, but rather a bowl. If you look further to the northeast the bowl turns into a pinyon and juniper plain. Beyond the plain there is a slickrock dome with a thin, trapezoidal-shaped dome on its left side. You want to end up at the base of the trapezoidal-shaped dome.

Work your way to the dome by negotiating several cliff bands and finding a way across a shallow, slickrock-lined canyon. Once at the trapezoidal-shaped dome (you have avoided a canyon this way) go south around the end of the slickrock monolith, then southeast for fifteen min-utes across broken ground back to the start. A 100-foot-tall white tower perched in a canyon to the right is called the White Knight.

South Fork of Coal Wash—Hike #27

Season	Any. Winter without excessive snow is okay.
Time	Part 1—4 to 6 hours (10 miles)
	Part 2—6 to 8 hours (12 miles)
Elevation gain	850′
Water	There are sulphur springs in the South Fork of Coal Wash. Bring your own water.
Maps	The Blocks. San Rafael Knob. Sid and Charley (San Rafael Knob) [San Rafael Desert]
Circle trip	Yes
Skill level	Part 1—Easy route finding. Class 3 scrambling. This is a moderate hike.
	Part 2—Intermediate route finding. Class 3 scrambling. This is a long day hike.

Walking along the rim of a canyon and then hiking in the bottom of the same canyon can provide interesting insights into the true beauty of an area. Perceptions are radically changed. Indistinguishable walls seen from a distance are found to contain pinnacles, hanging valleys, arches, and caves as one moves closer. Deep in a canyon, distant views are often blocked by sheer walls that hide slickrock domes and towers far above.

The route comes in two parts. Part 2 is an extension of Part 1, providing an option for those interested in doing a longer hike. The route follows a mining track on the west rim of the South Fork of Coal Wash, with impressive views of The Blocks, Chimney Rock, Joe and His Dog, and an arch high on a canyon wall. The track drops into Coal Wash and returns to the start by hiking up its bottom.

Part 1: Go north down the track. In a half hour you will see a 100-foot-high pinnacle to the left next to the canyon wall. (The pinnacle is at the northeast end of the buttress marked elevation 7112 on The Blocks map.) Remember the pinnacle. Past the pinnacle the track divides in the middle of a meadow. Follow the main track to the left (SW).

> **Digression:** The track to the right (N) goes to the edge of Coal Wash. With fine views, this is a good destination for those wanting a short, scenic hike.

After an hour watch for an arch on the skyline to the left. It is easy to miss. (It is shown on the Sid and Charley map.) To the right (E), across the canyon, are The Blocks. The pinnacles forming a V are Joe and His Dog.

The track deteriorates as it enters a wash and seems to end. Go down the wash (NE). The track comes and goes as you drop into the South Fork of Coal Wash. Go right (S). In forty-five minutes there is a short side canyon coming in on the right (SSW) with the pinnacle at its head. Remember it? Hike up the canyon and scramble up a steep slope. Continue west to the original track.

Part 2: Instead of exiting at the pinnacle continue up the South Fork of Coal Wash. In five minutes the canyon divides. Go right (S). The left fork goes east up the canyon and by Chimney Rock (Hike #29). In another ten minutes the canyon divides again, the main course going to the left (S). Go right (SW). At this juncture there is a small pinnacle on the wall to the south. Ascend the steep slope to the right of the pinnacle (Class 3) until you reach the canyon rim.

> **Rock-climber's note:** Instead of exiting by the pinnacle, go up the canyon to the right (SW). There are several Class 4 sections, none with exposure problems. There is a sulphur spring and a small natural bridge that you can walk over. Above the bridge the canyon divides, with neither fork providing an outlet. Both are worth a short diversion to check them out. To exit the canyon go to the top of the natural bridge; then go uphill (E) to a ledge system. Follow it down the canyon for several hundred yards until you can continue up slabs by some small openings. Once below the last cliff band go right until a Class 4 exit is found; then join the original route.

From the rim you will see the Navajo wall you started under to the west. To get back to the start, go generally southwest around the heads of several small canyons. Join the track close to the start.

Swasey Cabin and the Broken Cross Road Section

Access to Hike #28
Access is from Interstate 70.
Metric map—San Rafael Desert

This road goes south from Interstate 70 to the Swasey Cabin. From Green River go west on Interstate 70 for 35.5 miles until one-half mile past milepost 123. The only access is from the eastbound lanes. Locate a hard-to-see underpass. Drop off the interstate to the south, just west of the underpass, and go through a wire gate. (The road to the north, through the tunnel, is the Dutchmans Arch/Devils Racetrack road.) Depending on how recently the road has been graded, it can be either a light- or medium-duty road and is well suited for mountain bikes. There is camping throughout the area.

0.0	Mileage starts at the wire gate just south of I–70. The road initially goes west.
0.3	Road divides. Go right.
0.9	Brush corral to the right.
1.1	Wire gate.
1.6	"Tee." Stay left to go to the Swasey Cabin.
	Go right to go to the Devil's Box pictograph and petroglyph panels.

Side road

0.0	Mileage starts at the "Tee" and goes right.
0.1	Track divides. Stay left (W), going toward the Devil's Box.

0.3	Track divides. Stay with the main track to the left as it goes into the box canyon.
0.4	The pictograph and petroglyph panels are on a wall to the right (N). They are hard to see. They are to the left (W) of a vertical gray streak.
0.5	The Devil's Box pictograph. It is on the north wall. **End of side road**
2.3	"Y." Stay with the main road to the right (W).
3.1	Start of Swasey Cabin and Upper Eagle Canyon **Hike #28.** You can park near the Swasey Cabin. There is a BLM-maintained outhouse to the east of the cabin.

★ | **Swasey Cabin and Upper Eagle Canyon—Hike #28**

Season	Any
Time	3 to 4 hours to the arch and back (5 miles)
Elevation gain	500′
Water	There is water in a developed spring behind the Swasey Cabin. There is no other water on the route. Bring your own water.
Maps	San Rafael Knob. (San Rafael Knob) [San Rafael Desert]
Circle trip	No
Skill level	Easy route finding. Class 1 walking. The hike is suitable for all.

Festina lente (make haste slowly) as you savor the upper reaches of Eagle Canyon. It is steep walled and lined with cottonwoods, junipers, and pinyon pines. A large arch, a sulphur spring, and an old mine site will make the hike interesting to all.

The route starts at the Swasey Cabin and follows a 4WD road into the bottom of Eagle Canyon. Several options are given for exploring the canyon.

Historical note: The Swaseys were a pioneer Mormon family who moved into the San Rafael Swell area in the 1870s. They started to use the Head of Sinbad area, the plain surrounding the cabin, in the 1880s, sleeping in nearby caves. The cabin was built in 1921. They called it the Cliff Dweller Cabin. It has recently been stabilized by the BLM.

The pinnacle behind the Swasey Cabin is the Broken Cross. Behind it, to the southwest against a cliff band, are a small spring and a corral. Behind these is a cave that was used to keep food cool. A quarter mile south of the cabin, against the cliff band, are the remnants of an old brush corral.

The legacy of the Swasey family will endure in the names they gave to many of the features in the San Rafael Swell. Sids Mountain, Sids Leap, Sids Draw, and the Sid and Charley pinnacles are named for Sid or Charley Swasey. Joe and His Dog is named for Joe Swasey. Rods Valley is named for Rod Swasey. Swazy on the top of Sids Mountain was also named for the Swasey family. Swazy is an erroneous variant of Swasey used on the U.S.G.S. topographic maps. Besides using their own names, the Swaseys were responsible for naming many other features, including Eagle Canyon, Ghost Rock, and Cliff Dweller Flats.

From the Swasey Cabin follow a 4WD track west as it goes down a beautiful canyon. In an hour you will intersect Eagle Canyon. To find the arch walk north down the canyon on the jeep road for fifteen minutes. There is a developed sulphur spring another fifteen minutes down

The Swasey Cabin and the Broken Cross.

the canyon from the arch on the left (LDC) tucked into a shady alcove of trees. You will smell it before you see it! The more energetic can continue down Eagle Canyon to I–70. It will add two hours to the hike.

If you turn left (S) in Eagle Canyon it will take a half hour to reach the mining area at the head of the canyon. There are several fine pinnacles along the route. The head of the canyon is heavily sculpted and exceptionally photogenic. Either way you go, return the way you came.

Dutchmans Arch/Devils Racetrack Road Section

Access to Hikes #29 through 31
Access is from Interstate 70.
Metric map—San Rafael Desert

This is a short track going north from Interstate 70. From Green River go west on Interstate 70 for 35.5 miles until 0.5 mile past milepost 123. The only access is from the eastbound lanes. Locate a hard-to-see underpass. Drop south off the interstate just to the west of the underpass and go through a wire gate. Drive north through the tunnel that goes under the interstate to another wire gate. (The road to the south goes to the Swasey Cabin at the Head of Sinbad.) This is a medium-duty track. There is quite a bit of sand in the area, making it unsuitable for mountain bikes. There is camping throughout the area.

0.0	Mileage starts at the wire gate just north of I–70 and goes north.
0.2	"Tee." Go left (NW).
	Go straight (N) to go to an overlook above Cane Wash. The first right past the intersection goes to a good Barrier Canyon Style pictograph panel.
0.4	Track to the left (S) going toward I–70.
0.6	The small Dutchmans Arch.

1.0	Track coming in on the right. Continue straight.
1.1	The start of **Hikes #29 through 31.** The track divides. Take the main track to the right (N) and park between several fifteen-foot-high formations. The track turns into a 4WD track in a third of a mile. There are several decent campsites in the area.

★ | ## The Best Views in the Swell—Hike #29

Season	Any. Since Part 1 follows a 4WD road it is advisable to do the hike during the off-season or midweek. This road must be walked to enjoy it to the fullest.
Time	Part 1—3 to 4 hours (7 miles)
	Part 2—5 to 7 hours (10 miles)
Elevation gain	Part 1—300'
	Part 2—800'
Water	Seasonal. Bring your own water.
Maps	The Blocks. San Rafael Knob (San Rafael Knob) [San Rafael Desert]
Circle trip	Part 1—No
	Part 2—Yes
Skill level	Part 1—Easy route finding. Class 1 walking. Anyone can and should do this part of the hike.
	Part 2—Moderate route finding. Class 3+ scrambling. A moderately long day.

Oh boy, is this hike a pleasure! Easy walking along the rim of an escarpment combines with eye-popping views of the Sids Mountain area to make this route mandatory for the San Rafael Swell aficionado.

The hike comes in two parts. Part 1 is an easy walk along an old mining road—often called the Dutchmans Arch road. It takes you past the heads of several canyons—Cane Wash, Coal Wash, and Bullock Draw—with views aplenty! The route finishes at the end of the track. Load a lunch and a camera. Bring the kids.

Part 2 starts at the end of the mining track. The route goes cross-country to the middle of The Blocks and up an unnamed tributary of the South Fork of Coal Wash. It then passes under Chimney Rock with an optional ascent of this Navajo tower.

Part 1: The mining track will be described in detail to help you locate landmarks and become oriented. (The times mentioned are cumulative.) Hike up the track to the northwest. After several minutes the track goes up a steep section. At the top look west. The monolith is Chimney Rock. After five minutes pass a wire gate. For twenty-five minutes the track goes gently uphill. Suddenly it starts down. You will obtain the first of the far views to the north. Straight ahead, in the far distance, is the Devils Monument tower.

The track goes down a rough slickrock section. At the bottom of the slickrock, if you go right (NE) for fifty yards, you will be at the top of Cane Wash (Hike #31).

For thirty-five minutes the track has generally been going north. Keep an eye out for a drill pipe to the left (W). (This is shown on The Blocks map.) It is fifty yards off the track and is partially hidden by a tree. Four minutes after the drill pipe the track goes to the edge of the North Fork of Coal Wash; then it turns from north to west, hugging the rim of the canyon. The dominant Navajo monolith to the northwest is elevation 7079. It is adjacent to the Twin Priests pinnacles which are barely visible from this angle. In ninety seconds the track goes away from the rim. There are several large cairns to the right (N). They mark the start of the Devils Racetrack cattle trail (Hike #30). It follows the rim to the north.

Continue west on the track until it ends at a slab area with a drill pipe. (This is shown to the northwest of elevation 6884 on The Blocks map.) For those not continuing on, return the way you came.

Part 2: Go west toward The Blocks. You will be going toward a 175-foot-high spire. (This is shown as elevation 6882 on The Blocks map.) From the left side of the spire, looking west, there are three of The Blocks lined up like battleships. Hike to the one furthest to the left (S). (This is shown as elevation 6854 on The Blocks map.) From its eastern shoulder hike a straight line (SE) toward Chimney Rock. In eight to ten minutes you will intercept a deep canyon. It is a tributary to the South Fork of Coal Wash. If you aren't sure you are in the right spot, look for a sixty-foot-tall pinnacle sticking out of a slab halfway up the canyon wall. Follow the rim north. As it turns southeast there is a steep gully 200 yards before the pinnacle. Descend the gully to the canyon floor. There is one moderate (Class 3+) section near the top.

At the bottom turn left (E). As you go up the canyon there are bits and pieces of an old mining road and several seasonal springs. After fifteen minutes, in an area of pinnacles, caves, and alcoves, the canyon divides. Go right, toward a spectacular, 150-foot-tall, freestanding pinnacle. Once even with the pinnacle clamber up behind it (N). This area is fun just for its small caprock spires. Zigzag north up colorful cliffs and past several caves (Class 3+) to the rim. The views of the canyon, the pinnacle, and The Blocks are superb.

Hike southeast for forty-five minutes across a pinyon and juniper plain, passing Chimney Rock on its north side. When you intersect a track go left (E). It goes back to the start.

> **Rock-climber's note:** Can Chimney Rock (7406) be climbed? You bet. Start on the north side. Ascend a steep gully (Class 4) for 100 feet and work up to a red ledge. Traverse the ledge to the left (E). It is wide except for one narrow spot that has horrendous exposure. Beginners may want to be roped. Scramble up an easy gully to a slot. Climb straight up to the summit. The first fifteen feet are the crux (5.3, 15') and can be somewhat protected with a sling through a hole. After that it is easier (Class 4, 80'). Beginners will want a rope. Downclimb the route. The climb takes one hour.

The Devils Racetrack, Bullock Draw, and the Golden Gate—Hike #30

Season	Any. Spring and fall are best.
Time	6 to 8 hours (12 miles)

Elevation gain	1000′
Water	Seasonal. Upper Bullock Draw has a good, but sulphur-tainted, spring. Bring your own water.
Maps	The Blocks. San Rafael Knob. (San Rafael Knob) [San Rafael Desert]
Circle trip	Yes
Skill level	Moderate route finding. Class 3 scrambling. Most of the hike is in washes, on easy terrain, or along a track.

Just the name of the hike is intriguing enough to make one want to check it out. Don't worry, no Satanism is involved, unless cattle and cowboys. . . .

The route goes along the Dutchmans Arch road until it intersects the historic Devils Racetrack cattle trail. It then drops into the head of Bullock Draw, down this fine canyon to a break in a cliff band, and rejoins the Devils Racetrack after passing two pinnacles and two arches.

Go northwest up the same mining track, the Dutchmans Arch road, as do Hikes #29 and 31. Part 1 of Hike #29 has a good description of how to get to the start of the Devils Racetrack. Follow those directions.

> **Historical note:** The Devils Racetrack cattle trail has been used since the turn of the century to take stock from the top of the Swell into the Coal Wash area.

From the cairns follow the Devils Racetrack as it goes north along the west rim of the North Fork of Coal Wash. It may be vague at times. Persevere, it is never lost for long. The rim you are following narrows down. There is a wire gate at the narrowest part. Do not continue along the Devils Racetrack. Instead, descend a slope to the west. All water courses here will lead to the head of Bullock Draw. At a large fall follow the rim to the right (LDC) for a quarter mile until a side canyon is reached. Scramble down it into the main canyon.

At a tall, skinny fall stay on a ledge to the left (LDC) for a quarter mile until a steep slope goes to the bottom. Go down the canyon for an hour. The canyon gets shallower. You will see a set of monoliths to the right (N). The first in line is elevation 7079, abutting the Twin Priests. Past this a large unnamed wash comes in on the left (SSE). At its head there is a monolith, one of The Blocks.

Fifteen minutes from this junction intersect a small wash coming in on the right (LDC)(NE). This is an important intersection. (It is southwest of elevation 6712 on The Blocks map.) To make sure you are in the right place note its characteristics. You have been walking on slickrock in the bottom of the wash. At the end of the slickrock there is a slightly overhung pothole, three feet wide by ten feet long. To the northwest a third of a mile is a red tower. To the west is a wall with a short pinnacle high on its east side.

Go northeast up the wash. For the first three to four minutes walk on slickrock up a shallow canyon. In another five minutes the canyon divides. Go left (NE). The wash peters out after a bit. Hike through a prominent break in the canyon wall to the north. On the far side of the break are the Golden Gate pinnacles.

> **Rock-climber's note:** The 175-foot-tall Golden Gate pinnacles have the potential for several fine climbs. Though the Twin Priests have no potential routes, elevation 7079 has two moderate routes on the southeast side that are destined to become classics.

Hike up to the south side of the pinnacles. To the north is Joe and His Dog. To join the Devils Racetrack go east up a long uphill plain. Note the arch high atop elevation 6708 to the right. Just past the arch you will intersect the Devils Racetrack. At one point it goes close to the rim of Coal Wash. Slipper Arch is down in and on the far side of Coal Wash. Follow the Racetrack for two hours back to the start.

Upper Cane Wash, Upper Saddle Horse Canyon, and the Upper North Fork of Coal Wash— Hike #31

Season

Any. Since the hike follows several 4WD tracks it is advisable to do it during the off-season or midweek.

Time	6 to 8 hours (12 miles)
Elevation gain	650'
Water	Seasonal pools and springs. Bring your own water.
Maps	The Blocks. San Rafael Knob. (San Rafael Knob. The Wickiup.) [San Rafael Desert]
Circle trip	Yes
Skill level	Easy route finding. Most of the walking is on old mining roads. There are two Class 3 scrambles. This is a moderate hike.

"Contrast . . . a juxtaposition of dissimilar elements in a work of art." Webster's definition describes this hike perfectly. From the smooth pinyon plains on the top of the Swell, this hike plunges you into a trio of wide, Wingate-walled canyons rimmed with Navajo towers and spires. This is a good hike for those who want to cover a lot of country, but do not want to struggle with difficult terrain.

The route starts by following the Dutchmans Arch road. It then drops into the top of Cane Wash and intersects a track that goes through a pass into Saddle Horse Canyon. From there you go over another pass into the North Fork of Coal Wash, which is followed back to the start.

Go northwest up the Dutchmans Arch road. Part 1 of Hike #29 has a description of how to get to the head of Cane Wash. Follow those directions. From the apex of the canyon go right (LDC)(E) for several hundred yards along its rim; then go down a steep chute. At the bottom of the chute traverse left on ledges until an easier slope is reached. Any water course you end up in will take you into Cane Wash. After an hour of easy hiking you will intersect an old mining track. After twenty more minutes you will pass an oil seep, and eight minutes later a track comes in from the left (N). It is hard to see. If you miss it you will run into the Indian caves 100 yards further down the canyon. These are a series of small caves at wash level. Backtrack 100 yards to the start of the track. (This track is included in the Oil Well Flat/Saddle Horse Canyon Road Section at mile 1.6 + 100 yards.)

Follow the track north. In one minute the track divides. Go right. It takes an hour to reach a pass. (The pass is shown to the west of elevation 6482 on The Blocks map.) Devils Monument and Joe and His Dog are to the northwest. To the east in the distance is the Wickiup.

After a half hour of downhill hiking, near the floor of Saddle Horse Canyon, the track divides. Go left (S). In a half hour the track goes through a pass. (The pass is shown to the southeast of elevation 6622 on The Blocks map.) Follow the track down the other side into the North Fork of Coal Wash; then go down the wash (W) for several hundred yards until you intersect a canyon to the left (S).

> **Digression:** Slipper Arch is down the canyon (W) on the right (LDC). One-hour round trip.

Go south up the canyon. There is a vague track for a short distance. After fifteen minutes the canyon divides. Go right. After another twenty minutes the canyon divides. Go right. After yet another ten minutes the canyon divides. Go left. Continue up the steepening canyon. There are several drops to negotiate as well as a boulder-strewn ravine. Near the top ascend a steep slope to the right of center. From the top go southwest. Within fifteen minutes intersect the Dutchmans Arch road. Go left (S). It will take a half hour to get back to the start.

Sinbad Country, Swasey Cabin, and Devils Canyon

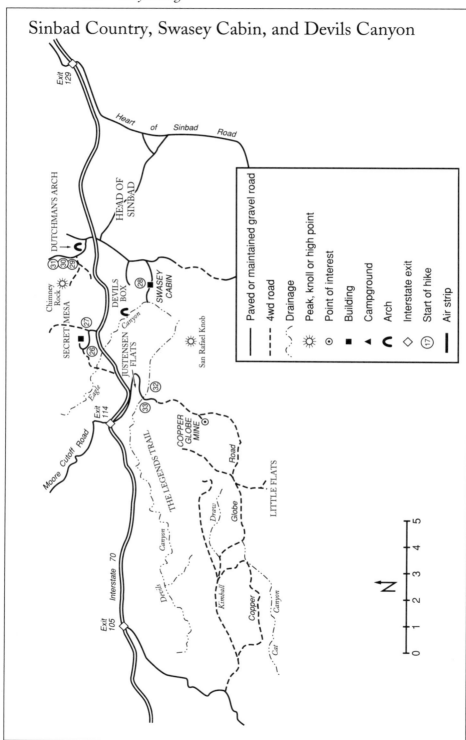

Legend

——	Paved or maintained gravel road
- - - -	4wd road
∿	Drainage
☼	Peak, knoll or high point
⊙	Point of interest
■	Building
◄	Campground
⊂	Arch
◇	Interstate exit
⑰	Start of hike
		Air strip

Exit 129

Heart   of   Sinbad   Road

HEAD OF SINBAD

DUTCHMAN'S ARCH

③① ③⓪ ㉙

Chimney Rock ☼

DEVILS BOX

SECRET MESA

㉗

㉖

JUSTENSEN FLATS

SWASEY CABIN

㉘

San Rafael Knob ☼

Eagle

Exit 114

Moore Cutoff Road

㉜

㉝

THE LEGENDS TRAIL

COPPER GLOBE MINE ⊙

Globe Road

LITTLE FLATS

Devils   Canyon

Kimball   Draw

Copper

Cat   Canyon

Interstate 70

Exit 105

N

0 1 2 3 4 5

4 | Devils Canyon

Devils Canyon is a small area in the west-central part of the San Rafael Swell. The area is bounded by Interstate 70 on the north, Muddy Creek on the west, the Copper Globe area on the south, and the San Rafael Knob on the east. The area contains Devils Canyon and a number of small side drainages. Though Interstate 70 runs close by in several places, it is not an intrusion. Devils Canyon provides a true wilderness experience.

Tight narrows make Devils Canyon difficult to negotiate. This kept out the miners and the cowboys. A lack of water deters wildlife and apparently discouraged the Indians as they left no signs of passage in the canyon. Devils Canyon is included in the Devils Canyon Wilderness Study Area. For some inexplicable reason upper Devils Canyon and the San Rafael Knob were left out.

Copper Globe Road Section

Access to Hikes #32 and 33
Access is from Interstate 70.
Metric map—San Rafael Desert

This road goes south from Interstate 70, past Justensen Flats, to the bottom of Devils Canyon. From Green River go west on Interstate 70 for forty-four miles to Exit 114. This exit has an overpass and is used for the Moore Cutoff road. Cross the interstate to the south and take the paved frontage road east to the start of the gravel Copper Globe road. The road is for light-duty vehicles to Justensen Flats at mile 2.0 and is for medium-duty vehicles to the intersection with Devils Canyon at mile 3.5. Past Devils Canyon it is for 4WDs only. This is a good mountain bike road until Devils Canyon. After that it is sandy. Bikes can be locked to trees near the Devils Canyon-Copper Globe road junction. There is good camping in the Justensen Flats area.

0.0	Mileage starts at a cattle guard just south of Interstate 70. The road goes east.
0.3	Through a road cut.
1.0	Justensen Flats sign.
1.1	End of the gravel road. Continue east-southeast on the main, graded road. There are many spur roads and tracks leading to campsites.
2.0	Starting down a steep hill. This is the end for light-duty vehicles. There is a faded sign on a tree pointing to Devils Canyon.
2.1	The road turns west.
3.5	The start of Devils Canyon—East—and the San Rafael Knob **Hike #32** and Devils Canyon—West—and the Legends Trail **Hike #33.** The junction with Devils Canyon.

★ | **Devils Canyon—East—and the San Rafael Knob—Hike #32**

Season	Any. No snow.
Time	6 to 8 hours (10 miles)
Elevation gain	1100'
Water	Seasonal potholes in Devils Canyon. Bring your own water.
Maps	San Rafael Knob. Copper Globe. (San Rafael Knob) [San Rafael Desert]
Circle trip	Yes
Skill level	Moderate route finding. Class 3+ scrambling. Though there is considerable elevation gain, it is gradual. This is a moderate hike.

If you do only one hike in the San Rafael Swell, this should be it. Be forewarned, it is like eating almond roca; once you are on top of the knob and can see the whole

Swell and what it has to offer, you will keep coming back! Guaranteed.

The route goes up Devils Canyon, ascends the San Rafael Knob, the highest point on the Swell, and finishes by going down an unnamed tributary back to Devils Canyon. To keep you from being confused, there are many slickrock knobs in the area. The San Rafael Knob is not one of them. It is the peaklike monolith seen to the southeast as you go down the Copper Globe road.

From the Copper Globe road, where it crosses Devils Canyon, go east into the canyon. If you find yourself going down a track to the south, you are going the wrong direction. The canyon doesn't look like much at this point.

As you go up the canyon you will be confronted occasionally by falls. These can all be passed easily, but often you will have to backtrack for several hundred yards and work up steep slopes or gullies to the canyon rim. Always drop back into the main canyon before proceeding up the canyon. The canyon divides several times. Go right at each intersection. You will be going generally east then southeast. Above the first fall there is a natural arch to the left. After two hours you will be able to see the knob to the south. Exit the canyon and hike to the north side of the knob.

The easiest way to ascend the knob is to work your way up its northwest side on ledges and steep slabs. Below the final cliff band traverse to the south side of the knob and scramble up easy slabs to the top (7921).

The Swell is below you:

> *North:* The largest and closest dome beyond Interstate 70 is Chimney Rock. To the right of it, far in the background, is Window Blind Peak. Harder to see, but visible, are Pinnacle #1, Joe and His Dog, elevation 7079, and Devils Monument. Mexican Mountain is hidden.
> *Northeast:* The yellowish cliffs closest to you belong to upper Eagle Canyon. The flat area behind the cliffs is the Head of Sinbad near the Swasey Cabin.
> *East:* In the far distance are the La Sal Mountains near Moab.
> *Southeast:* A monolith with a road running toward it is Temple Mountain. The tall tower, elevation 7595 on the

map, is Turkey Tower. The pinnacled fin to the right and in the distance is Family Butte. In the far distance are the Henry Mountains near Hanksville. The big butte in the distance is Factory Butte.

Southwest: The always white-topped ridges of the Wasatch Plateau.

Northwest: The coal-fired Hunter Power Plant in Castle Valley, south of Castle Dale.

Walk to the south end of the summit ridge and look southwest. There is a meadow with a track running through it. Descend the way you came; then work your way to the track. Go down it to the west. After five minutes the track crosses a wash. Either go down the wash, which has a little scrambling and is untracked, or continue down the track, which is faster. After an hour the canyon and track rejoin. Stay on the track as it curls slowly north and joins the Copper Globe road.

Try to do this hike on a warm clear day so you can enjoy the summit.

★ | ## Devils Canyon—West—and the Legends Trail (AN)—Hike #33

Season	Early spring, spring, or fall. Summer, after a good rain, will be fine.
Time	2 to 3 days; 2 days if you simply hike Devils Canyon and the Legends Trail. Add an extra day for exploring the many narrow side canyons coming into Devils Canyon (16 miles).
Elevation gain	1400'. It is all on the last day, hiking from Devils Canyon to the start of the Legends Trail.
Water	There is no permanent water in Devils Canyon until near its end. If you plan on exploring side canyons, start with a two-day supply of water. A perennial spring is located near the bottom of the canyon, a half hour before you exit the canyon.
Maps	Copper Globe. (San Rafael Knob) [San Rafael Desert. Salina.]

| Circle trip | Yes |
| Skill level | Moderate route finding. Easy Class 3 scrambling. Familiarity with low-impact camping techniques is essential. |

Enigma Canyon might be a more appropriate name for Devils Canyon. Why? Although it has the easiest access to one of the remotest and finest canyons in the Swell, Devils Canyon is rarely explored. Also, the miles of tight, narrow, side canyons are a puzzle in themselves. They can be a challenge to figure out.

The route goes down Devils Canyon, through its narrowest part, then exits up a unique side canyon. After a short cross-country stretch, the route joins the Legends Trail, an old pack trail that is now used by wild horses. The trail goes to the junction of Devils Canyon and the Copper Globe road.

From the junction of the Copper Globe road and Devils Canyon, go west down the canyon. After an hour you will reach the first fall, the start of the narrows. You can traverse along the rim on a path to the right, but it is better to enter the canyon. Within two minutes a side canyon comes in on the left (LDC)(S).

> **Digression:** To get into the side canyon climb a slickrock chute (5.0, 15′) above a sandy landing. This is a great, narrow canyon.

As you work your way down the canyon, a half dozen side canyons will be encountered. All of them are worth exploring. Some are short and easy; others are exceptionally narrow and challenging to negotiate. Let your sense of adventure run rampant here.

It takes five to seven hours to reach the spring area if you do not explore side canyons. There is a watering trough above the spring and camping in the area. The spring goes underground after a quarter mile and does not reappear downstream.

The canyon walls now consist of mud and shale. From the spring go down the canyon for thirty minutes. The first side canyon to the left (LDC)(S) is the exit canyon. At its mouth it is forty feet wide with vertical mud and shale walls. It looks like it ends in 150 yards.

> **Digression:** Note the incredible folding of the sandstone

Through the narrows of Devils Canyon.

layers on the north side of Devils Canyon near the exit canyon.

Go south up this unique narrow canyon. It does twist and turn! After seven minutes the canyon divides. Go right. After another nineteen minutes the canyon divides. The main channel goes right. Go left.

The canyon becomes shallower and divides often. Take your pick. Go generally southeast. Once out of the canyon you will be at the top of a hill. Discrepancies here won't matter. Before you is a juniper and pinyon plain. Follow a compass course southeast. For the next hour go cross-country, in and out of gullies and over hills. Do not be intimidated. As long as you go southeast, you will intersect an old mining track. You will not miss it. Go left, northeast, then east on the mining track. Several side tracks enter. Ignore them. The track follows the rim of a canyon for a short while. It deteriorates on rocky sections, but is always easy to find again. At a hilly section, as you near the rim of an escarpment, the track becomes hard to follow. Persevere. At the rim of the escarpment the track joins the Legends Trail. (You are now a half mile southeast of elevation 7192.)

Author's note: I could not find a historic reference or name for this trail. I call it the Legends Trail, as that is all there is left—a trail and a tale. There are places where some construction was done. In one place there is an old brush corral. The trail is now heavily used by wild horses, hence the abundance of side trails.

Go north, following the rim of the escarpment on a track. In ten minutes the track deteriorates into a horse trail. Follow it, generally going northeast. After a short, steep drop (where horses apparently have problems) the path divides. Stay with the main path to the right. The trail traverses along the left side (LUC) of a valley. There are many side tracks. Try to stay on the main trail. Usually the trails that diverge also converge.

Pass an old brush corral that is to the right. Eleven minutes past the corral the trail goes into a canyon going west. Don't go west into the canyon. Instead, go north up a gully. After several minutes the gully intersects an old mining track and the horse trail. Go right (E). Follow the horse trail, not the track, across a pasture. (You will be just north of elevation 7185.)

At the end of the pasture cross an old reservoir. The Legends Trail crosses a shallow valley then reaches the rim of an escarpment. The trail switches back down the face of the escarpment on a sandy slope. Wild horses have left a maze of tracks here. At the bottom of the escarpment the trail deteriorates at a small sand dune. Note the horse corral to the right as you cross the dune. A short, steep canyon to the north goes into Devils Canyon. The Legends Trail goes south. Go east off the trail and follow the south side of a slickrock ridge. The ridge has a bright red boulder that looks like ET on its flank. Follow the ridge north as you round its east end. In ten minutes, after passing a small white pinnacle and a steep gully that are to the right, go east down easy slopes to the Copper Globe road. There are many possibilities. Follow the road north back to the start.

Mussentuchit Badlands and the Moroni Slopes

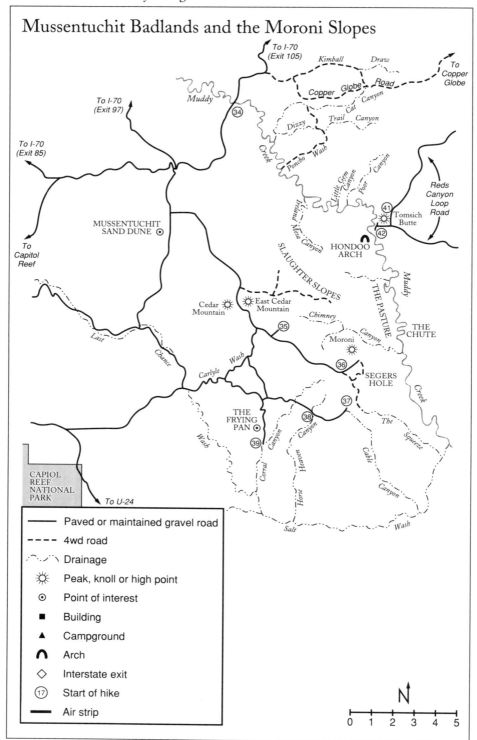

Paved or maintained gravel road

- - - - 4wd road

⌒‿⌐⌐⌐ Drainage

☼ Peak, knoll or high point

⊙ Point of interest

■ Building

▲ Campground

∩ Arch

◇ Interstate exit

⑰ Start of hike

━━ Air strip

5 | Mussentuchit Badlands, Cedar Mountain, and the Moroni Slopes

The Mussentuchit Badlands, Cedar Mountain, and the Moroni Slopes areas are located in the southwestern part of the San Rafael Swell. The area is bounded by Interstate 70 on the north, Muddy Creek on the east, Highway 24 (west of Hanksville) on the south, and the Cathedral Valley/Caineville Wash road on the west. These areas are combined into one chapter. They are accessed by the same road.

The Mussentuchit Badlands are in the northern part of this section. Early ranchers said of this barren area that one "must not touch it." Over the years this warning evolved into Mussentuchit. It is a wonderful, colorful, and sculpted area of buttes, bentonite hills, and volcanic outcroppings. Muddy Creek runs through the Badlands and Devils Canyon drains into it. To some the badlands may appear to be a wasteland, but most will find it intriguing and energetic. It is a photographer's heaven. The area is known for the Mussentuchit Sand Dune, a favorite escape for the ORV crowd. It is in one small area and does not impact the badlands themselves. This is not a wilderness study area, though wilderness designation is being pursued.

The Cedar Mountain area, in the center of this section, consists of Cedar and East Cedar mountains. Cedar Mountain is a large mass webbed with igneous intrusions in the form of dikes and sills. It is the lord of the Mussentuchit Badlands, its summit providing an unequaled panorama. Due to its rugged slopes, human encroachment has been limited. East Cedar Mountain is the king of the Chimney Canyon area. It is visible from the San Rafael Knob, Reds Canyon, and Keesle Country. Though routes to the summits of these fine desert peaks are not detailed, the trailhead used for hiking to them is noted in the road section. This area has been omitted as a wilderness study area.

The Moroni Slopes are the southwestern terminus of the Swell. Though from a distance they appear to be a sage-covered plain, this is deceiving. The slopes are cut by a myriad of complex and forceful canyons. The Moroni Slopes are the place for present and future "hard man" canyoneering. Expert canyoneers will relish Cable Canyon and The Slides and Segers Hole and The Squeeze, two of the most dynamic narrow canyon hikes in the Swell. The delicate Corral Canyon and the ponderous Horse Heaven Canyon are seldom-traveled works of art. This area has vast potential for future exploration.

It is beyond me why the Moroni Slopes are not being considered for wilderness designation. Perhaps Those Who Decide have only seen the slopes from a distance and have never experienced their charm.

Mussentuchit Badlands Road Section

Access to Hikes #34 through 39
Access is from Interstate 70.
Metric map—Salina

This road goes south from Interstate 70 and ends at the top of the Moroni Slopes, after first passing through the Mussentuchit Badlands and the Cedar Mountain area. From Green River go west on Interstate 70 for sixty-one miles to Exit 97. There is a cattle guard just south of Interstate 70. The road is for medium-duty vehicles. Be forewarned that there are short sand traps throughout the region. If in doubt survey them on foot first. Due to the sandy nature of these roads, mountain bikers will have trouble. Places to camp are available everywhere.

The following road section is the most complicated in the guide. Be meticulous in following directions.

0.0 | Mileage starts at the cattle guard just south of Interstate 70 and goes south.

0.1	Sign to Mussentuchit Flat and the Middle Desert Road.
7.9	Wire gate.
8.1	Stock pond on the left.
8.2	"Tee."

Side road

The road to the left (E) goes to the Lone Tree Crossing on Muddy Creek and the start of Hike #34.

0.0	Mileage starts at the "Tee" and goes east.
0.6	Note the black dike to the left.
1.9	"Y." Stay to the left (N). Watch for sand traps beyond the intersection.
4.5	Start of Upper Muddy Creek and Cat and Dizzy Trail Canyons **Hike #34.** You are on a bridge at the Lone Tree Crossing of Muddy Creek.

If you cross the bridge and continue north on the track you will intersect I–70 at Exit 105. As this road is for medium-duty vehicles and is impassable at times due to water in South Salt Wash, it is not used as the primary access road to the Mussentuchit area.

End of side road

The road to the right (W) goes to Mussentuchit Flats, Cedar Mountain, and the Moroni Slopes. (You are at mile 8.2.) Follow the road west for several hundred yards, go through a wire gate, and intersect a graded road going north-south. There is a sign to Mussentuchit Dunes, Cedar Mountain, and U-10. You will restart your mileage at this junction.

0.0	At the sign go south.
0.1	Wire gate.
1.2	"Tee." Stay left (S).
2.1	Marked junction. Go to the left (E) toward Cedar Mountain and the Moroni Slopes.

Side road

The road to the right (S) goes to the Mussentuchit Sand Dune and Last Chance Wash. Though a route through Last Chance Wash is not detailed, the wash will be of special interest to mountain bikers. (See mile 10.9 below.)

0.0	Mileage starts at the sign to Last Chance Wash and goes south.
1.5	Track on the right going to a huge climbing sand dune. This is the Mussentuchit Sand Dune, a designated ORV area.
2.9	Stock pond on the right.
3.9	Stock pond on the left.
4.8	Cattle guard.
6.0	Cottonwoods on the right.
6.3	"Tee." Stay left (SE).
	The track to the right goes west up Last Chance Wash.
8.0	Cattle guard.
10.3	The track divides before a cattle guard. Go left (S).
	If you go straight (W) across the cattle guard the track joins the Cathedral Valley/Caineville Wash road in about six miles. You can then go south to Cathedral Valley and to Highway 24. It is an exceptionally beautiful drive. It is for medium-duty vehicles.
10.9	The track goes across Last Chance Wash. Park here. Mountain bikers can go down the ever-deepening Last Chance Wash to its confluence with Salt Wash. The riding is generally easy on the hard-packed wash bottom, though there is challenging riding through several boulder areas. Just before reaching Salt Wash, as the canyon ends, there is a small petroglyph and pictograph panel to the left (LDC). The round trip takes four to five hours. **End of side road**
7.7	"Tee." Stay to the right (S).
9.4	Cattle guard. At the top of a rise between East Cedar and Cedar mountains.
	Though routes to the tops of these fine desert peaks are not detailed, both are short Class 3 scrambles. East Cedar Mountain is shorter (two hours round trip), while Cedar Mountain is longer and more scenic (three hours round trip).
10.0	"Y." Two major road sections start at this point. The road to the right (S) goes to Hikes #37 through 39. It is presented after the following road section.
	The road to the left (SE) goes to Hikes #35 and 36.
0.0	Restart your mileage at the "Y." Go left (SE).

1.4	The start of Top of Chimney Canyon **Hike #35.** There is a vague track to the left (N). Follow the track for 0.2 mile until it ends at a turnaround. Park here. (This is shown just north of elevation 6025 on The Frying Pan map.)
2.9	Water tank on the left.
3.0	"Tee." Go left (E). The road gets rougher and is for medium-duty vehicles.
3.2	What appears to be two chimneys on the hillside to the left. They are really fancy cowboy cairns.
4.9	The start of Segers Hole and The Squeeze **Hike #36.** You are at a four-way intersection at the edge of a cliff. (This is shown just north of elevation 6681 on The Frying Pan map.) There is a track going straight down the cliff. Park at the top of the cliff.
	The road to the right (S) goes to Hikes #37 through 39.
0.0	Mileage starts at the "Y" and goes south. (This is the same "Y" as at mile 10.0 above.)
1.8	"Y." Go left (SE).
2.4	"Tee." Stay to the right (SE).
	The track to the left (ENE) goes to the Last Chance Well.
3.2	Drill pipe on the right.
4.0	"Y." Go right (W) to Corral Canyon Hike #39.
	Go left (E) to the start of Horse Heaven Canyon Hike #38 and Cable Canyon and The Slides Hike #37.
	Side road
0.0	Mileage starts at the "Y" and goes east.
3.2	The start of Horse Heaven Canyon **Hike #38.** The Moroni Slopes Catchment is on the right (S). There is no parking area, so park by the side of the road.
4.2	Watering trough on the right.
4.3	Horse Heaven Reservoir on the right.
4.9	The start of Cable Canyon and The Slides **Hike #37.** There are two drill pipes in a flat area to the left. Park here. The track, no longer graded, continues for a quarter mile to a grand overlook. There is great camping in the area. (The end of the road is shown on The Frying

Pan map. Cable Canyon starts just to the west of elevation 6602.)
End of side road

4.2	"Y." There is a drill pipe to the right. Stay left (S).
	The 4WD track to the right (NW) goes to Last Chance Wash.
4.9	Drill pipe on the left.
5.8	Drill pipe on the left.
6.1	The Frying Pan catchment. It is worth a look.
6.5	Corral Canyon starting on the left.
7.0	The start of Corral Canyon **Hike #39.** The graded track ends. Park here. The track continues, but it is for 4WDs and mountain bikes only.

Upper Muddy Creek and Cat and Dizzy Trail Canyons—Hike #34

Season	Early spring, late summer, or fall. Spring can be buggy and wading in winter can be cold.
Time	6 to 8 hours (12 miles)
Elevation gain	800′
Water	Muddy Creek. Both Cat and Dizzy Trail canyons have springs. Bring your own water.
Maps	Ireland Mesa. Big Bend Draw. Mesa Butte. [Salina]
Circle trip	Yes
Skill level	Easy route finding. Class 2 walking. This is a moderate hike. Wading shoes are necessary.

The person who named these canyons must have been
prescient. He or she was firmly tuned in to the 1960s.
Why else would you name them Cool Cat Canyon and
I'm So Dizzy Trail Canyon? Luckily calmer minds shortened the names to their present configurations.

The route goes down Muddy Creek from Lone Tree
Crossing, past the confluence of Muddy Creek and

South Salt Wash, to Cat Canyon. It goes a short way up Cat Canyon to Dizzy Trail Canyon, which is followed to its top. A track is then followed as it traverses rolling hills to the top of Cat Canyon, which is descended back to Muddy Creek. This hike belongs in the Muddy Creek chapter, but it starts from the Mussentuchit Badlands. The route not only makes for a good day hike but also helps tie the upper part of Muddy Creek to the lower section accessed from Tomsich Butte (Hike #41).

The Lone Tree Crossing of Muddy Creek.

From the bridge at Lone Tree Crossing, go down the creek. The first part of the hike is across a flat tamarisk plain next to the creek. South Salt Wash comes in on the left (N) after fifteen minutes. You will have to wade the creek three or four times. In an hour the wash enters the canyon. Cat Canyon intersects Muddy Creek on the left (NE), seventy-five minutes from Lone Tree Crossing. It is the first side canyon on the left.

> **Digression:** Continue down Muddy Creek. It will take ninety minutes to two hours to reach Poncho Wash. It is the first side canyon on the left (N) after Cat Canyon. (See Hike #41 for more information if you plan on proceeding down the canyon.)

Go up Cat Canyon for eight minutes until it narrows and divides. Cat Canyon continues on the left. Go right

(E) up Dizzy Trail Canyon. In ten minutes you will reach a spring area, then thrash through tamarisks for several minutes. From here up, stay with the main water course. Twenty-five minutes from the spring area the canyon opens and becomes a wash. The path of the wash gets confusing. There is a twenty-foot-tall, gray square tower sitting by itself on a rise. Go to the right side (LUC) of the tower and drop back into the wash. Again stay with the main wash. In fifty minutes a track intersects the wash on the left. You will not miss the track because it then uses the wash as a track. Exit Dizzy Trail Canyon by taking the track to the left (N). Follow the track for forty-five minutes across rolling hills until it drops into Cat Canyon. It is the first big wash encountered after leaving Dizzy Trail Canyon. Go down Cat Canyon (SW). Halfway down you will run into a series of springs and a watering trough. Cat Canyon will return you to Muddy Creek.

Top of Chimney Canyon—Hike #35

Season	Any. No snow.
Time	4 to 5 hours. This does not include time for exploring side canyons (7 miles).
Elevation gain	500'
Water	There are small springs in the head of the entrance and exit canyons. There is no water in the bottom part of the canyon.
Maps	The Frying Pan. Ireland Mesa is optional. [Salina]
Circle trip	Partial
Skill level	Easy/moderate route finding. Class 3+ scrambling. The route is mostly Class 1, but there are several short drops to negotiate.

The fast track, a toboggan ride, a water slide. These are often the quickest ways to reach an objective. The fastest way to reach the top part of Chimney Canyon is to do this hike.

The route starts at the base of East Cedar Mountain and follows a sinuous course down a narrow canyon into the top part of Chimney Canyon. It does not continue down Chimney Canyon. To descend Chimney Canyon to Muddy Creek without prior knowledge—having gone up it—is dangerous. This route should be in the Muddy Creek chapter, but access is from the Cedar Mountain side.

From the parking area go northeast toward a distant square-topped tower for 200 yards. (You can only see the top of the tower.) Intersect the top of a shallow canyon. Descend the canyon, generally going north. There are many side canyons joining the main canyon. This is not a problem while descending. Coming back up can be confusing, so memorize your route. Note the first side canyon you encounter to the left (LDC)(NW) at a thirty-foot-tall fin. The route goes up this canyon on the way out.

After a narrow section you will be stopped by a large fall. (It is the same fall that stops rock climbers who are going up the canyon in Hike #42.) You cannot get around the fall. You can circle to the left (LDC)(N) and intersect several side canyons that are worth exploring. To do this backtrack to the start of the narrow section. Follow ledges to the left (LDC) into a bowl area. There is a lot to explore.

On your return, go right (LUC) at the thirty-foot-tall fin mentioned above. Immediately past the fin the canyon divides. Go right (NW). In four minutes the canyon divides again. Go left. Two minutes past a spring area (many tamarisks) note a track on the hill to the left running under a cliff. There is a log holding a section of it in place. Go around the next bend to an area of developed springs; then go back down the canyon for twenty-five yards. (This is labeled East Cedar Mountain Spring on The Frying Pan map.) On the right (LDC) is the track going steeply uphill. Follow it until you top out.

This is the perfect place to do an overnight hike. There is much to do. The canyon is isolated and quiet. You will have to bring your own water.

★ | Segers Hole and The Squeeze (AN)—Hike #36

Season	Any. No snow. Warm weather preferred. There is a flash flood potential in both canyons.
Time	7 to 9 hours (12 miles)
Elevation gain	1000′
Water	Seasonal potholes. Bring your own water.
Maps	The Frying Pan. Hunt Draw. These canyons are shown but are not labeled on the maps. On the Hunt Draw map The Squeeze is the southernmost canyon entering Muddy Creek from the west before it joins Salt Wash. (This is just north of elevation 5343.) The unnamed return canyon is the northernmost canyon entering Salt Wash before it joins Muddy Creek. (This is just south of elevation 5729.) [Salina. San Rafael Desert.]
Circle trip	Yes
Skill level	Moderate route finding. Class 3+ scrambling. A short rope will be helpful. The route is for intermediate and above canyoneers. It is a tiring day hike. Bring wading shoes.

For those doing the second digression, a rope, wading shoes, and an inner tube are required. It is for rock-climbers and expert canyoneers only.

Segers Hole is the hamburger; The Squeeze is the relish. And relish this hike you will! Both offer scenery and excitement. Segers Hole is a large bowl surrounded by Navajo walls. The Squeeze is one of the narrowest canyons on the Swell and is a challenge to negotiate.

The route starts near Moroni, the highest point on the Moroni Slopes. It then goes across Segers Hole on an abandoned mining track and joins The Squeeze, a long canyon that goes to the mouth of Muddy Creek. The route does not go all the way through The Squeeze as there are overwhelming obstacles partway down. It does go through The Squeeze area itself. After exiting the canyon the route traverses the face of the Moroni Slopes and intersects an unnamed canyon going back to Segers Hole.

Go west then southeast down the steep track into Segers Hole. In a half hour the track divides. Go right (SE). Note the volcanic plug to the right. Ten minutes later the track divides again. Go right (generally south). The track goes into and out of the top of a canyon (the top of The Squeeze) and goes southeast, then east. Follow the main track. If you lose it keep going east. You will find it again. You will be following the south rim of The Squeeze. Do not drop into it yet. The track goes to the left (N) side of a dome and ends. (The dome is elevation 6247 on the Hunt Draw map.) Continue east, passing the dome on a shelf. It will drop you, slick as a whistle, into The Squeeze.

Chimney, jump, and squeeze down the canyon. There are many obstacles, but none are hard. A short rope may be helpful for dogs and packs. There are logs jammed high overhead in several places. At one point crawl under a logjam. It is an important landmark. Twenty feet past the logjam there is a narrow slot to the right. Don't go up the slot; instead, continue down the canyon for two minutes, past a narrow, sand-floored section. The canyon makes an abrupt right turn. Stop at the corner. Do not continue down the canyon.

> **Digression:** The adventurous can continue down the canyon for a way yet. The obstacles get harder to negotiate. At one point you will have to rappel twenty-five feet from a log. Leave the rope because you cannot climb back up without it. Beyond the rappel there is a pool to wade; then the obstacles become insurmountable.

From the corner go right (LDC)(S) up a red, then white, ledge for 200 yards. It turns to the west. Follow the ledge up (W) for 200 yards around a short corner. Ascend a bush-choked gully to the left (S). Pick your way through short cliff bands until you get to the rim of the canyon.

Go generally west along the curving rim of the canyon. In a half hour the rim comes to a point. The goal is to get to the bottom of the canyon that is on the left (LUC)(SW). To do this drop west along a ridge, past several short cliff bands, to a saddle. From the saddle drop to the southwest along ledges and steep slabs. Zigzag down as terrain dictates. There are several possibilities.

> **Digression:** Can you go down the canyon? Yes, with difficulty. There is exposure, loose rock, two rappels, and

the potential for swimming. This is for rock-climbers or expert canyoneers only. It will add three hours to an already long day. It is exciting and worthwhile.

The first drop you encounter is into a pool. There is a small arch to use as an anchor for a rope. The first person down will have to determine the depth of the pool.

The second drop is taller. It can be bypassed on a ledge to the right (LDC). Follow the ledge as far as possible. There is one tricky section (5.0) as you descend toward a pool. Ten feet above the pool do a friction traverse on the left (LDC). There is a rock to anchor a rope to if the slab looks too hard. It will allow you to rappel straight down, but into the pool.

The next obstacle is a twenty-foot rappel from a boulder into a deep pool. The drop after the pool is by an arch and cannot be rappelled. You can pass the arch on the right (LDC). Once you have scrambled down below the arch the canyon gets less interesting. Exit the canyon through cliff bands to the left (NE). There are many places to do this. After attaining the rim, follow it up the canyon (WNW). Descend back into the canyon at the same place you did originally.

Go west up the canyon. In several minutes the canyon seems to end at four dead-end slots. Go up the ledges to the left of the third slot from the right (LUC). Continue up the canyon, staying with the main course. Note an arch to the left. The canyon divides at a slickrock sheet just before a dome that has two pinnacles on its left side. Go into the short canyon to the right (NW), staying above the inner canyon. (This is shown a quarter mile southeast of elevation 5849 on the Hunt Draw map.) At its top stay to the right. Follow bits and pieces of a track. If you lose the track, go north. You will intersect the original track on which you came in.

★ ## Cable Canyon (AN) and The Slides (AN) —Hike #37

Season | Any. No snow. Warm weather preferred. There is a flash flood potential in both canyons.

Time	Part 1—5 to 7 hours (8 miles)
	Part 2—9 to 11 hours (11 miles)
Elevation gain	Part 1—1000′
	Part 2—1400′
Water	Perennially full potholes in the main canyon. Bring your own water.
Maps	The Frying Pan. Hunt Draw. The canyons are on the map but are not labeled. They are the first two drainages to the east of Horse Heaven Reservoir on the Frying Pan map. [Salina. San Rafael Desert.]
Circle trip	Yes
Skill level	Moderate route finding, mainly finding ways around obstacles. Class 5.0 climbing. There are two rappels. You should be familiar with setting up and executing rappels safely. There is much bouldering—short, hard moves without exposure. You will need at least a 100-foot rope and forty feet of sling material. One inner tube per group is recommended. Every group should have an advanced canyoneer or a competent rock-climber in it. The route is a tad hairy at times; no beginners. Wading shoes are essential.

Chant your mantra as you descend into the dark depths of these canyons. Cable Canyon contains all the necessary ingredients for a first-rate adventure: great hiking through a beautiful canyon, two rappels, one swim, many short climbing problems, and seemingly endless stretches of tight narrows.

The route has two parts. Part 1 goes down The Slide, a steep gully, into a narrow canyon. The route returns by going up another long, narrow canyon, one of the most beautiful canyons on the Swell. Part 2, which gets better and better, continues down the canyon. At a big drop it exits the canyon to the face of the Moroni slopes. After ascending the Slopes the route descends back into the canyon and returns up the same canyon as does Part 1.

Part 1: From the two drill pipes go east over a small rise. In several minutes reach the rim of a canyon. Follow the rim to the left (N) for a hundred yards until a narrow, steep gully—The Slide—is reached. There is a ten-foot-tall pinnacle (white with a brown top) near the head of The Slide. Descend it. There are several chockstones to negotiate.

Contemplating a drop in The Slide.

Downclimb a twenty-foot drop on the right (LDC)(5.4, 20') or rappel it. There is a half-inch cable wrapped around a chockstone to use as an anchor for a rappel.

The second big drop in The Slide can be rappelled (25'), or you can bypass the drop on a thin ledge to the right (LDC)(Class 4, 30', slightly intimidating).

The Slide opens for a bit, then closes down again. Two

hours from the start there is a twelve-foot drop into a pool. Backtrack for 100 yards. Slip through a brush-filled slot to the left (LUC)(W). After 100 yards the slot opens into a small clearing. This is where Parts 1 and 2 diverge.

To continue with Part 1, go up a canyon to the south-southwest. This long, narrow canyon has many small obstacles, none seriously hard. At an impassable fall backtrack for five minutes and exit the canyon to the left (LDC)(N) by climbing up a steep slab (Class 4, 25′) that is broken into five-foot steps. This is the first possible exit. Once above the steep section of the slab go north and northwest up gentler slabs and across ledges (several cairns, Class 3) until you can descend back into the main canyon.

From the top of the fall continue up the canyon, always staying with the main watercourse. At an arch the canyon divides. Go to the left. Exit the canyon through a steep, narrow slot; then go north-northwest to the rim of Cable Canyon, near the top of The Slide. You may pass a brush corral.

Part 2: Before continuing down the canyon make sure you become familiar with this area. You will need to recognize it from the east rim of the canyon later. From the small clearing go south down a short, narrow slot. The pool can vary from waist deep to deep enough to swim. You may have another pool to wade or swim as well. Past the pools the next big obstacle to negotiate is a chockstone which is passed with a forty-foot rappel. A forty-foot sling will be needed to wrap around the chockstone. You can get by with a shorter sling around a smaller chockstone, but it is low and will make it hard to start the rappel safely. You will not be able to backtrack after the rappel.

There is a ten-foot drop below the rappel. After a long stretch of easy narrows there is a beautiful set of deep potholes you cannot descend. (This area is just west of elevation 5486 on the Hunt Draw map.) Backtrack to the first possible exit and leave the canyon completely by working up to the rim (NE) on ledges. There are several possibilities here.

Follow the rim of the canyon uphill (NW). In thirty-five minutes you will be directly east of the swim hole.

Continue up along the rim, drop onto a saddle, and go to its far (NW) side. Do not go around the red cliff. There is yellow sandstone here and a steep intersecting canyon with a small pinnacle on one wall. Go down the canyon (W). Two-thirds of the way down is the second Slide, a section of steep slickrock. Walk down the slab (Class 4, 50′). Some may want to be belayed. There are other slopes you can descend in this area.

Once back in the main canyon go down it and join with the exit canyon used in Part 1.

Horse Heaven Canyon (AN)—Hike #38

Season	Any. No snow.
Time	7 to 9 hours (11 miles)
Elevation gain	1500′
Water	There is no reliable water on the route. Bring your own water.
Maps	The Frying Pan. Cane Spring. Horse Heaven Canyon is shown but is not labeled on The Frying Pan map. It begins at the Moroni Slopes Catchment and starts as a wash going southwest then south. [Salina. San Rafael Desert.]
Circle trip	Optional
Skill level	Easy route finding. Class 4 climbing. A short rope may be handy for helping beginners over several small obstacles. This is a long day hike.

Well hidden in the folds of the Moroni Slopes, Horse Heaven Canyon has rarely been explored. An abysmal start high on the Moroni Slopes and a nondescript end at Salt Wash have combined to keep this colorful and heavily sculpted canyon concealed from canyoneers.

The route is straightforward. It goes down Horse Heaven Canyon to Salt Wash and returns the same way. Not only is this a beautiful canyon, it is the only narrow canyon on the Moroni Slopes that is relatively easy to negotiate. You can backpack through Horse Heaven Canyon, something you cannot do in Cable Canyon, The Squeeze, or Corral Canyon.

The route starts at the Moroni Slopes Catchment. Go south. Within minutes drop into a shallow valley and follow it down for seventy-five minutes until you reach a big drop and the head of the real canyon. To get into the canyon go east up a steep slope. From a saddle at the top of the slope, descend a colorful hillside to the east for 250 yards to the apex of a short side canyon. Go down it. Once past the initial brown cliff band go left (N) around a corner. There are cairns through this section. Snake down ledges and slabs to the bottom.

Pass the first fall on the right (LDC). You can either jump or be lowered over the next fall (Class 4, 8′). The next fall can be passed to the right (LDC), after first backtracking for a hundred yards or so. The fall after this can be easily jumped.

Once out of the slickrock part of the canyon and into the mud-walled portion it will take a half hour to reach Salt Wash. Once there note the volcanic dike going through the 250-foot-high red wall (North Caineville Reef) to the south. Factory Butte is visible to the east.

To return you can go up the face of the Moroni Slopes to the east side of the canyon. After negotiating the initial jumble leading to the Moroni Slopes there are no major obstacles. All in all you will be better off returning the way you came.

Corral Canyon—Hike #39

Season	Any
Time	2 to 3 hours (5 miles)
Elevation gain	250′
Water	There are springs partway down the canyon. Bring your own water.

Maps
Circle trip
Skill level

The Frying Pan. [Salina]
No
Easy route finding. Class 3 scrambling. The route is mostly Class 1, but there are several obstacles to negotiate. This is a good hike for youngsters.

Corral or Coral Canyon? Either is an appropriate description of this colorful and compact canyon. It was once used to hold cattle.

The route goes down a mud-walled canyon to a drop that cannot be passed. En route you pass an arch and a series of springs that form several gorgeous pools.

From the end of the track go southeast down a moderate slope into the canyon. There are several possibilities. Avoid the short cliff bands. It takes a half hour to get to the arch and the first springs, which continue intermittently. As you go through a long stretch of yellow slickrock there are several good-sized pools. The canyon ends at a long section of rapidly falling potholes. They will be a challenge to future canyoneers. Return the way you came.

6 | Muddy Creek

The Muddy Creek area is located in the south-central part of the San Rafael Swell. It is bounded by Devils Canyon on the north, the Mussentuchit Badlands on the west, Salt Wash on the south, and Sinbad Country on the east. Though dominated by Muddy Creek and its thirty-mile-long canyon, the area is exceptionally complex. There are a score of side canyons, towering buttes, slender pinnacles, and stalwart towers. Arguably, the finest multiday hike in the Swell (The Chute of Muddy Creek, Chimney Canyon, and the Pasture Track Hike #42) is contained within this area. Certainly one of the most technical canyons to descend (Quandary Canyon and Lower Muddy Creek Hike #46) is part of the Muddy Creek area. The Reds Canyon Loop road is a popular drive. With breathtaking scenery and many mine sites to explore, it can be busy during the summer. Muddy Creek itself is in a wilderness study area. Much of the country adjacent to Muddy Creek has inexplicably been left out.

The Muddy Creek area has no signs of Indian occupation, but they certainly must have used the area. Pictograph and petroglyph panels are found in the surrounding areas—on the Moroni Slopes, at the Rochester panel where Muddy Creek enters the western part of the Swell, and at the Head of Sinbad.

Miners left their mark throughout the area. Several big mines were developed, notably the Lucky Strike, Tomsich Butte, and Hidden Splendor mines. For a time the Hidden Splendor Mine was the largest uranium producer in the Swell. The legacy the miners left, a network of roads, now provides easy access to such canyons as Chimney, Quandary, Knotted Rope, Cistern, and Ramp.

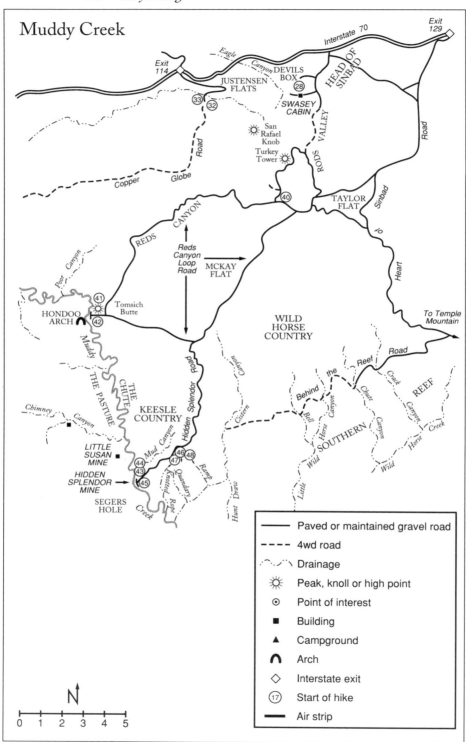

Muddy Creek

Exit 114

Exit 129

Interstate 70

Eagle
Canyon

DEVILS BOX

JUSTENSEN FLATS

28

SWASEY CABIN

HEAD OF SINBAD

33
32

San Rafael Knob

Turkey Tower

RODS VALLEY

Road

Copper   Globe

Road

40

TAYLOR FLAT

Sinbad

CANYON

REDS

Poor Canyon

Reds Canyon Loop Road

MCKAY FLAT

Jo

Heart

41
42

Tomsich Butte

HONDOO ARCH

Muddy

WILD HORSE COUNTRY

To Temple Mountain

THE CHUTE

THE PASTURE

Chimney   Canyon

THE

KEESLE COUNTRY

Hidden Splendor Road

Cistern

Canyon

Behind

the

Reef

Road

Crack

Chute

Canyon

REEF

Canyon

Creek

LITTLE SUSAN MINE

Mud Canyon

44

46 48
47

Bell

Horse

Wild

SOUTHERN

Canyon

Wild

Horse

HIDDEN SPLENDOR MINE

43

45

Knotted

Quandary

Ramp

Rope

Little

Wild

SEGERS HOLE

Creek

Hunt Draw

	Paved or maintained gravel road
- - -	4wd road
	Drainage
☼	Peak, knoll or high point
⊙	Point of interest
■	Building
▲	Campground
∩	Arch
◇	Interstate exit
⑰	Start of hike
▬	Air strip

N

0   1   2   3   4   5

Heart of Sinbad (AN) Road Section

Access to Hikes #40 through 53
Access is from Interstate 70 and Highway 24.
Provides access to the Reds Canyon Loop and the
   Hidden Splendor Mine roads.
Provides alternate access to the Temple Mountain and
   the Goblin Valley/Southern Reef roads.
Metric map—San Rafael Desert

   This road goes between Interstate 70 in the north to
Temple Mountain in the south. From Green River go
west on Interstate 70 for twenty-nine miles to Ranch
Exit 129. (The road going north of the exit is the Cottonwood Wash road. It provides access to the Mexican
Mountain and Sids Mountain areas). The road, good for
light-duty vehicles, ends on Highway 24, twenty miles
north of Hanksville at milepost 137. There are several
sandy sections that you may want to walk first before negotiating. Though the road is suitable for mountain
bikes, the terrain is not that interesting. Camping is available throughout the area.

0.0	Mileage starts at the cattle guard just south of Interstate 70. The road goes generally south, but starts by going west. There are signs at major intersections. These are sometimes missing, so do keep track of mileage.
0.1	Sign to U–24, Goblin Valley, and Temple Mountain.
1.0	Track to the left going to an old reservoir.
1.8	Road turns south.
3.0	Cattle guard.
3.8	''Tee.'' Stay to the left (S). Road to the right (W). It goes to the Head of Sinbad (Swasey Cabin) area.
4.1	Cross a wash.
4.9	Marked junction. Stay to the left (S). To the right (NW) is the Head of Sinbad.
6.5	Track left to a gravel pile.
9.9	Marked junction. To the right is Reds Canyon and Tan Seeps. Go right (SW).

To the left (S) is an alternate road going to Goblin Valley, U–24, and Temple Mountain.

10.1 First view of Family Butte (also called the Seven Sisters) to the west. The large tower to the right is not named on the maps. It is Turkey Tower (AN). The peaklike monolith to the right of Turkey Tower is the San Rafael Knob.

13.0 Track on the right (N). It is the exit road for Bike/Hike #40. This 4WD track goes to the Head of Sinbad area.

13.5 Major Marked Junction. There are both old and new signs. This junction comes up often. Remember it as the Major Marked Junction. Go to the left (SE) toward Temple Mountain and Goblin Valley.

To the right (W) is Reds Canyon and McKay Flat. (See the Reds Canyon Loop Road Section for details.) It provides access to **Hikes #40 through 48.**

16.1 Marked junction. Go straight. The road to the left (N) goes to I–70.

18.2 Barren area and miscellaneous tracks to the left. Good camping spots here overlooking Temple Mountain.

20.4 A place in which to pull off on the left. Great views of Temple Mountain.

21.8 Mine ruins and a large area in which to pull off on the right. The escarpment to the south is the backside of the Southern Reef. In the next several miles mining roads to the right lead to good views and camping.

25.0 "Tee." A road coming in on the right (SW). This is the Behind the Reef road. (See that road section in the Temple Mountain and the Southern Reef chapter for details.) The Behind the Reef road goes to **Hikes #50 through 53.**

25.1 Start of Temple Mountain Circumambulation **Hike #49.** The Temple Mountain parking and camping area is to the left (N). Park near a small, concrete block structure.

25.3 Track on the left (N) goes to the Temple Mountain mining area.

25.7 Good camping on the left.

25.8 Road changes from dirt to asphalt.

26.2 Barrier Canyon Style pictograph panel under an overhang on the left (N). It can be seen from the road.

27.0 "Tee." Track on the left (NE). The track provides access to the mouth of North Temple Wash and Farnsworth Canyon. (See the Temple Mountain Road Section in the

Temple Mountain and the Southern Reef chapter at mile
5.0 for details.)

27.1 Marked Goblin Valley junction. Go straight (SE), staying
on the pavement to intersect Highway 24 in 5.1 miles.
   Go right (SW) onto the Goblin Valley/Southern Reef
road. This road leads to **Hikes #54 through 56.** (See the
Goblin Valley/Southern Reef Road Section in the Temple
Mountain and the Southern Reef chapter for details.)

Reds Canyon Loop Road Section

Access to Hikes #40 through 48
Access is from the Heart of Sinbad road.
Provides access to the Hidden Splendor Mine road.
Metric map—San Rafael Desert

This is a loop road that starts at mile 13.5 on the
Heart of Sinbad road. This is at the Major Marked Junction. It is a graded road that is for light-duty vehicles.
The road is excellent for mountain bikes, though traffic
can be a problem on summer weekends. Camping is
available throughout the area.

0.0 Mileage starts at the Major Marked Junction and goes
right (W). There is a sign to Reds Canyon and Tan Seeps.
You will make a large counterclockwise loop and will end
up back at the Major Marked Junction. Normally you
can follow BLM signs. Unfortunately these have a habit
of disappearing from time to time, so do keep track of
mileage.

0.1 Cattle guard. Just past the cattle guard there is a track on
the right (N). Follow the track for 200 yards to Tan
Seeps. There is a well, a horse corral, and several out-
buildings.

1.0 Marked junction. To the right (W) is Reds Canyon. Go
right. This is the start of the actual loop.
   To the left (SW) is McKay Flat. If you are just going to
the Hidden Splendor Mine it is faster to go left for 8.3

miles to the junction with the Hidden Splendor Mine road.

2.0   The start of Turkey Tower and the Swasey Cabin **Bike/ Hike #40**. There is a track to the right (N). Park off the main road. This is a 4WD road that goes under Turkey Tower and eventually to the Head of Sinbad.

2.9   Down a long hill.

7.9   Sulphur Spring Canyon is on the right (N). There is a track going up the wash into the canyon. This is for 4WDs, but it is worth walking. As you go up, the canyon divides. Stay left. Toward the end of the canyon it branches into three bowls. The middle branch contains the sulphur spring and has a pinnacled ridge at its head. One-hour round trip.

10.1   "Y." Go left (SW).

The road to the right (NW) goes to the Lucky Strike Mine. It is in a beautiful setting. The road is good for light-duty vehicles. Two-mile round trip.

11.6   Drill pipe on the left.

11.9   Canyon to the right (N). It has a white tower and large overhangs. There is a track going up the wash and into the canyon. It leads to a mining area surrounded by towers, pinnacles, and overhangs. The track is for 4WDs, but it is worth the walk. Two-mile round trip.

12.6   Mine ruins on a hillside to the right.

13.3   The butte straight ahead is North Butte. In the background is Hondoo Arch.

15.4   The start of Upper Muddy Creek **Hike #41**. It is at an unmarked junction with a vague track to the right (W). This is on the north side of Tomsich Butte. Park near the slowly disappearing remains of an old truck. Ten years ago it was a complete vehicle. If it vanishes completely you can still recognize the junction. Look northwest across a barren, brown plain for a small cabin at its west end.

Tomsich Butte is to the southwest. Rock climbers can climb to the top on the north side. From the truck go up an old mining track that diagonals to the west. At the base of a Wingate wall, near several tunnel openings, go east on the track. This goes to a flat area with many tracks. To the south-southwest there is one weakness through the lowest cliff band, a left-leaning, twenty-foot-high crack to the right of a large boulder. Ascend the crack (Class 5.2, 20′). (You can use Friends, a mechanical climbing device, to protect it.) Traverse right for several hundred yards on a ledge until you reach a moderate exit at a boulder. The true summit (5805) is at the southeast corner.

15.5	Mine ruins to the right.
15.7	Starting down a steep hill along the side of a Moenkopi wall. This section of road is dangerous when wet or snowy. Watch for fallen rocks.
16.0	End of the Moenkopi wall. At a "Tee." The main road goes left (E).

Side road
   The road to the right (W) goes to Hondoo Arch and the Dirty Devil Mine area and the start of Hike #42.

0.0	Mileage starts at the "Tee" and goes right (W).
0.2	Top of a hill. Hondoo Arch is straight ahead.
0.3	Bottom of the hill. Classic mine scene up a short wash to the right.
0.4	Two cabins to the left.
0.5	The start of The Chute of Muddy Creek, Chimney Canyon, and the Pasture Track **Hike #42**. The road divides. Go straight (W) to a cabin and a four-hole outhouse. Park in this area. You can also start Hike #41 here by hiking north up Muddy Creek.

End of side road

16.2	Cross the mouth of Penitentiary Canyon. A short hike goes east up the canyon. In eight minutes there is a spring area to the left. Stay right, in the main wash. After another ten minutes there is a seventy-five-foot-tall mud pinnacle. Minutes past the pinnacle there is a short, narrow side canyon to the right (LUC). One-hour round trip. Good for all, especially the kids.
17.6	Cattle guard.
20.3	Cattle tank on the right.
21.1	Marked junction. Stay on the main road to the left (NE). The Hidden Splendor Mine road is to the right (S). (See that road section for details.) The Hidden Splendor Mine road goes to the start of **Hikes #43 through 48.**

21.9	There is a canyon/valley starting on the right. Hike down the valley (S). In a half hour you will reach the Cistern Tank. This is the start of Upper Cistern Canyon, which goes to the backside of the Southern Reef.
24.2	Cattle reservoir on the right. The track to the south goes near the head of Ding Dang Dome. Mountain bikes and 4WDs only. Thirty miles round trip.
25.8	Cattle guard.
29.4	''Tee.'' This is the end of the loop. Go right (E).
30.3	Back at the Major Marked Junction. To go to Temple Mountain go right (SE). To go to Ranch Exit 129 on I–70 go left (N).

★ **Turkey Tower (AN) and the Swasey Cabin—Bike/Hike #40**

Season	Any. No rain or snow.
Time	4 to 6 hours. The time includes exploring mine sites and the Swasey Cabin area (18 miles).
Elevation gain	350'
Water	None. Bring your own water.
Maps	San Rafael Knob. Turkey Tower is shown as elevation 7595 on the map. (San Rafael Knob) [San Rafael Desert]
Circle trip	Yes
Skill level	Easy route finding. Moderate bike riding with no pushes or carries. Wear walking shoes for exploring the mine ruins and the Swasey Cabin area.

This mountain bike tour is one of the best in the Swell. It has a mixed bag of ingredients: an impressive spire, endless Wingate walls and towers, panoramic views, and a historical perspective. The route follows a 4WD road as it winds under Turkey Tower, then under Wingate walls to the Swasey Cabin at the Head of Sinbad. It returns down the Heart of Sinbad road. There is the potential for 4WD traffic, though this should not be a deterrent. There are only a couple of rough spots, but

Turkey Tower

they can be negotiated by mountain bikes and 4WDs. The rest of the route is quite easy. Since this is a road, it is presented below as a road section. There is enough detail to keep you oriented.

0.0   Mileage starts at mile 2.0 on the Reds Canyon Loop road. Take the track to the right (N).

0.8	A track enters on the left (W). There is a short hike going up the wash to a mine site under Family Butte. The wash is soft, so you will have to walk. One-mile round trip.
1.8	Mine ruins to the left.
1.9	The tall spire in front of you is Turkey Tower. The road goes up a steep hill and traverses northeast under the spire.
	Rock climber's note: This 250-foot-tall spire has a handful of potential routes on it. The track goes within a five-minute walk of its base.
3.9	At the backside of Turkey Tower.
6.4	Stock reservoir to the right.
6.6	"Tee." You are in the bottom of Rods Valley. To get back to camp quickly go right (S).
	To go to the Swasey Cabin go left (N). Restart your mileage here.
0.0	Mileage starts at the "Tee" and goes left (N).
1.2	Mine site to the left.
1.5	Wire gate and a brush fence. The going gets tougher.
2.5	At the top of a rise. The Head of Sinbad and I–70 are in front of you (N).
3.3	A track comes in on the left (W). The Broken Cross Pinnacle is clearly visible. Go west on the track. It goes to the Swasey Cabin area. (See Hike #28 in the Sids Mountain chapter for details on exploring the area.) Return the way you came, back to the "Tee." Pick up your mileage at that point.
6.6	At the "Tee." Go south.
7.3	Reservoir on the left.
7.4	Drill pipe on the left.
8.7	Wire gate.
9.2	Intersect the Heart of Sinbad road at mile 13.0. Go right (W).
9.7	At the Major Marked Junction. Go right (W).
9.8	Cattle guard. Tan Seeps is to the right (N).
10.6	McKay Flat and Reds Canyon sign. Stay to the right (W).
11.6	Back at the start of the ride.

Upper Muddy Creek—Hike #41

Season	Early spring, late summer, or fall. Insects can be intolerable along the river in the spring and early summer.
Time	Part 1—7 to 9 hours with both digressions. This is a very long day hike or a more reasonable overnight hike (16 miles).
	Part 2—2 to 3 days with all but the Slaughter Point digression (28 miles). For the Slaughter Point digression add 7 to 9 hours (11 miles).
Elevation gain	Part 1—300'
	Part 2—500'. If you go to Slaughter Point you will gain 1950'.
Water	Part 1—Muddy Creek. Poor Canyon has perennial springs. Little Gem Canyon (AN) has a spring at its head.
	Part 2—Muddy Creek. No water is available in Ireland Mesa Canyon or Poncho Wash.
Maps	Tomsich Butte. Ireland Mesa. (Wild Horse) [San Rafael Desert. Salina.]
Circle trip	No
Skill level	Part 1—Easy route finding. Class 2 walking. Wading shoes are necessary. If you do this as an overnight hike, low-impact camping skills are essential.
	Part 2—As above. The Slaughter Point digression is for advanced canyoneers only. A short rope may be useful.

Upper Muddy Creek, north of Tomsich Butte, is a deep, Wingate- and Navajo-walled, flat-floored canyon. Because of the ease of access, side canyons to explore, and excellent camping along Muddy Creek, this area has become a popular area with backpackers.

The route comes in two parts. Part 1 goes up Muddy Creek to Poor and Little Gem canyons. Part 2 continues up Muddy Creek from Little Gem Canyon to Ireland Mesa Canyon and Poncho Wash, a short, narrow side canyon. Both routes return the way you came.

Part 1: From the truck body look northwest across a barren, brown plain. Muddy Creek is at the far end, past

Moenkopi cliffs behind a lonely cabin near Muddy Creek.

a lonely cabin. A track starts at the truck and goes down the south side of the plain, to the north of Tomsich Butte. Follow the track to Muddy Creek. A side track goes to the Torval Albrecht cabin, the lonely cabin.

Go up Muddy Creek, wading it many times. In forty minutes you will pass a tower that is sitting in the middle of a dry meander. This is a rincon called the Merry-Go-Round. You won't miss it. As you pass its west side Poor Canyon intersects on the right (N).

> **Digression:** Poor Canyon takes two hours to explore. There are intermittent springs, several huge caves, and an abundance of cottonwoods. Good camping is had throughout the canyon. A mining track is visible in places. After forty-five minutes the canyon divides. A spring can be found 200 yards up the canyon to the left, near its end.
>
> The canyon to the right shows evidence of mining activity. Note the core samples strewn along the track. The canyon continues for fifteen minutes beyond the end of the track but gets much rougher and ends in a fall.

Twenty-five minutes up Muddy Creek from Poor Canyon, Little Gem Canyon intersects on the right (NE).

> **Digression:** Little Gem Canyon lives up to its name. It has a fine overhang for camping on the left ten minutes up and ends in a spring pool.

Return the way you came.

Part 2: From Little Gem Canyon go up Muddy Creek for a half hour. The first noteworthy feature is Prickly Pear Bend, another dry meander with a seventy-foot-tall fin in the middle of it. Two canyons come into the bend, one to the south and one to the southwest. Both are short, narrow, and come to a dead end quickly.

One hour past Prickly Pear Bend you will reach Ireland Mesa Canyon coming in on the left (SSE). To ensure that you are at the right canyon, go up the wide wash. As you enter the canyon there is a diamond-shaped cave on a wall to the left (LUC). There is good camping in the area. Poncho Wash and the hike to Slaughter Point are presented below as digressions, both starting at the mouth of Ireland Mesa Canyon. For those continuing up the canyon there are many excellent campsites.

> **Digression:** To get to Poncho Wash proceed up Muddy Creek. After thirty-five minutes there is a short, narrow canyon to the right (LUC) at a sharp left-hand bend in the creek. Twenty minutes past the bend, Poncho Wash comes in on the right (NNE). It is also a short, narrow canyon. (For details on continuing up Muddy Creek see Hike #34.)

> **Digression:** The hike up Ireland Mesa to Slaughter Point is done as a day hike. It is for advanced canyoneers only unless you only plan on exploring the lower parts of Ireland Mesa Canyon. Plan on seven to nine hours round trip.
>
> Before starting up Ireland Mesa Canyon walk 200 yards northeast down Muddy Creek. Carefully check routes through the bottom cliff band. The route drops through this cliff at the end of the hike.
>
> Go up Ireland Mesa Canyon. After fifteen minutes it divides. Go left (SE). In another twenty minutes the canyon divides again. Go left (E). This is not an even division. The canyon to the right seems like it is the main canyon, but it dies shortly. The canyon to the left starts as a grey slickrock area and has much rubble in it.
>
> After five minutes the canyon ends at a fall. Backtrack 100 yards and exit to the right (LUC)(E) up a steep hillside. Do not continue up the canyon. Instead, proceed east up the steep slope and exit the canyon. Look for an

easy place to negotiate the final cliff band. It is loose (Class 4+, 12'). Careful.

Once on the rim you will be on Ireland Mesa. (You are just south of elevation 5735 on the Ireland Mesa map.) Go southeast. While hiking up the mesa note what its north end looks like—narrow and slowly going uphill. You will be walking to the end of the mesa at the conclusion of the hike.

Don't be pedantic. Stay on the top of rounded ridges instead of going in and out of gullies. As long as you go generally southeast you will intersect a canyon going north-south. Go south following another rounded ridge. (You will pass the east side of elevation 5905 on the Ireland Mesa map.) Once again you will reach the edge of a canyon. Drop into it. To do this easily go right (W). Drop into a short side canyon that goes into the main canyon. You are in Ireland Mesa Canyon again.

Go up the canyon to the left (SE), always following the main canyon. There are several falls to negotiate. After forty-five minutes the canyon divides at a colorfully banded butte. Go left (E). As you round the northwest corner of the butte the canyon divides again. The main canyon goes right. Go left (N). The canyon dies in a quarter mile. Exit the canyon to the left (N) up broken ground onto a saddle.

On the other side of the saddle is another canyon. To get to Slaughter Point drop into this canyon and hike up it (E) until it ends at an escarpment. Go up a steep slope to the left (N) and follow the rim for several minutes until on top (6770).

Descend the canyon that is to the northwest. There are many options for getting into it. After you have been in the canyon for forty-five minutes, or by the time you reach the first big fall, exit to the left (LDC). Variations here are not important. You will end up on Ireland Mesa. Go to the north end of the mesa. Muddy Creek is far below.

Go to the northwest end of the escarpment. The mouth of Ireland Mesa Canyon is below you. Drop west along the ridge, using discretion. When the route west looks impractical, go right (E). You will be on a steep slope between two brown cliff bands. Go east as far as possible to the edge of a cliff. Muddy Creek is below you. Drop through the lower brown cliff band. Descend easier rock and negotiate the final cliffs to the river.

★ **The Chute of Muddy Creek, Chimney Canyon, and the Pasture Track—Hike #42**

Season | Early spring and late summer through fall. The hike can be done well into November, weather permitting, providing the water is not too cold to wade. There is a flash flood potential in The Chute of Muddy Creek.

Time | Part 1—8 to 10 hours or 2 shorter days (15 miles)
Part 2—2 days (22 miles)
Part 3—3 to 4 days. This includes a day for day hiking in Upper Chimney Canyon (28 to 36 miles).

Elevation gain | Part 1—300′ elevation loss
Parts 2 and 3—900′ elevation gain

Water | Muddy Creek. There are seasonal springs in the lower and upper parts of Chimney Canyon, though its midsection is dry. There is a perennial spring at the miner's cabin in Upper Chimney Canyon. There is no reliable water along the Pasture Track.

Maps | Parts 1 and 2—Tomsich Butte. Hunt Draw. (Wild Horse) [San Rafael Desert]
Part 3—Tomsich Butte. Hunt Draw. The Frying Pan. Ireland Mesa is optional. (Wild Horse. Emery.) [San Rafael Desert. Salina.]

Circle trip | Part 1—No
Parts 2 and 3—Yes

Skill level | Part 1—Easy route finding. Class 2 walking, often up to knee deep in the creek. This is a long day hike. Wading shoes (see 'How to Use the Guide') are mandatory. Even when hot out, the narrows can get chilly. Be prepared.
Parts 2 and 3—As above. Moderate route finding. Class 4 climbing. A thirty-five-foot rope will be useful for beginners, dogs, and packs. Knowledge of low-impact camping techniques is essential.

Beethoven and Mozart, Shakespeare and Longfellow, Rembrandt and Picasso. Each different, each in a class by himself. If we were to add canyon names to this distinguished list, Muddy Creek and Chimney Canyon would fit like a glove. They are the showcase canyons of the San Rafael Swell.

The hike comes in three parts. Part 1 goes down The Chute, or narrows, of Muddy Creek on a one-way trip that exits at the Hidden Splendor Mine. You will need to arrange a car shuttle or leave mountain bikes at the mine. (See the Hidden Splendor Mine Road Section for directions to the mine.)

Part 2 goes through The Chute, then up the lower narrows of Chimney Canyon, and returns by way of the Pasture Track, an abandoned mining road. Part 3 continues up Chimney Canyon where day hikes take you into several extraordinary side canyons, and returns via the Pasture Track.

Part 1: Go down the canyon. The arch to the right, high on the Wingate wall, is Hondoo Arch.

> **Historical note:** According to San Rafael Swell historian Owen McClenahan, the name Hondoo is derived from the fanciful similarity between the arch and a knot on a cowboy's lariat, which the Spanish call a hondoo.

Follow a mining track south as you crisscross the river. It is easiest to put your wading shoes on from word go. The deeper into The Chute you progress the more time will be spent in the water. Unless you are doing the hike during spring runoff, the water is no more than knee deep. If the river is muddy, a probe is a good idea. There are deep holes. It is interesting to watch the canyon walls as the river cuts its way through the Moenkopi Formation, Sinbad Limestone, and finally into Coconino Sandstone.

> **Digression:** After the first narrow section there is a side canyon to the right (LDC)(W) cutting through the Moenkopi Formation. It is worth a half hour side trip.

It will take four to six hours to reach a logjam—logs jammed twenty-five feet above your head. This is the narrowest section of The Chute. It will take another hour or so to exit the narrows and reach the mouth of Chimney Canyon. Past Chimney Canyon you will have to ford the river occasionally, but the long-distance wading is over. It will take ninety minutes to reach the Hidden Splendor Mine from Chimney Canyon. As you near the mine you will see a track winding its way up a cliff to the left (LDC)(E). Go up the track to the mine site.

The narrowest part of The Chute of Muddy Creek.

If you are doing the hike in two days, remember that there are no campsites in The Chute itself. You can either camp at the head of The Chute or at its mouth.

It is sixteen miles from the Hidden Splendor Mine back to the Hondoo Arch area along the Hidden Splendor Mine and Reds Canyon roads. This will take two to three hours on a mountain bike.

Part 2: Turn right (NW) into Chimney Canyon. There is a ten-foot-high boulder on either side of Muddy Creek at the confluence with Chimney Canyon. After hiking up the canyon for 200 yards the way is blocked by a short, twin-tiered fall. The first fall is Class 4, eight feet. The second fall is Class 4, twenty feet. A rope will reassure beginners. There is a spring area and good camping several hundred yards above the falls.

Go up Chimney Canyon for forty minutes. There are intermittent springs along the way. Watch for a fence line crossing the shallow canyon and an old mining track going south. The springs end at the fence.

> **Digression:** The track goes south along the rim of Muddy Creek to the Little Susan Mine (Hike #43). It is a worthwhile side adventure.

You will exit Chimney Canyon at the fence by going to the right (LUC)(NE). The Pasture Track parallels Muddy Creek, but 700 feet above it. First, you need to connect with the track. Pick your way northeast. You can go in and out of a dozen gullies, or find a cattle track that meanders around them always at the same elevation. The latter is longer but easier and is recommended. As you turn north you will see why it is called The Pasture. The track itself runs along the top, or west side, of the pasture area, well below the Wingate Sandstone and the Chinle Formation. The cow path turns into the Pasture Track. The track itself disappears at times. Simply continue contouring.

Two hours from Chimney Canyon is a side canyon coming in on the left (W). There are old mine workings at the head of the canyon and a small seasonal spring fifty yards down the canyon from the Pasture Track.

Fifteen minutes past the side canyon the track makes a hard right turn and goes into a gully going southeast. This turn is nearly impossible to see. Look for a cairn on a peninsula to the right (LUC). Walk toward the cairn. If you don't see the turn you will run into a very steep slope in five minutes, with the track 100 feet below. Slide down the slope—not fun with a pack on—or backtrack to find the Pasture Track. Once at Muddy Creek it is 50 minutes and five creek crossings back to the start. There is camping, without water, along the Pasture Track. It will take four to five hours to hike from Chimney Canyon to the Hondoo Arch area.

Part 3: Continue up Chimney Canyon. The next hour takes you up a wide wash with towering Wingate and Navajo walls. If you are cutting corners (do), you will cross an abandoned airstrip that is not on the map. The miner's cabin is just ahead.

The canyon divides at the cabin. There is a perennial spring behind the cabin and camping throughout the area. There are day hikes up both forks of the canyon.

To get into the South Fork, the canyon behind the cabin, hike southwest up the narrow mouth of the canyon and tackle a short wall, or go north in the main canyon until the wall can be passed on ledges. Cattle find their way up, so you shouldn't have any problems.

Once above the wall the canyon divides. Go right (W). There are many campsites in an area of spring-fed pools shaded by cottonwoods. The canyon ends at a pool and a hanging garden.

To explore the North Fork of Chimney Canyon go north from the cabin. In ten minutes there is a short, wide canyon to the right. It is not very interesting. In twenty minutes the main canyon divides at a red, holey-walled buttress. Go left (SSW). In ten minutes, before reaching a large, balanced dirt clod, note the Ghouls Wall (AN). There are monstrous and imaginative shapes formed in the eroding sandstone. This is the best wall of its type I have seen. After another ten minutes the canyon ends at a fall.

> **Rock-climber's note:** The canyon ends only for non-climbers. A special treat awaits. The next section of canyon is difficult to enter from either end. Because of this it is pristine. There have been no cattle or miners leaving their usual marks of passage.
>
> Backtrack from the fall for several hundred yards until the wall to the right (LDC)(S) reaches its lowest height. Find the easiest place to ascend the eroded wall (5.3, 20′). Above the fall the canyon divides. Go right. The canyon ends in a fine set of narrows and a small grotto.
>
> To continue up the canyon, backtrack 300 yards from the start of the narrow section. To the right (LDC), just

Hidden alcove in Chimney Canyon.

before a mud prow, ascend broken ground (5.0, 30'). At the top of the prow go southwest, traversing slabs for 150 yards until a slab/crack with sagebrush in it is reached. Above the slab work up for several hundred feet to a white ledge under a Navajo wall.

Traverse west under the wall on the white ledge until it ends. East Cedar Mountain is in the background. There is a trapezoidal-shaped monolith in a bowl below you to the southwest. (This monolith is shown as elevatic 5928 on The Frying Pan map.) You want to drop intc the canyon and pass the monolith on its right (N) side. To do this backtrack for 100 yards and go down slabs and ledges. As you drop, circle to the left (LUC) toward the monolith. There are many variations possible here, all Class 3+. (See Hike #35 for details on exploring this area.) This is a four- to eight-hour day hike, depending on how much time is spent exploring side canyons.

Back to the canyon division that is ten minutes down the canyon from the Ghouls Wall. Go left (LDC)(N). This short canyon complex is the music of Chimney Canyon. Plan on an hour or so to explore these lavishly vegetated masterpieces. Because of the intense beauty of these side canyons, please do not camp in them. Let's leave them absolutely unscarred.

Return the way you came, back to the miner's cabin and down Chimney Canyon. As with Part 2, exit northeast at the fence to join the Pasture Track.

Hidden Splendor Mine Road Section

Access to Hikes #43 through 48
Access is from the Reds Canyon Loop road.
Metric map—San Rafael Desert

This road goes south from mile 21.1 on the Reds Canyon Loop road to the Hidden Splendor Mine. There is a sign at the junction. The road is good for light-duty vehicles. This is a popular road for mountain bikers. Camping is available throughout the area.

0.0	Mileage starts at the Hidden Splendor Mine sign and goes south.
5.2	Old gray car on the left. The area to the left (E) is Sinbad Country. Wild horses are often visible.

Top of a hill. Good views into the Muddy Creek drainage. The area to the right (W) is called Keesle Country. Although no hikes are delineated, this is a great area for wandering.

The start of Quandary Canyon and Lower Muddy Creek **Hike #46,** Upper Knotted Rope Canyon and a Hidden Splendor Overlook **Hike #47,** and Cistern and Ramp Canyons **Hike #48.** There is a vague track to the left (ESE). It is north of a Wingate-walled buttress to the south. It may take some close looking to find the track. The track is impassable to vehicles. Park next to the main road.

9.8 | The start of Chimney Canyon from the Hidden Splendor Mine **Hike #43**, Mud Canyon **Hike/Bike #44**, and Lower Muddy Creek **Hike #45.** You are at the Hidden Splendor Mine, below a silver water tank. Park here. There is camping throughout the area.

 The Hidden Splendor Mine is also called the Delta Mine. At one time it was the largest uranium producer on the Swell.

Chimney Canyon from the Hidden Splendor Mine—Hike #43

Season	Early spring and summer through fall
Time	5 to 6 hours (10 miles)
Elevation gain	350'
Water	Muddy Creek. There is a spring a short distance above the fall in Chimney Canyon. Bring your own water.
Maps	Hunt Draw. (Wild Horse) [San Rafael Desert]
Circle trip	Yes
Skill level	Easy route finding. Class 4 climbing. The hike is Class 1+, mostly along mining tracks, except for eight- and twenty-foot-tall falls in Chimney Canyon. A rope may be needed for belaying beginners. Wading shoes are recommended.

You'll be singing "zippity do da . . . what a wonderful day" as you fly through the middle portion of Muddy Creek. It is a high-walled, wide-bottomed canyon filled with cottonwoods. The track above Muddy Creek that goes by the Little Susan Mine provides outstanding views of Keesle Country. The route is presented as a day hike. It can also be used as access to Chimney Canyon for those wanting to do an overnight hike without having to wade through The Chute.

The route goes up Muddy Creek from the Hidden Splendor Mine to Chimney Canyon. It then goes up the lower, narrow section of Chimney Canyon and follows an abandoned mining track above Muddy Creek, past the Little Susan Mine, and through an unnamed, mud-walled canyon back to Muddy Creek.

From the silver water tank at the Hidden Splendor Mine go west on a road. It crosses a landing strip and de-teriorates as it drops through the Moenkopi Formation to Muddy Creek. Follow mining tracks as you go up the creek. You will have to wade it several times. In thirty minutes, as the canyon makes a U-turn and goes from south to north, there is a side canyon entering on the left (S). The floor of the side canyon is filled with rounded stream rocks. This is the exit canyon. Fifteen minutes past this Mud Canyon comes in on the right (E) (Hike #44).

Chimney Canyon enters on the left (LUC)(NW) after another thirty-five to forty minutes. There are two ten-foot-high boulders on each side of Muddy Creek imme-diately below the opening into the canyon. Go up the canyon. In 200 yards there is a twin-tiered drop. The first fall is Class 4, eight feet. The second fall is Class 4, twenty feet. Beginners will want a rope. Go up the can-yon for forty minutes until a fence is reached. (See Hike #42, Part 3, for more information on continuing up Chimney Canyon.)

Past the fence there is an old mining track going south. Follow it. Note the black dike to the left. If you look up the canyon, you can see it for several miles.

After an hour you will reach the Little Susan Mine. The buildings are well preserved. Continue following the track. It goes into the top of and down the mud-walled exit canyon.

★ | # Mud Canyon (AN)—Hike/Bike #44

Season	Any
Time	5 to 6 hours (9 miles)
Elevation gain	600'
Water	Muddy Creek. There is no water in Mud Canyon. Bring your own water.
Maps	Hunt Draw. Mud Canyon is shown but is not labeled on the map. It starts immediately north of elevation 5030. (Wild Horse) [San Rafael Desert]
Circle trip	Yes
Skill level	Easy/moderate route finding. Class 3+ scrambling. There are several chockstones to surmount. Other than those, this is a Class 1+ hike. Wading shoes (see ''How to Use the Guide'') are recommended.

For those who are tired of soaring Wingate walls and smooth, vertical expanses of rock, Mud Canyon will be a welcome relief. It has soaring mud walls, replete with pinnacles, towers, and narrows all carved into the Moenkopi Formation. This is a busy hike. There is always something to see or do.

The route starts at the Hidden Splendor Mine and goes up Muddy Creek to Mud Canyon, which it ascends. Near the head of Mud Canyon the route exits and goes cross-country to the Hidden Splendor Mine road. Either hike or bike back to the start.

Before starting the route, if you plan on riding a mountain bike, drop it off. From the silver water tank at the Hidden Splendor Mine go back up the main road for 2.0 miles and cache your bike. There are small gullies within 100 yards of the road, so this should not be a problem. Discrepancies here won't matter.

From the silver water tank at the Hidden Splendor Mine follow a road west, cross an abandoned airstrip, and descend into the canyon. Go up the canyon, often following a mining track. Cross the river at least four times. The first side canyon to the right (LUC) after the mining track ends is Mud Canyon. It starts as a wash coming in from the east. After thirty minutes Mud Canyon divides. There is a ten-foot-high, brown square tower at wash level on the right. Go left.

Thirty minutes past the tower the canyon divides at a brown mud fin. Go left, following the grey canyon floor.

> **Digression:** Go right, following the red canyon floor. This narrow canyon ends in an alcove. Fifteen minutes round trip.

Fifteen minutes past the mud fin the canyon divides equally at a horizontally layered buttress. Go right. At a fall you will have to exit the canyon. To exit, backtrack for 200 yards. Scramble up a steep, loose slope to the left (LDC)(S). Below a dark brown cliff band traverse left (E) at a comfortable level for five minutes (do not drop back into Mud Canyon.) Go around a corner and exit through the first easy break in the cliff band. Once on top go southeast. Drop in and out of several shallow canyons, all easy to negotiate. Variations here won't matter. Intersect the Hidden Splendor Mine road. If you are walking, it is fifty minutes back to the start. If you are riding, it is a ten-minute downhill whiz.

★ | ## Lower Muddy Creek—Hike #45

Season	Early spring, summer and fall. There is a flash flood potential in this section of Muddy Creek.
Time	4 to 5 hours (8 miles)
Elevation gain	200′
Water	Muddy Creek. Bring your own water.
Maps	Hunt Draw. (Wild Horse) [San Rafael Desert]
Circle trip	No
Skill level	Easy route finding. Class 2 walking. This is a hike most can do—a good family hike. Wading shoes are essential.

Muddy Creek, where it exits the Swell in the south, cuts through the reef in an awesome display of Wingate and Navajo walls. The creek meanders down a wide, cottonwood-lined canyon and past an area of mine ruins.

A tall pinnacle and a short box canyon are encountered along the way.

The route follows Muddy Creek from the Hidden Splendor Mine, through the Southern Reef, and returns the same way.

From the silver water tank at the Hidden Splendor Mine follow a track south that descends to Muddy Creek. Go down the canyon, following the mining track when possible. There are mine ruins and an encampment to visit before the wading starts. The water is shallow, mid-calf at most, but there are some holes. If the river is muddy, a walking stick for probing will be helpful.

After ninety minutes to two hours, toward the end of the canyon, watch for a side canyon to the left (LDC)(E). This short canyon (Knotted Rope Canyon), partially blocked by tamarisks, has a fantastic spring-fed pool at its head. Classic.

Muddy Creek exits the reef in another five minutes. Turn around here. The creek continues for many miles, but it is not as interesting as it heads across the flats.

★ **Quandary Canyon (AN) and Lower Muddy Creek—Hike #46**

Season	Warm weather. No recent rains. No snow. There is a flash flood potential in both canyons.
Time	8 to 10 hours. Plan on more time if your group is large (11 miles).
Elevation gain	1200′
Water	There are perennially full potholes in Quandary Canyon. Bring your own water.
Maps	Hunt Draw. Quandary Canyon is shown but is not named on the map. It is the second canyon to the east of the Hidden Splendor Mine and starts to the southeast of elevation 6245. (Wild Horse) [San Rafael Desert]
Circle trip	Yes

Skill level

Difficult route finding. Class 5.4 climbing. Ability to handle ropes, set up a rappel, downclimb an unprotected thirty-foot chimney/chute, negotiate tight narrows, and swim short distances in bitterly cold water. Quandary Canyon is for expert canyoneers and rock-climbers only. Bring an eighty-foot climbing rope and one inner tube per group. Wading shoes are essential. Every member of the party should carry a thirty-foot rope for lowering packs. Youth groups should not be testing their mettle in this canyon.

Quandary Canyon presents the expert canyoneer with many challenges. It is a deep, narrow, Navajo-walled canyon that penetrates the Southern Reef. It is a difficult, technical, and exceptionally rewarding canyon to negotiate.

The route starts at the top of the reef and descends Quandary Canyon in steep steps. From the base of the reef the route returns by way of Lower Muddy Creek. This hike belongs in the Southern Reef chapter, but it is accessed from the Muddy Creek side.

A competent team of rock-climbers will have no problems doing this route. Dogs will have an exceedingly rough time because there are bottomless narrows that climbers can easily chimney through; dogs though, will have to be hauled or carried. Leave them behind on this trip. Several large potholes must be swum and, less experienced climbers will need to be belayed over numerous obstacles. There should be one experienced climber in every party to take up the rear. He or she will have to descend some slightly intimidating rock without protection.

You can save yourself two miles of hiking along the road by leaving a car or a mountain bike at the Hidden Splendor Mine.

From the Hidden Splendor Mine road go east-southeast on the track for ten minutes until a blue car is reached. Go southwest up a wash into a wide canyon, following a faded mining track. The track goes diagonally up a hill. Under a notch in a Wingate wall the track turns southeast, goes through a road cut, and enters a remarkable bowl. Once in the bowl go south. The bowl is a good destination for those looking for a short hike.

At the far side of the bowl the real canyon starts. It narrows immediately. The first fall has a rock bollard to drape a rope over, or it can be downclimbed (5.4, 12').

At the second fall there is an eight-by-eight-inch twelve-foot-long timber that can be used as a rappel anchor. Reset it to your satisfaction. Rappel down the twelve-foot drop. This can also be downclimbed on a rotten ledge to the left (LDC)(5.8, 12'). Below the fall the canyon opens. There is a track here. Figure that one out! Follow the track through an open area. It ends at a drill pipe. Below is an undocumented natural bridge. Go under it and continue down the canyon past another small natural bridge.

The next obstacles, a deep pothole and a fall, are bypassed to the right (LDC)(5.0, 30') by going up a steep slab, traversing down, and dropping back into the canyon. Beginners may want a rope.

Next is a chimney/chute (5.4, 30') that ends in a narrow pool. You will have to lower inexperienced climbers. There is no protection possible. The last person down will be at risk. The pool could be deep, so the first person down should be prepared (no cameras, inner tube ready). Immediately after the pool there are a couple of short potholes to swim or wade. Tight, challenging narrows follow.

After a short easy section there is a deep pothole. Backtrack fifty yards, and pass it on the left (LDC)(E) by going up a steep gully. At the top of the gully there is a steep gully/chimney going west back into the canyon. Do not go down this gully. Rather, go southeast over a small saddle and traverse along the top of a large, steep slab. Intersect a wall running east to west. Go west, climb under a large chockstone, and join the original canyon.

The next section of canyon contains many easy obstacles. It ends at two large perennial pools before intersecting a wash that marks the base of the reef. Go right, generally south-southwest, until Muddy Creek is reached. Hike up the creek back to the Hidden Splendor Mine.

A natural bridge in Quandary Canyon.

Digression: Instead of returning by way of Muddy Creek you can follow the face of the reef to the left (NE) and go up Ramp Canyon. It takes fifty minutes, walking along the face of the reef, to reach the mouth of Ramp Canyon. (See Hike #48 for details.)

Upper Knotted Rope Canyon (AN) and Hidden Splendor Overlook—Hike #47

Season	Any. No snow.
Time	3 to 5 hours (6 miles)
Elevation gain	700'
Water	None. Bring your own water.
Maps	Hunt Draw. Knotted Rope Canyon is shown but is not labeled on the map. It is the first canyon to the east of the Hidden Splendor Mine and is south-southwest of elevation 6245. (Wild Horse) [San Rafael Desert]
Circle trip	No
Skill level	Moderate route finding. Class 4 climbing. Beginners may want a rope going through Wayne's Wriggle.

Knotted Rope Canyon does not go through the reef. It does provide access to a large bowl that has seen mining activity and to the top of the Wingate-walled escarpment that stands high above the Hidden Splendor Mine. The canyon is named for a knotted rope that hangs through Wayne's Wriggle, the crux of the route. It allows access to the top part of the canyon.

The route uses the same start as Quandary Canyon, scales a wall, and gains the rim of the escarpment directly above Hidden Splendor. Return the way you came. This hike belongs in the Southern Reef chapter, but it is accessed from the Muddy Creek side.

Use the Quandary Canyon Hike #46 description to gain the bowl at the end of the mining track. As you near the end of the bowl, Quandary Canyon starts to the south as a narrow canyon. To the southwest is a steep gully going up the canyon wall. It looks like the top is blocked by a boulder and an overhang. Scramble up the loose gully. At its top is a chimney with a hole. This is Wayne's Wriggle. Pieces of an old knotted rope are lying about. Wriggle through the hole (Class 4, 20') if you aren't too big.

From the rim Quandary Canyon is to the south. To the southwest is a Wingate cliff band. Knotted Rope Canyon is on the other side of this. To reach Knotted Rope Canyon go west, then south, along the rim of the escarpment. There are miner's cairns all along the rim. The views are something else. If you drop into the upper part of the canyon you will see bundles of four-by-four-inch posts and lengths of pipe. Apparently the miners tried to pump water up from Muddy Creek.

Take a picnic on this hike, find a comfortable spot, and enjoy the views.

★ **Cistern and Ramp Canyons (AN)—Hike #48**

Season	Any. No snow. There is a flash flood potential in both canyons.
Time	Part 1—4 to 6 hours (10 miles)

	Part 2—5 to 7 hours (10 miles)
Elevation gain	850'
Water	Cistern Canyon has a perennial spring at its head. Bring your own water.
Maps	Hunt Draw. Ramp Canyon is shown but is not labeled on the map. It is the first canyon going through the reef to the west of Cistern Canyon. (Wild Horse) [San Rafael Desert]
Circle trip	Part 1—No
	Part 2—Yes
Skill level	Part 1—Easy/moderate route finding. Class 3 scrambling.
	Part 2—Moderate/advanced route finding. Class 5.1 climbing. A forty-foot rope will be needed for beginners, dogs, and packs. Wading shoes may be needed in Ramp Canyon.

Cistern and Ramp canyons, svelte and sinuous, are both Wingate- and Navajo-walled canyons that pierce the Southern Reef. Cistern Canyon is one of the easiest narrow canyons on the Southern Reef to hike, while Ramp Canyon has an onerous obstacle to overcome.

The hike comes in two parts. Part 1 goes along the backside of the reef, then drops through Cistern Canyon to the face of the reef. Return the way you came. Part 2 continues along the face of the reef and ascends Ramp Canyon back to the start. This is the preferred route, but Ramp Canyon has one tricky section (5.1, 25') that is best left to rock-climbers and advanced canyoneers. This hike should be in the Southern Reef chapter, but access to it is from the Muddy Creek side.

Part 1: From the Hidden Splendor Mine road go east-southeast along the track. (This is the same track you take at the start of Hikes #46 and 47.) In ten minutes you will reach a blue car. To the southeast there is an opening in the escarpment. It marks the head of Ramp Canyon. Cistern Canyon is the first canyon to the east of Ramp Canyon. To get to it follow the track toward Ramp Canyon until you are close to its head; then go northeast up a steep slope, paralleling a Wingate-walled buttress, but well below it. From the top of the slope follow a steep, shallow, red-walled gully east down to the mouth of Cistern Canyon.

Hike south down Cistern Canyon. The spring at the top of the canyon is called Bullberry Spring. The canyon itself has small challenges, but no big problems. Exit the reef. From the base of the reef go southwest in a wash until a northeast-southwest-running, striated brown cliff band (Summerville Formation) is reached. There is a wash running under it. The reef has more colors in it in this area than in any other section. For those doing Part 1, return the way you came.

Part 2: Go right (SW) along the face of the reef. There is a maze of small washes, hills, and cliffs. Ramp Canyon is easy to miss. It is the second major drainage you will pass. To tell if you are going up the correct canyon, hike up it for 10 minutes to see if the following description matches what you are seeing:

> Go up a rock-scattered wash to the north-northwest. After 100 yards enter the reef. There is a triangular-shaped peak to the left (NW), high on the reef. The canyon takes a sinuous course as it winds through the various sandstone layers of the reef. After five minutes it takes an abrupt left turn and goes west-southwest. You are hiking along a unique, straight corridor with a 45-degree, dirty white slab to the right (N). The corridor lasts for 250 yards, then turns right for ten yards and ends at a thirty-foot-high slickrock slab. Ascend the slab (Class 3). The canyon continues a serpentine course up. By this time you should have decided if you are in the right canyon.

A twin-tiered fall is passed on a steep slope to the left (LUC). There are more obstacles, all fairly easy to negotiate, until you reach a huge chockstone blocking the canyon. It is passed on the left (LUC) along a thin dike or ramp. There are several choices here. The lowest ramp is the easiest (5.1, 25′). Beginners and dogs will need a rope.

> **Warning:** At least two people have fallen off the ramp. Luckily both were being belayed with a rope and were unharmed. Be careful.

The canyon finishes on easier terrain. At its head follow the mining track back to the blue car.

Corridor near the entrance to Ramp Canyon.

A longer alternative to this hike would be to continue along the face of the reef to the southwest; then hike up Muddy Creek to the Hidden Splendor Mine.

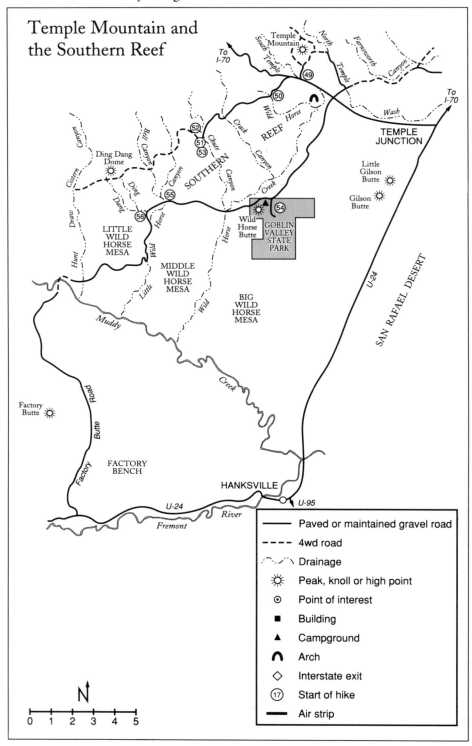

Temple Mountain and the Southern Reef

Temple Mountain

To I-70

North Temple

Farnsworth Canyon

South Temple

Wild Horse

REEF

Temple

Wash

To I-70

TEMPLE JUNCTION

Creek

Chute Canyon

SOUTHERN

Canyon

Little Gilson Butte

Gilson Butte

Cistern Canyon

Bell Canyon

Ding Dang Dome

Ding Dang

Creek

Draw

Hunt

Wild Horse Butte

GOBLIN VALLEY STATE PARK

LITTLE WILD HORSE MESA

Little Wild

MIDDLE WILD HORSE MESA

Wild Horse

BIG WILD HORSE MESA

Muddy

Creek

U-24

SAN RAFAEL DESERT

Factory Butte

Factory Butte Road

FACTORY BENCH

Factory

HANKSVILLE

U-95

U-24

River

Fremont

	Paved or maintained gravel road
- - - -	4wd road
	Drainage
☀	Peak, knoll or high point
⊙	Point of interest
■	Building
▲	Campground
∩	Arch
◇	Interstate exit
⑰	Start of hike
▬	Air strip

N

0 1 2 3 4 5

7 | Temple Mountain and the Southern Reef

Temple Mountain and the Southern Reef are located in the southeastern corner of the San Rafael Swell. The area is bounded by Temple Mountain on the north, Muddy Creek on the west, Wild Horse Mesa and Goblin Valley on the south, and the San Rafael Desert on the east.

The Temple Mountain area encompasses just the one mountain. It was an important mountain in the early 1900s because of the radium it contained. Radium was used extensively in Europe as a panacea. It allegedly cured such maladies as gout, consumption (tuberculosis), and a variety of cancers. It was used in baths, given as shots, or taken orally. In 1911 one gram of radium was worth $210,000. It was later found that radium was useless as a cure-all. As demand declined mining stopped on Temple Mountain.

After World War II the demand once again increased for Temple Mountain and San Rafael Swell ore. This time it was mined for its uranium content. At Temple Mountain you can plainly see the differences in the two eras: old stone houses are juxtaposed next to frame buildings, war surplus vehicles rot next to hand-excavated mine shafts. The mining stopped in the early 1960s, though mining claims are kept current. Temple Mountain is not in a wilderness study area.

The Southern Reef is similar to the Eastern Reef. It is an uplift penetrated by many deep canyons. Most of the hikes described go through the reef in one canyon, circle behind it, and return via another canyon. Quite convenient. Little Wild Horse Canyon (Hike #55), is by far and away the most popular hike on the San Rafael Swell. Some of the Southern Reef is included in the Crack Canyon Wilderness Study Area.

The book *Stone House Lands* by Joseph Bauman details the history of the reef areas of the San Rafael Swell. It starts at the Swell's geologic beginning 200 million years ago. From there chapters are devoted to the Indians, the

Spanish and American explorers, the Mormon settlers, the days of lawlessness when the Hole-in-the-Wall gang inhabited the Swell, the uranium miners, and the latest on the battles to make the Swell a wilderness area or a national park. This is essential reading for those interested in the San Rafael Reef.

Temple Mountain Road Section

Access to Hike #49
Access is from Highway 24.
Provides access to the Goblin Valley/Southern Reef
    and the Behind the Reef roads.
Provides alternate access to the Heart of Sinbad road.
Metric map—San Rafael Desert

    This road goes west from Highway 24 to Temple Mountain. From Exit 147 on Interstate 70 go south on Highway 24 for twenty-five miles until you reach a sign to Goblin Valley State Park. It is at milepost 137. This is twenty-five miles north of Hanksville. The road is paved and is good for any vehicle. There is camping throughout the area. The Temple Mountain road is also covered in the Heart of Sinbad Road Section.

0.0	Mileage starts at the cattle guard to the west of the highway. Go west on a paved road.
5.0	"Tee." Stay on the pavement.

Side road
    A track to the right (NE) goes to the mouth of North Temple Wash and Farnsworth Tanks.

0.0	Mileage starts at the pavement and goes northeast. This is a medium-duty vehicle road.
0.4	Track going to the left (N) up a wash toward a canyon. This is a good canyon for those looking for a short hike.

0.8	Track to the left.
1.0	"Tee." The track continuing to the right (E) along the base of the reef is for medium-duty vehicles.
	The track to the left (NW), going up North Temple Wash, is for 4WDs. It goes to a mine site on the backside of Temple Mountain.
1.4	At a shallow wash. This is the end of the medium-duty road.
	Walk along the track (E) for ten minutes. To the left (N) is Farnsworth Tank, a stock reservoir. In another 10 minutes there is a track coming in on the left. Follow this track northwest. It goes into Farnsworth Canyon. You can walk through the lower, narrow section of the canyon in two hours round trip. To make this a circle trip go west as you exit the top of Farnsworth Canyon. Follow mining roads into the head of North Temple Wash, the next canyon to the south. Hike back through the reef. The hike takes four hours. **End of side road**
5.1	Goblin Valley junction. Follow the pavement west.
	The Goblin Valley/Southern Reef road starts here and goes to the left (SW). (See that road section for details.)
6.0	Barrier Canyon Style pictograph panel under an overhang to the right (N). It is visible from the road.
6.4	Road changes from asphalt to dirt.
6.5	Camping on the right.
6.9	Track on the right. It goes to the Temple Mountain mining area.
7.1	The start of Temple Mountain Circumambulation **Hike #49.** The Temple Mountain parking and camping area is to the right (N). Park near the small concrete block building.
7.2	"Tee." Road coming in on the left (SW). This is the Behind the Reef road. It goes to Hikes #50 through 53. (See that road section for details.)
	If you are going northwest from here, to the Hidden Splendor Mine, Reds Canyon, or the Muddy Creek area, see the Heart of Sinbad Road Section in the Muddy Creek chapter for details. You are now at mile 25.0 on the Heart of Sinbad road.

Temple Mountain Circumambulation—Hike #49

Season	Any
Time	3 to 4 hours without stops. With exploring plan on a good portion of the day (7 miles).
Elevation gain	300′
Water	None. Bring your own water.
Maps	Temple Mountain. (Temple Mountain) [San Rafael Desert]
Circle trip	Yes
Skill level	Easy route finding. Class 2+ walking. Though most of the hike is on mining roads, rock slides have obliterated some sections.

> **Warning:** The area around Temple Mountain has many open mines. These are unmarked and uncovered. Watch your children. Do not enter the mines. They contain potentially lethal, stagnant air.

The flanks of Temple Mountain are as colorful as an artist's palette. With vividly tinted walls and old uranium mine workings, there is much to see, explore, and photograph.

The hike goes around Temple Mountain on mining tracks at a high enough level to afford good views of the surrounding Sinbad Country.

From the parking area work your way around Temple Mountain in a counterclockwise direction, initially going north to northeast. You will be following old mining tracks. In a flat area covered with old mine workings follow the main track (sometimes questionable as to which is which) to a saddle on the right (E) side of the mountain. From the saddle go left (W). The track deteriorates quickly and ends abruptly. Pick your way across boulder and talus slopes for ten minutes until the track is regained, above several more mines.

> **Rock-climber's note:** The climb to the top of Temple Mountain is technically not difficult (5.0, 200'), but the route described contains much loose rock and has frightening exposure. Experts only.
>
> From the saddle described above look north at the southeast face of Temple Mountain. You will see two

The west side of Temple Mountain.

large, long, green/copper streaks. The immediate goal is to get to the top of the streak to the left (W). After crossing the boulder slope mentioned above, ascend a steep slope (W) above the mines. Near the ridge start traversing right (NE) under a pointed white tower. Continue northeast under a pinnacle until above the green/copper area. There is a dished area above with several steep gullies going up. Ascend any of these, zigzagging a bit, staying with easier rock (some 5.0). There is a lot of loose rock for the next several hundred feet.

From the top of the ridge the small red tower above you is Class 4, and is ten feet lower than the true summit. Scramble west along the ridge to the true summit (6773). This is Class 4, exposed, hairy, and loose. Downclimb the route. This is the easiest route on Temple Mountain. It is dangerous.

The track continues, mostly unbroken. There are mine ruins scattered everywhere. They all have bits and pieces of tracks going to them, making exploration easy. The west end of Temple Mountain, with several pinnacles and a kaleidoscope of colored formations, is perhaps the nicest part.

Mountain biker's note: You can do a fine bike ride around Temple Mountain. Follow the main road north, then northwest as you go clockwise around the mountain. There are short side roads here and there, so it may take a little looking. After getting to the backside of the mountain, at a miner's cabin, follow the track east into North Temple Wash. This will take you back to the Temple Mountain road. Plan on two hours.

Behind the Reef Road Section

Access to Hikes #50 through 53
Access is from the Temple Mountain and the Heart of Sinbad roads.
Metric map—San Rafael Desert

This road goes southwest from the Temple Mountain road, along the north side of the Southern Reef, to the top of Chute Canyon. The Behind the Reef road starts at mile 7.2 on the Temple Mountain road and at mile 25.0 on the Heart of Sinbad road. An extension of the road, no longer suitable for cars, provides access to Little Wild Horse, Bell, Ding, Dang, and Cistern canyons. (This extension is described in Bike/Hike #52.) The road is for light-duty vehicles and is excellent for mountain bikes. There is camping throughout the area.

0.0	Mileage starts at the junction with the Temple Mountain road, 0.1 mile west of the Temple Mountain parking area, and goes southwest.
0.1	Cross South Temple Wash.
1.0	Top of a rise.
1.6	The start of Wild Horse Canyon **Hike #50.** Track going left (S) toward a break in the escarpment. Park off the main road.
1.7	Road turns west.
2.1	Wash/track to the left. The track goes to what appears to be the next break in the escarpment. It goes back to Wild Horse Canyon.

2.8	Top of a rise.
4.1	Track to the left (S). It is 100 yards before the bottom of a hill and goes to a break in the escarpment. This is Crack Canyon. To hike to the crack, the narrowest section of the canyon, takes 2.5 hours round trip. An alternate and more scenic route is described in Hike #51. For those doing Hike #51 you can cache mountain bikes here.
4.4	Top of a rise.
5.8	Cross a wash.
6.0	Cross a wash as the road makes a sharp U-turn. You are going into the top of Chute Canyon.
6.2	Cottonwoods and a good campsite are on the left.
6.2 + 100 yards	The start of Behind the Reef **Bike/Hike #52.** There is a track to the right (LDC)(SW) going up a hill. Park off the road.
6.6	The start of Chute and Crack Canyons **Hike #51** and Chute Buttress—An Ascent **Hike #53.** There is a silver shack on the left. Park here.

Wild Horse Canyon—Hike #50

Season	Any
Time	4 to 6 hours (9 miles)
Elevation gain	300′
Water	Seasonal potholes. Bring your own water.
Maps	Temple Mountain. (Temple Mountain) [San Rafael Desert]
Circle trip	Yes.
Skill level	Easy route finding. Class 2 walking. This is a good day hike for all.

After hiking down Wild Horse Canyon don't be surprised if you catch yourself grinning from ear to ear. Though there are more spectacular canyons in the San Rafael Swell, the combination of easy walking, heavily varnished walls, a narrow section, and several sets of Barrier Canyon Style pictograph panels make this hike a joy.

The hike goes down Wild Horse Canyon to South Temple Wash, which it follows back to the Temple Mountain road. This is followed back to the Behind the Reef road.

Those with mountain bikes can leave them in the vicinity of the pictograph panel at mile 6.0 on the Temple Mountain road and ride back to the start.

There is an alternate start to the hike at mile 0.3 on the Goblin Valley/Southern Reef road. This provides shorter access to the narrows and to the lower pictograph panel. (See that road section for details.)

Follow the vague track going south into Wild Horse Canyon. After twenty minutes the canyon narrows considerably. In another four minutes, at the end of a slickrock area and behind a prominent twenty-foot-high boulder, there is a small pictograph panel to the left (LDC).

Continue down the canyon. After an hour the canyon walls start to subside. At this point keep your eyes peeled to the left (LDC)(N). At the top of a slickrock slab, 100 feet above the wash, are two shallow overhangs. The one to the left appears to be partitioned into three or four segments, while the one fifty yards to the right has a black streak running down the middle of it. The sectioned overhang has an unsullied, petite set of Barrier Canyon Style pictographs. If the canyon tapers down and you enter a shallow, narrow section, you have missed the panel.

After enjoying the pictographs continue through a corridor-like section of canyon. In a wash area, ninety seconds after exiting the narrows, South Temple Wash comes in from the left (LDC)(E). Go east up the wash. After fifteen minutes you will enter a short, red, shallow, narrow section. Several minutes later the wash divides. Go right (LUC)(N). It takes a half hour to intersect the Temple Mountain road near the pictograph panel.

Barrier Canyon Style pictographs in Wild Horse Canyon.

Chute and Crack Canyons—Hike #51

Season	Any. No snow. There is the potential for flash floods in both canyons.
Time	5 to 7 hours (11 miles)
Elevation gain	600'
Water	None. Bring your own water.
Maps	Little Wild Horse Mesa. Horse Valley. Goblin Valley. Temple Mountain. (Temple Mountain. Wild Horse.) [San Rafael Desert]
Circle trip	Yes
Skill level	Easy/moderate route finding. Class 4 climbing. There are several short obstacles to surmount in Crack Canyon, otherwise this is a Class 2 hike.

The Chute and Crack canyons hike is second only to Little Wild Horse and Bell canyons in popularity. Both of these canyons are sheer-walled and wonderful. Chute Canyon has a track running its length while Crack Canyon contains a classic narrow section. Only the jaded will not enjoy this hike.

The route goes down Chute Canyon, across the face of the Southern Reef, and joins Crack Canyon just below the narrow section.

Those with mountain bikes can leave them at mile 4.1 on the Behind the Reef road, at the head of Crack Canyon, and ride the 2.5 miles back along the road to the parking area.

There is an alternate start to the hike. You do the same route, but you go up Crack Canyon first. (See the Goblin Valley/Southern Reef Road Section at mile 5.0 for details.)

From the parking area at the silver shack go down Chute Canyon for ninety minutes until you exit the canyon proper. Go up the first wash encountered on the left (N). After five minutes watch for a single pictograph at eye level on the left. Three minutes past the pictograph the canyon divides. Go right. Another fifteen minutes of walking will bring you to a spring area below an easily passed six-foot-tall fall. Two minutes later the canyon divides at a gray prow. Stay to the right. Forty-five seconds past the gray prow the canyon divides again. The main canyon goes to the left. Go right (NE) up a three-foot-wide wash that goes up a hill. In 200 yards the wash tapers off. Go east across the face of the reef. As long as you go east (a touch north thrown in is okay) you will intersect a red-and-brown-walled canyon.

Gain the bottom of the canyon and go up it (N). You will quickly reach a white slickrock and pothole area. This lasts for several hundred yards. Enter a bowl surrounded by white slickrock domes and cliffs. A quarter of the way through it turn east, go up a rise, and onto a saddle. Below you is Crack Canyon. Descend moderate slopes and slabs. Discrepancies won't matter. If you have been going generally east you will intersect Crack Canyon.

Go up the canyon (N). Several obstacles must be negotiated, but none are too hard. As you exit the canyon join a track going north. Follow this to the Behind the Reef road. It is 2.5 miles back to the silver shack.

★ | **Behind the Reef—Bike/Hike #52**

Season	Any. No snow or recent rains. There is the potential for ORV use in this area.
Time	5 to 6 hours (3 to 4 hours bicycling, 2 hours hiking) (20 miles)
Elevation gain	750'
Water	There is water in Bullberry Spring at the head of Cistern Canyon. Bring your own water.
Maps	Little Wild Horse Mesa. Horse Valley. Hunt Draw. (Temple Mountain. Wild Horse.) [San Rafael Desert]
Circle trip	No
Skill level	Easy route finding. Class 1 hiking. Moderate/hard bike riding. There are several long uphill sections and pushes, but no carries. The fit will have no problems. Wear walking shoes.

This is a choice route for mountain bikers. It combines long hills with exceptional scenery, mine ruins, wild horses, and several possible digressions.

The route uses an abandoned mining track to traverse along the north, or backside, of the Southern Reef. The track goes from the head of Chute Canyon to Cistern Canyon and provides alternate access to Little Wild Horse, Bell, Ding, Dang, and Cistern canyons. The track is an extension of the Behind the Reef road.

From the main road go up the mining track to the southwest. The first hill is the worst on the route. It has a soft base. Don't be discouraged. At the top of the hill the track divides. Go right. It takes forty-five minutes to reach the first break in the Wingate wall, which is shortly after passing a freestanding, pinnacled fin to the left. This is the head of Little Wild Horse Canyon.

Twenty minutes past the head of Little Wild Horse Canyon you will descend a hill into the top of Bell Canyon.

> **Digression:** You can do a loop hike by going down Bell Canyon and up Little Wild Horse Canyon. (See Hike #55 for details.)

As you continue west you will pass a photogenic cabin

on a knoll. Twenty-five minutes past Bell Canyon descend into the head of Ding Canyon. To the west is an
impressive peak, Ding Dang Dome, named after con-
certed efforts to ascend it failed. (This is shown as elevation 6107 on the Little Wild Horse Mesa map.) It is the
dominant feature on the backside of the Southern Reef.

It will take ten minutes to reach the head of Dang
Canyon, after circling around the north side of Ding
Dang Dome.

> **Digression:** A short loop hike goes down Dang Canyon
> and up Ding Canyon. As this is a short hike, it is the
> most logical one to do in conjunction with the bike ride.
> (See Hike #56 for details.)

Past the dome the track deteriorates drastically. Bike on
for another mile and then start walking.

Continue following the track. It will take an hour to
reach Cistern Canyon. At its head is Bullberry Spring. (It
is mentioned in the Muddy Creek chapter, Hike #48.)

Return the way you came.

Chute Buttress—An Ascent—Hike #53

Season	Any. No snow.
Time	4 to 5 hours (5 miles)
Elevation gain	1300'
Water	None. Bring your own water.
Maps	Horse Valley. Temple Mountain. Chute Buttress is shown but is not labeled on the map. It is elevation 6508 on the Horse Valley map. (Temple Mountain. Wild Horse.) [San Rafael Desert]
Circle trip	No
Skill level	Moderate route finding. Easy Class 4 climbing. There are no exposure problems on the climb. It is a good climb for beginners if they have competent leadership. A forty-foot rope may be helpful.

Chute Buttress is the highest point on the Southern

Reef. Its summit provides an exciting platform for viewing the surrounding country.

The route goes up a short unnamed canyon, ascends Chute Buttress, and returns the same way.

From the silver shack cross the road and hike southwest up an abandoned mining track. The track ends in eight minutes at a short fall that leads into a canyon. Go up the canyon (W). There is much scrambling, mostly around big boulders.

The canyon ends in a bowl. Do not go straight (W) up an obvious gully. Go up a gully to the southwest. The gully ends on slickrock. Ascend slabs and ledges until a ridge is topped.

Go right (N) along the top of the ridge. At one point you need to traverse under the ridgetop before dropping onto a saddle. From the saddle continue north. After several minutes you will traverse under a twenty-to-forty-foot-tall, dark brown cliff band on its east side. Look for a slot going through the cliff band to the left (W). If you go past the slot the cliff band gets higher and is not climbable.

From the top of the cliff band you are on your own. Snake your way north to the summit (6508). A bench mark from 1952 is at the top. There are tremendous views from the summit.

Return the way you came.

Goblin Valley/Southern Reef Road Section

Access to Hikes #54 through 56
Access is from the Temple Mountain and the Heart of Sinbad roads.
Provides access to the Factory Butte road.
Metric map—San Rafael Desert

This road goes southwest from the Temple Mountain

road to Goblin Valley. It then goes west along the south side of the Southern Reef and ends at Muddy Creek. The road starts at mile 5.1 on the Temple Mountain road and at mile 27.1 on the Heart of Sinbad road. A sign points to Goblin Valley. The road is for any vehicle and mountain bikes. There is camping throughout the area.

0.0	Mileage starts on the pavement, at a sign pointing to Goblin Valley, and goes southwest.
0.2	Track on the right.
0.3	Track on the right (W). The track provides alternate access to Wild Horse Canyon Hike #50. Drive 0.3 mile west until the track ends. To the west, on the reef, there is a large cave. Wild Horse Canyon is to the left (S) of this. Negotiate a wash and several hills until you reach Wild Horse Canyon.
0.8	Track on the right.
2.8	Road on the left.
5.0	A track to the right (W) goes down a hill to a clump of cottonwoods. This is an alternate start to Chute and Crack Canyons Hike #51. Go 0.4 mile down the hill. Park under the cottonwoods next to a corral. Hike west, cross a wash (Wild Horse Creek), and continue west for ten minutes over small hills. The first large wash you reach leads into Crack Canyon.
5.1	Mollys Castle view area.
6.0	Marked junction. Go left (S) to Goblin Valley **Hike #54.** Go right (W) to get to Hikes #55 and 56.

Restart mileage at this junction. The road is for light-duty vehicles to mile 5.3. Beyond that it is for medium-duty vehicles. This is a good mountain bike road.

0.0	Mileage starts at a sign to Wild Horse Mesa and Muddy Creek and goes west.
0.3	Wild Horse Mesa is on the left (S).
0.5	The break in the reef on the right (N) is the mouth of Crack Canyon.
1.1	Track on the left.
1.5	Cattle guard.
1.7	Track on the left.

2.0	Into a wash. There are cottonwoods on the right. The wash leads north into Crack Canyon.
2.3	Cross a wash. The wash goes north into Chute Canyon.
3.9	Fence.
4.9	Track on the left.
5.2	High Clearance Vehicles Only sign. Pay attention to it.
5.3	The start of Little Wild Horse and Bell Canyons **Hike #55.** The road dips into and out of a wash. There is parking and camping to the north in the lower part of the wash.
5.3 + 100 yards	Parking area on the left.
6.5	The start of Ding and Dang Canyons **Hike #56.** A wash comes in on the right (N) just before the main road turns from west to south. A vague track goes up the wash, and there are several small cottonwoods near its mouth. Park off the main road.
9.0	Out of the wash and up a hill.
9.4	Top of a hill.
9.8	Water trough to the left.
10.2	Rough road section.
12.5	Track to the right. There is good camping at the end of the track.
12.7	Across a wash.
13.1	Into the Bentonite Hills. This is a favorite area for photographers. Though ORVs leave tracks, don't you.
13.4	Track to the right.
14.4	Across a big wash. This is Hunt Draw. It leads north to Cistern Canyon.
14.6	Corral and cabins on the left. They are partially hidden by trees. Worth a look.
15.8	Track to the right. It goes to, but not across, Muddy Creek. There is camping along the track. You can hike up Muddy Creek for forty-five minutes and enter the Southern Reef. This provides alternate access to Lower Muddy Creek Hike #45.
15.8 + 25 yards	The road divides. Go left to cross the creek.
15.9	At the Muddy Creek Crossing. Walk the creek before trying to cross it. Most should turn back. It is a long walk to Hanksville.

To continue across Muddy Creek and past Factory Butte see the Factory Butte Road Section further along in the chapter.

★ Goblin Valley—Hike #54

Season	Any
Time	2 to 3 hours (5 miles)
Elevation gain	150'
Water	None on the hikes. Water is available at the campground. Bring your own water.
Maps	Goblin Valley. (Temple Mountain) [San Rafael Desert]
Circle trip	Yes
Skill level	Easy route finding. Class 1+ walking. The hikes are along well-marked trails.

Goblin Valley State Park is special and unique. It encompasses a small area of wondrous figures carved by wind and water in a layer of Entrada Sandstone. These "goblins," delicate yet firmly a part of the larger whole, are a delight for those of all ages. Imaginative children and adults will enjoy the area.

As this is a state park, there is a $3.00 entrance fee for day use. Campers pay $8.00 per night. There are campsites, a picnic area overlooking Goblin Valley, bathrooms, water, and showers. The park is open year around.

The park has two developed trails. The marked Curtis Bench Trail starts a half mile past the campground along the main road on the right side. It is suitable for everyone and will take about two hours to complete. It is well marked. It goes south up a hill and along a track. At the top of the hill the track turns into a trail. Follow the blue cairns. As the trail goes past Goblin Valley it divides. The trail to the right goes on for a quarter mile to an overlook. The trail to the left goes down into Goblin Valley. From Goblin Valley follow the main road back to the start.

Playing in Goblin Valley.

The Carmel Canyon Trail starts near the end of the main road at Observation Point. It is suitable for everyone and will take about an hour to complete. It can be done in conjunction with the Curtis Bench Trail. From the marked trailhead the path goes northeast along a ridge top. As it drops into Carmel Canyon follow the blue cairns. They will lead you on a circle hike that ends back at the main road, several hundred yards north of the start.

This area is a must for everyone visiting the San Rafael Swell.

★ **Little Wild Horse and Bell Canyons—Hike #55**

Season	Any. No snow.
Time	4 to 6 hours (8 miles)
Elevation gain	500'
Water	Seasonal potholes in both canyons. Bring your own water.
Maps	Little Wild Horse Mesa. (Wild Horse) [San Rafael Desert]
Circle trip	Yes

Skill level Easy route finding. Class 3 scrambling. This is a moderate hike. Though usually dry, there can be water in Little Wild Horse Canyon. Wading shoes are recommended.

Little Wild Horse Canyon is by far and away the most popular canyon in the San Rafael Swell—with good reason. It is a high-walled, tight narrows canyon, spectacular at every twist, turn, and corner. Colors and textures run rampant here—a photographer's delight. The Navajo narrows of Little Wild Horse Canyon last for a mile or more.

The route goes up Little Wild Horse Canyon. After exiting the canyon it traverses west along the backside of the Southern Reef on the Behind the Reef road to Bell Canyon, which it descends back to the start.

Go up the wash to the north. In fifteen minutes the wash divides. Bell Canyon is to the left (LUC)(SW). Go up Little Wild Horse Canyon to the right (NNW). For the next hour twist and squeeze through the remarkable narrows. They politely open occasionally to give you a rest and a place to reload your camera. There are small obstacles to overcome, but nothing serious. For the less fit, or those with children, go as far as you are comfortable. Hiking through the first narrow section is a treat everyone will enjoy.

As you exit the head of the canyon you will see mining debris and sections of a mining track. Follow the track north to the Behind the Reef road. Go left (W) on the road for thirty minutes. The head of Bell Canyon starts at the next break in the escarpment. To the west, on a knoll, is a picturesque miner's cabin. Go south down Bell Canyon. It has small obstacles to circumvent. Bell Canyon goes back to the mouth of Little Wild Horse Canyon.

From child to senior, fat to fit, everyone will enjoy these canyons.

Ding (AN) and Dang (AN) Canyons—Hike #56

Season	Any. No snow.
Time	3 to 4 hours (7 miles)
Elevation gain	450'
Water	Ding Canyon has seasonal potholes. Bring your own water.
Maps	Little Wild Horse Mesa. Ding Dang Dome and Ding and Dang canyons are shown but are not labeled on the map. Ding Dang Dome is elevation 6107, west of Bell Canyon. Ding Canyon is to the southeast of Ding Dang Dome. Dang Canyon is to the south of it. (Wild Horse) [San Rafael Desert]
Circle trip	Yes
Skill level	Easy/moderate route finding. Class 5.0 climbing. There are no exposure problems, but a short rope will be needed to get dogs, packs, and beginners over obstacles in Dang Canyon. Wading shoes are recommended.

Svelte, serpentine, and scintillating—Ding and Dang canyons are shorter versions of Little Wild Horse and Bell canyons. They cut through Navajo Sandstone as they breach the Southern Reef. A challenge to negotiate, their floors are rarely trodden.

The route goes up Ding Canyon. At its head, on the backside of the reef, a mining track is followed to the top of Dang Canyon, which is descended back to the start.

From the parking area go up the shallow wash for twenty minutes. The wash divides at a fifty-foot-high, brown-and-green-layered cliff that is wonderfully folded. Go to the right (N) up Ding Canyon. At the top of the canyon go left (W) between a Wingate wall and the pointed, peaklike Ding Dang Dome. A mining track runs between them. Dang Canyon starts on the west side of the dome. Go down it (S), negotiating a series of chockstones on the way. Follow the main wash as you exit. It turns east and snakes back to the mouth of Ding Canyon.

Factory Butte Road Section

**Access is from Highway 24 and the Goblin Valley/
 Southern Reef road.
Metric map—Hanksville**

This road goes north from Highway 24 to Muddy
Creek. Although it is not used as primary access to any of
the described hikes, it can be used as alternate access to
Lower Muddy Creek, the Southern Reef, and the
Moroni Slopes. From Hanksville go west on Highway 24
for 10.5 miles. The Factory Butte road is unmarked,
though there is a stop sign. It is good for medium-duty
vehicles. The first several miles of the road are gravel, but
the road deteriorates past Factory Butte. The road is suitable for mountain bikes. As the road is infrequently trav-
eled and has a gravel base, you can use it for camping in
inclement weather, knowing your car will not sink in the
mud.

0.0	Mileage starts at the stop sign just north of Highway 24 and goes north.
3.7	Stock reservoir on the left.
9.5	''Y.'' The main road goes right. Go left.
10.0	High Clearance Vehicle Only sign.
10.5	''Tee. Top of a hill. The Southern Reef is before you. Go right to the Muddy Creek Crossing. Do not go down the hill if it is wet or snow covered. The road turns into a slick clay with which even 4WDs will have problems. If in doubt walk it first.
	The track to the left goes to Salt Wash, North Caineville Reef, and the base of the Moroni Slopes. It is for 4WDs only. It becomes impassable to most vehicles in 0.5 mile.
13.7	At the Muddy Creek Crossing. This is the same crossing as at mile 15.9 in the Goblin Valley/Southern Reef Road Section.

8 | The Eastern Reef

The Eastern Reef is what most people associate with the San Rafael Swell. Paralleling Highway 24, between Interstate 70 west of Green River and Hanksville, this unique 1000-to-1500-foot-high escarpment has lured many into its abundant folds.

Long lines of boaters going to Lake Powell have gazed at its jagged white face. Uranium miners have probed every hidden cranny. Cowboys fenced in box canyons for their cattle. A pre-automobile generation used its pot-holes, tanks, and springs to water their stock and themselves. The Hole-in-the-Wall gang found secret canyons to hide and rest in. The Fremont Indians left petroglyph panels in Three Finger Canyon. Desert Culture Indians left Barrier Canyon Style pictographs in Old Woman Wash and South Temple Wash.

The dozen or so canyons that go through the Eastern Reef provide good day hiking. Though there is only one multiday hike described, Eardley Canyon, Straight Wash, and Greasewood Draw Hike #57, the guide can be used to design your own.

While this chapter of the guide concentrates on the canyons that go through the Eastern Reef and can be tied into other through canyons, creating circle trips, there is much to explore between the major canyons. In the northern section of the Eastern Reef, just south of Interstate 70 where the face of the reef is steep, there are many short canyons, some leading into the bowels of the reef, others leading to its crest. In the southern part of the Eastern Reef, north of Temple Mountain near Old Woman Wash, the face of the reef is not as steeply tilted. It provides endless possibilities for marvelous slickrock walking, dome climbing, and canyon exploring.

This guide does not describe every canyon that goes through the reef, though it does describe the major ones. Backpackers may wonder if they can do an extended hike

The Eastern Reef

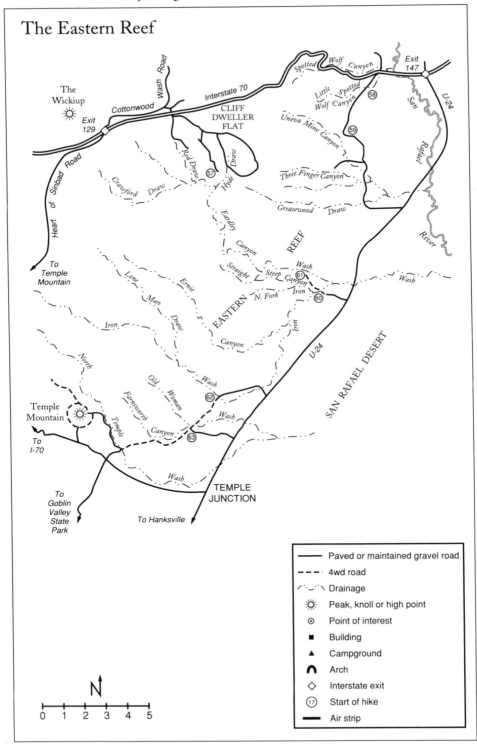

The Wickiup

Exit 129

Exit 147

Exit 58

Exit 59

Cottonwood Wash Road

Interstate 70

CLIFF DWELLER FLAT

Spotted Wolf Canyon

Little Spotted Wolf Canyon

Uneva Mine Canyon

San Rafael River

U-24

Heart of Sinbad Road

Red Draw

Hyde Draw

57

Three Finger Canyon

Crawford Draw

Earnley Canyon

Greasewood Draw

To Temple Mountain

Lone Man Draw

Ernie Draw

Straight

Steep

EASTERN

REEF

Wash

61

Wash

Iron

N. Fork

60

Iron

Iron

Canyon

U-24

SAN RAFAEL DESERT

North Wash

Old Woman

Farnsworth

62

Wash

Temple Mountain

Temple

Canyon

63

To I-70

Wash

TEMPLE JUNCTION

To Goblin Valley State Park

To Hanksville

	Paved or maintained gravel road
	4wd road
	Drainage
☼	Peak, knoll or high point
⊙	Point of interest
■	Building
▲	Campground
∩	Arch
◇	Interstate exit
17	Start of hike
	Air strip

N

0 1 2 3 4 5

behind the reef. Yes, you can hike behind the reef from Little Spotted Wolf Canyon to Straight Wash. Water will be a seasonal concern.

The Eastern Reef is a part of the San Rafael Reef Wilderness Study Area.

Cliff Dweller Flat Road Section

Access to Hike #57
Access is from Interstate 70.
Metric map—San Rafael Desert

This short road goes south from Interstate 70 to Cliff Dweller Flat. From Green River go twenty-nine miles west on Interstate 70 to Ranch Exit 129. Go north. The road turns east immediately. In 3.7 miles there is a four-way intersection. A sign to the right (S) points to Hyde Draw. Take this road under Interstate 70 to a cattle guard. This is a medium-duty vehicle road and is a fair road for mountain bikes. There is camping in the area.

0.0	Mileage starts at the cattle guard just south of the underpass and goes east.
1.7	"Y." Go right (S). The main road goes left (E).
2.6	Drill pipe on the left.
2.7	Start of a landing strip. It is hard to see. The road is straight. You are on Cliff Dweller Flat.
3.1	Wood troughs to the left.
4.2	The start of Eardley Canyon, Straight Wash, and Greasewood Draw **Hike #57**. End of the road. On a plateau overlooking a large meadow (Arsons Garden). (This is a quarter mile southeast of elevation 6689 on the Arsons Garden map.) There are great views and good camping.

★ | # Eardley Canyon, Straight Wash, and Greasewood Draw—Hike #57

Season	Any. Summer could be intolerable for those doing Part 2. There is a flash flood potential in Eardley Canyon.
Time	Part 1—2 days (14 miles) Part 2—2 to 3 days (22 miles)
Elevation gain	Part 1—1600' Part 2—2000'
Water	Eardley Canyon, below the rincon, has several springs. As you get closer to the narrows the more likely you are to find water. The only perennial water is in the large pool at the bottom of Eardley Canyon. Part 2 hikers will get to the pool. Part 1 does not go that far. If in doubt, carry your own water. Greasewood Tank at the mouth of Greasewood Draw is a seasonal pothole.
Maps	Arsons Garden. Greasewood Draw. Drowned Hole Draw. (Tidwell Bottoms. The Wickiup.) [San Rafael Desert]
Circle trip	Part 1—No Part 2—Yes
Skill level	Part 1—Easy route finding. Class 3+ scrambling. Extensive boulder hopping. Possible pothole wading. A short rope for lowering packs may be helpful. Wading shoes are recommended. Knowledge of low-impact camping techniques is essential. The route is not for beginners. Part 2—As above, plus moderate route finding. Class 5.0 climbing with loose rock and frightening exposure. A short rope will prove useful. There is a 2000-foot vertical rise on the last day. It is rough with a pack. The route is for advanced canyoneers and rock-climbers only.

Eardley Canyon is the crème de la crème of the Eastern Reef. It is a deep, narrow, Coconino-walled canyon with long sections lined with cottonwoods. At the bottom end of the canyon there are many large pools. The price of admission is high. Though there are areas of easy walking, most of the canyon is boulder lined or choked. If you aren't boulder hopping, you will be trying to find your way around huge boulders or down small drops. This can be tiring with a pack on. Beginners will have a rough time of it.

The route comes in two parts. Part 1 goes down Eardley Canyon to a narrow slickrock and pothole area near the mouth of the canyon. This part of the canyon is exceptional. Large potholes and falls keep you from going all the way through the canyon. Return the way you came. Part 2 exits the canyon immediately above the narrows. It joins Straight Wash, which goes through the reef. A short stretch north along the face of the reef leads to Greasewood Draw. This is followed back through the reef and up its face to Cliff Dweller Flat.

Part 1: Before starting, walk to the southwest rim of the parking circle. To the northeast is the meadow area of Arsons Garden. Hyde Draw Reservoir, usually empty, is in the middle of the meadow. To the east is the top of Greasewood Draw as it joins the Arsons Garden meadow. This is the canyon Part 2 hikers come up. To the southeast, running through the meadow, is Hyde Draw. It empties into Eardley Canyon but cannot be used as access due to a large fall. To the south is Eardley Canyon. Visually follow Eardley Canyon up (E) from where Hyde Draw joins it. The next small side canyon will be used to enter Eardley Canyon. It is to the southwest. (This is shown to the northwest of elevation 6341 on the Arsons Garden map.)

From the parking circle make your way to the right (W) side of the small side canyon. Follow the rim of the canyon until it joins Eardley Canyon. There is a talus slope leading into the side canyon. Descend this, with some snaking, until the bottom is reached. There are many variations.

Go south down the canyon. The first several miles would make an fine day hike. After a couple of hours, past a long slickrock section, pass a fall on a steep slope to the right (LDC). A half hour past the fall you will reach a rincon. This is an abandoned meander that has left a freestanding monolith. (The rincon is shown to the east-northeast of elevation 6116 on the Arsons Garden map.) One hour past the rincon the route is blocked by a huge pool formed by an earthen dam. If it is too deep to wade backtrack for a quarter mile. Ascend a steep slope to the right (LDC). Traverse back down the canyon and reenter it immediately below the pool. You will reach the narrows after another hour or so. Go through them as far as you can, without packs. There is poor camping in the area, though there are plenty of adequate nooks and crannies. Plan on a solid eight hours of hiking to this point. Advanced canyoneers will move much more quickly. Plan on six to seven hours.

There are other options. For camping stay near the rincon or below the earthen dam and do a day hike further down the canyon. For the less experienced wanting to do Part 2, exit the canyon to the south of the rincon, up a steep hill (Class 3+). Make sure you can see the whole route, top to bottom, so you aren't surprised by an impassable cliff at the top. The nicest part of the canyon is below the rincon.

Part 2: To reiterate, this is for advanced canyoneers and rock-climbers only. There is loose rock and terrifying exposure. Climbing skills to 5.0 are necessary.

From the start of the narrow section, near the bottom of the canyon, backtrack for five minutes, or a quarter mile. Ascend a steep, boulder-covered ramp (not a gully) on the left (LUC). It parallels the canyon before narrowing and going straight up the wall. There are cairns at the start. You will be snaking up ledges and ascending short, steep walls. From the top follow the rim down (SE) until you intersect Straight Wash. There is camping in the wash. The perennial pool is 250 yards up Eardley Canyon. (See Hike #61 for details.) There is no camping at the pool. Plan on eight to nine hours to this point.

Hike down Straight Wash (NE). In an hour you will exit the canyon and are at the face of the reef. Go left (N) as soon as the cliffs of Straight Wash allow. Walk in front of the reef until the third through canyon is reached. This is Greasewood Draw. To keep you oriented, the first through canyon north of Straight Wash is reached in a half hour. There is a track going into it. The second through canyon is reached in another twenty-five minutes after going down a short slope. There is a row of four-by-four-inch posts going east. The third through canyon is Greasewood Draw. It is reached in yet another half hour, after negotiating a short, yellow cliff band. Greasewood Tank is near the mouth of the canyon.

Now for the 2000-foot hump. Go west through the reef. Partway through, the wash divides. Go left (SW). From the back of the reef go north up a long, boulder-filled wash to a saddle. From the saddle go up a steep slope to the west. Many variations are possible. As things level off on top, continue west. You will rejoin Greasewood Draw, but do not drop back into it. Follow its north rim, using donkey and cow trails, for a couple of hours. When Greasewood Draw ends you will be in the Arsons Garden meadow below the parking circle. Zip past the top of Hyde Draw and ascend the last wearying slope.

Northern Reef Road Section

Access to Hikes #58 and 59
Access is from Highway 24.
Metric map—San Rafael Desert

This road goes northwest from Highway 24 and intersects Interstate 70 to the west of milepost 154. From Exit 147 on Interstate 70 go south on Highway 24. Start your mileage at the first cattle guard and go 6.9 miles until 0.3 mile south of milepost 154. The road, to the west, is unmarked. It is for medium-duty vehicles and mountain bikes. Camping is available throughout the area.

0.0	Mileage starts at Highway 24 and goes west.
1.3	Corral on the right.
1.7	Four-way junction. Follow the main road to the right (N).
3.6	Across a mud plain. When this is wet it is a quagmire. Careful.

4.1	Track to the left.
4.2	Unmarked four-way junction. Follow the main road straight (N).

Side road

To get to Three Finger Canyon and the start of Hike #59 go left (W). This is a medium-duty track. It is fine for mountain bikes.

0.0	Mileage starts at the four-way junction and goes west.
1.0	At a short, rough, uphill section.
1.4	There is a wash on the left with several goblins along its walls.
1.6	The start of Uneva Mine and Three Finger Canyons **Hike #59.** You are looking down a steep hill at a red, Entrada Sandstone slickrock area. Park here. The track below gets rougher. If you are just going to Three Finger Canyon, hike along the track to the west. The mouth of the canyon and the petroglyph panels take ten minutes to reach.

End of side road

5.1	Track coming in on the right. Stay left.
6.1	Around the right side of a small butte.
6.5	Track on the left (W) going to Uneva Mine Canyon.
6.6	Track on the left also going to Uneva Mine Canyon.
6.9	Track to the right (E) going to Shadscale Mesa. Stay left.
7.0	Track to the left.
7.9	The start of Little Spotted Wolf and Uneva Mine Canyons **Hike #58.** There is a vague track going up a wash to the left (W). There is a cottonwood 200 yards up the wash. Park next to the main road.
8.4	There is an arch to the left (W) near the skyline, below a prominent red knob. Hike up the steep gully that goes to the arch. There is another arch/bridge in the gully.
9.8	Cross a wash, negotiate an S-turn, go through a wire gate, and intersect I–70.

You can continue north in the wash, go under I–70, and join the Black Dragon Wash road. Campers won't fit through the tunnel. This is for 4WDs only.

Little Spotted Wolf and Uneva Mine Canyons (AN)—Hike #58

Season	Any. Spring and fall are best. Winter with little snow is okay.
Time	5 to 7 hours (7 miles)
Elevation gain	1000′
Water	Seasonal potholes. Bring your own water.
Map	Spotted Wolf Canyon. Neither canyon is labeled on the map. Little Spotted Wolf Canyon is the first through canyon to the north of the Moonshine Tanks. Uneva Mine Canyon is the first through canyon to the south of the Moonshine Tanks. (Tidwell Bottoms) [San Rafael Desert]
Circle trip	Yes
Skill level	Moderate route finding. Class 3 scrambling. There is one long uphill section.

It is always a pleasure to hike through the reef. Little Spotted Wolf Canyon makes it superlative. For the geologist this canyon clearly shows the layers of sandstone that were thrust up to form the reef over 50 million years ago.

The route starts by going through Little Spotted Wolf Canyon. Once through the reef the route continues behind it to Uneva Mine Canyon, taking you back through the reef. The route ends by walking north along the face of the reef.

Hike west up the small wash. A track appears. Follow the track as it goes up a steep hill to the right. From the top of the hill Little Spotted Wolf Canyon is to the west. Hike through this great canyon.

> **Digression:** It is worthwhile going just this far if you do not want to do the whole hike. Plan on a one-hour round trip. This is a short Class 1 hike that is suitable for everyone.

Once through the canyon some route-finding skills become necessary. The object is to go south up the 1000-foot-high hill that lies against the back of the reef. There are many options, all involving some snaking and steep scrambling. The goal is to end up at the top of the hill between the brown and yellow sandstone layers several hundred feet below the vertical Wingate walls at the top of the reef. Go in and out of many small canyons and washes as you work your way up to the saddle.

From the saddle you can see the Uneva Mine ruins far below (S). Go down the steep hill, staying above the yellow band for at least a quarter mile before dropping into a wash, thereby avoiding several cliff bands. From the mine site go east through the canyon. The mine itself is to the left (LDC). Once through the reef go north, paralleling its face. It is easiest to stay within several hundred yards of it. There are many small side canyons that are worth exploring, though they don't go through the reef.

★ Uneva Mine (AN) and Three Finger Canyons—Hike #59

Season	Any
Time	5 to 6 hours. Leave extra time for photographing the petroglyphs (6 miles).
Elevation gain	550'
Water	Seasonal in Three Finger Canyon. Bring your own water.
Maps	Spotted Wolf Canyon. Greasewood Draw. Both canyons are shown but are not labeled on the maps. Uneva Mine Canyon is the first through canyon to the south of the Moonshine Tanks on the Spotted Wolf Canyon map. Three Finger Canyon is the second canyon north of Greasewood Draw on the Greasewood Draw map. Both canyons have 4WD tracks going to their mouths. (Tidwell Bottoms) [San Rafael Desert]
Circle trip	Yes
Skill level	Easy route finding. Class 3 scrambling.

This hike is not exceptional for the terrain covered, but the perks along the way more than make up for this. There are a set of moonshine tanks, an old miner's encampment, a spectacular view slot, and several excellent panels of Fremont Culture petroglyphs.

The route goes up Uneva Mine Canyon, circles behind the reef, exits through Three Finger Canyon, and ends by traversing along the base of the reef.

To the west of the parking area, down a hill, is a red, Entrada Sandstone bowl. Do not go into the bowl, but rather, diagonal northwest toward the face of the reef, cutting across washes as you see fit. Once at the face go north. Try to traverse within 200 yards of the reef itself. It is up and down no matter what, but cattle trails tend to tie things together.

After thirty to forty minutes there is a short side canyon to the west that has a large red wall at its end. Hike up the canyon. Before a set of plunge pools there are a bunch of old barrel collars. They were used to hold barrel staves together. These lead me to believe that, with the tanks above, this was an area of moonshine tanks.

> **Historical note:** During prohibition bootleggers used the seasonal tanks along the face of the reef for making moonshine. The water was pure and they could see for great distances across the San Rafael Desert, watching for the law.

In twenty minutes you will reach Uneva Mine Canyon. It has a track starting into it. Go up the track into the canyon (W). Within ten minutes the start of the mining area is reached. At the top of the canyon you will reach the main mining area with three cabins perched on a knoll.

From the cabins follow the mining track south up a steep hill. When the track ends, after passing several mine sites, continue south up the canyon on steep, broken ground.

At a saddle go south, downhill. At the bottom of the hill a canyon comes in from the left (E) and appears to go through the reef. Follow the canyon down until stopped at a view slot. Just marvelous. Looking down from the view slot you will recognize the moonshine pools you visited earlier. Backtrack, then continue south behind the reef. Go uphill for 250 feet and once again descend. Three Finger Canyon enters from the east. Go down it. Toward its mouth, as it exits the reef, keep your eyes left (LDC)(N). There are several exceptional Southern San

Rafael Style petroglyph panels. A faint track going east quickly turns into a road. The road will take you back to the start.

North Fork of Iron Wash and Straight Wash Road Section

Access to Hikes #60 and 61
Access is from Highway 24.
Metric map—San Rafael Desert

This short track goes west from Highway 24 to the North Fork of Iron Wash and then to the mouth of Straight Wash. From Exit 147 on Interstate 70 go south on Highway 24. Start your mileage at the first cattle guard and go 12.6 miles until right at milepost 148. The road, to the west, is unmarked. It is for medium-duty vehicles to mile 1.6 at the Iron Wash crossing. After that it is a medium-duty and 4WD track to the mouth of Straight Wash. This is a good mountain bike road. There is camping in the area.

0.0	Mileage starts at Highway 24 and goes west.
1.1	Corral on the right.
1.4	Rough road section. It may stop some cars.
1.6	Through a tamarisk tunnel.
1.6 + 100 yards	The start of North Fork of Iron Wash, Steep Canyon, and Straight Wash **Hike #60.** You are at Iron Wash. Park here.
1.7	Bad uphill section. The track has rough sections from now on.
3.5	The start of Straight Wash, Eardley Canyon, and an Amazing Pool **Hike #61.** You are at the end of the track at a parking circle. There are cottonwoods to lock bikes to at the mouth of Straight Wash. Camping is available throughout the area.

North Fork of Iron Wash, Steep Canyon (AN), and Straight Wash—Hike #60

Season	Early spring, spring, or fall
Time	Part 1—4 to 5 hours (7 miles)
	Part 2—7 to 8 hours (12 miles)
Elevation gain	Part 1—300'
	Part 2—1400'
Water	Seasonal springs and potholes in all three canyons. Bring your own water.
Maps	Greasewood Draw. Arsons Garden. Old Woman Wash. The North Fork of Iron Wash is shown but is not labeled on the Arsons Garden map. It is the canyon east of elevation 4948. Steep Canyon is north of elevations 5510 and 6403 (Ernie). (Tidwell Bottoms. The Wickiup) [San Rafael Desert]
Circle trip	Part 1—No
	Part 2—Yes
Skill level	Part 1—Easy route finding. Class 1+ walking. This hike is suitable for everyone.
	Part 2—Moderate route finding. Class 3 scrambling. This is a long day hike.

The North Fork of Iron Wash is a wide, pleasant, Navajo-walled canyon that cuts deep into the reef. Steep Canyon, candy-striped, pinnacled, and pretty, is exactly that. It goes to the top of the reef. Straight Wash is shale-walled and ethereal in ambience.

The hike comes in two parts. Part 1 goes up the North Fork of Iron Wash and, after a short narrow section, ends at a fall. Part 2, after taking in the narrows of the North Fork of Iron Wash, goes partway up Steep Canyon. The route then goes through a pass and descends into Straight Wash a mile above the mouth of Eardley Canyon and its amazing pool. Straight Wash takes you back to the start.

Part 1: From the parking area at the Iron Wash crossing go south along the wash. There are intermittent springs in the area. Within fifteen minutes a side canyon comes in on the right. Go west up the side canyon. Two hundred yards after entering the canyon exit it to the right (LUC)(N), up an easy slope. Follow the rim of the canyon until a fall is passed.

Continue along the main wash. In a half hour, just after passing an old fence, the canyon divides. Go left (S). The canyon ends in fifteen minutes in a narrow section. There are several short box canyons that are fun to explore. Return the way you came.

Part 2: At the canyon division, past the old fence, go right (W). This is Steep Canyon. The first stretch is boulder choked. It gets better the further up you go. Bypass a fall on the right (LUC). Backtrack several hundred yards first. The canyon opens some above the fall before closing into a red-walled stretch. As you go up this portion of the canyon keep an eye on the vertical Wingate cliffs to the right. When even with the cliff's end, exit the canyon to the right (LUC)(N) by scrambling up a slope to a saddle at the end of the cliff. (This is just west of elevation 6162 on the Arsons Garden map.)

The canyon below (N) is Straight Wash. Go down a steep slope, angling right to avoid cliff bands; then descend a boulder-filled gully to Straight Wash. Go northeast down Straight Wash.

> **Digression:** After fifteen minutes you will pass the mouth of a narrow canyon that is to the left (LDC)(NW). This is Eardley Canyon (Hike #61). Hike up it for 250 yards to an amazing pool.

As you exit the canyon there is a track to the right (S). Follow the track west, then south back to Iron Wash.

★ ## Straight Wash, Eardley Canyon, and an Amazing Pool—Hike #61

Season	Any
Time	3 to 4 hours (5 miles)
Elevation gain	300'

Water	There is a perennial pool near the mouth of Eardley Canyon. Bring your own water.
Maps	Arsons Garden. Greasewood Draw. (Tidwell Bottoms. The Wickiup.) [San Rafael Desert]
Circle trip	No
Skill level	Easy route finding. Class 1+ walking. This is a short day hike suitable for all.

This is one of the most popular hikes in the Swell. Short, scenic, and exciting, it is worthy of attention. Straight Wash has a short stretch of narrows. Eardley Canyon contains the finest pool in the San Rafael Swell.

The route uses Straight Wash to penetrate the reef. It leads to the mouth of Eardley Canyon, which is ascended to a remarkable pool. Return the way you came.

From the parking area go west up the canyon. Thirty minutes into the hike note a side canyon coming in on the right (LUC)(NE). The side canyon is an important landmark for those wanting to do the digression. The narrowest section of the hike is two minutes past this. It starts with a short, white, slickrock area. Ten minutes after exiting the narrows look for a thin canyon entering on the right (LUC)(NW). It has some large boulders at its mouth. This is Eardley Canyon. Go up it for 250 yards until stopped by the amazing pool. Twenty-five yards in diameter and up to six feet deep, this is certainly the largest perennial pool in the Swell.

> **Author's note:** Bypassing the fall above the pool and re-entering the canyon upstream is not recommended except for advanced canyoneers. (See Hike #57 for details.)

Return the way you came.

> **Digression:** For those wanting to do a longer day hike, backtrack through the narrow area in Straight Wash. Go northeast up the wash mentioned earlier. It goes behind the reef. Partway up, the wash turns west. Continue north, paralleling the back of the reef. There is a little scrambling here (Class 3). After reaching the top of the wash descend into a yellow-floored canyon and follow it east to the face of the reef. Follow the reef south back to the parking area.

Ernie Canyon Road Section

Access to Hike #62
Access is from Highway 24.
Metric map—San Rafael Desert

This short track goes west from Highway 24 to Iron Wash. From Exit 147 on Interstate 70 go south on Highway 24. Start your mileage at the first cattle guard and go 18.1 miles until one-half mile south of milepost 143. A metal gate is located to the west of the highway. This is a medium-duty track and is suitable for mountain bikes. There is camping in the area.

0.0	Mileage starts at the metal gate just west of Highway 24 and goes west.
0.3	Track to the right. Stay left.
0.6	Across Iron Wash.
0.7	Lost Spring is to the right.
0.9	Track divides. Stay left (W).
	Go right (N) to get to the mouth of Ernie Canyon. For those seeking a short hike there is a good one going up Ernie Canyon. Follow the main track for two miles until a sandy wash is reached. This is Ernie Canyon. Hike up the canyon. It will take two hours to hike through the reef and back.
2.4	Track to the right. Stay left.
2.6	The start of Iron Wash, Lone Man Draw, and Ernie Canyon **Hike #62.** The track crosses Iron Wash. Drive up the wash (W) for 100 yards and park.

Iron Wash, Lone Man Draw, and Ernie Canyon—Hike #62

Season	Any but summer
Time	7 to 9 hours (12 miles)
Elevation gain	750'

Water	Seasonal springs in both canyons. Bring your own water.
Maps	Old Woman Wash. (Temple Mountain. The Wickiup.) [San Rafael Desert]
Circle trip	Yes
Skill level	Moderate route finding. Class 2 walking. This is a moderate day hike.

Both Iron Wash and Ernie Canyon go through the Eastern Reef. Both are Wingate- and Navajo-walled, deep, and impressive. Lone Man Draw is a singular Moenkopi- and Chinle-walled canyon that runs between Iron Wash and Ernie Canyon on the backside of the reef.

The route goes through the reef in Iron Wash, crosses the back of the reef in Lone Man Draw, and returns via Ernie Canyon.

Hike west up the sand-floored wash. There is a track to follow. After seventy-five minutes the canyon, after passing through the reef, divides at a green mud prow. The left fork is Iron Wash. Go right (N) into Lone Man Draw. The goal is to follow the back of the reef until you meet Ernie Canyon. In an hour pass the end of the vertical Wingate cliff band that is to the right (E). The wash divides. Go right. After this the wash divides often. Slight discrepancies will not matter. At some point you need to end up below the Wingate cliffs and at the base of a series of ribs running up to it. Ernie Canyon is on the other side of the cliffs to the east. Go north, staying under the ribs. They die as the hill you are following goes from north to east. You will be at the top of a ridge. Ernie Canyon is to the east below a huge, red, Wingate wall. Follow benches and shallow gullies east until you can drop into the canyon.

Go down Ernie Canyon. At one point there is a mine track on a hillside to the left. Past the track is a collapsed cabin on the right. Look for an arch high on the wall to the north of the cabin. After exiting the canyon traverse south along the base of the reef back to Iron Wash.

Old Woman Wash Road Section

Access to Hike #63
Access is from Highway 24.
Metric map—San Rafael Desert

This short track goes west from Highway 24 to Old Woman Wash. From Exit 147 on Interstate 70 go south on Highway 24. Start your mileage at the first cattle guard and go 20.6 miles until 0.2 mile south of milepost 140. A metal gate stands to the west of the highway. This is a medium-duty track and is suitable for mountain bikes. There is camping in the area.

0.0	Mileage starts at the metal gate just west of Highway 24 and goes west.
1.5	Track divides. Stay to the left (W).
1.6	The track is washed out. Most vehicles will have to stop here.
1.8	Track divides. Stay to the left.
2.0	Four-way intersection just before a wash. Turn right (N).
2.3	"Tee." The start of Old Woman Wash and Farnsworth Canyon **Hike #63.** A short track goes west to a chimney, the remnants of the Virginia Harris way station. Park here.

Old Woman Wash and Farnsworth Canyon—Hike #63

Season	Any
Time	Part 1—5 to 7 hours (9 miles)
	Part 2—6 to 8 hours (11 miles)
Elevation gain	Part 1—1000'
	Part 2—1200'

Water	Seasonal potholes. Bring your own water.
Maps	Old Woman Wash. Temple Mountain. (Temple Mountain) [San Rafael Desert]
Circle trip	Yes
Skill level	Part 1—Moderate route finding. Class 3 scrambling. This is a moderate hike.
	Part 2—Difficult route finding. Class 4+ climbing. A rope will reassure beginners at the hard spots.

As the Eastern Reef starts to taper down at its southern end, near Temple Mountain, its visual aspect is reduced. This is deceptive. The canyons going through this section of the reef—Old Woman Wash, Farnsworth Canyon, and North Temple Wash—are all long, deep, and impressive.

The hike comes in two parts. Both parts have a common start, going up Old Woman Wash to a panel of pictographs and petroglyphs. Part 1 then goes up the face of the reef, descends its backside, and returns to the front of the reef via Farnsworth Canyon. Part 2 continues up Old Woman Wash, exits the canyon to the north, goes behind the reef, and descends its face back to the start.

Parts 1 and 2—common start: From the way station, enter Old Woman Wash to the west.

> **Historical note:** Old Woman Wash was named for Virginia Harris, an old woman who ran a way station at the mouth of the wash during the uranium boom.

In twenty minutes the canyon divides. Go right. A Barrier Canyon Style pictograph panel is 100 yards to the right on a large wall. It is ten feet off the ground and very faded. Look close. The petroglyph panel is twenty-five yards to the left of the pictographs.

Part 1: From the pictographs look left (LUC)(WNW) across the canyon. A mining track goes diagonally up a hill and onto the face of the reef. Go up the track until it dies in a half mile. Work your way west. There are many options. Either follow shallow canyons or stay up on the slickrock. Once on top find a wide notch that is halfway between Old Woman Wash and Farnsworth Canyon. The notch perfectly frames Temple Mountain.

Descend a boulder-filled gully that starts at the notch

until you reach a mining track. Follow the track south until it drops into the head of Farnsworth Canyon. Go southeast down the canyon. At its mouth take a track north back to the start.

Part 2: From the pictograph panel continue northwest up the canyon for a half hour, bypassing several small falls. After entering a red-and-white-striped section of canyon, a large boulder blocks the way. Climb around it. Two smaller boulders block the way in another thirty yards. Do not go around them. Exit the canyon to the right (LUC)(NE) up a holey slab (Class 4, 15′). Go up to the next cliff band. Traverse under it (N). As the slope pinches off, climb east through a weakness in the cliff, a groove in a corner (Class 4+, 20′).

Continue north through several short cliff bands until you are on the face of the reef; then go northwest, roughly paralleling the canyon, until you reach the junction of the head of the canyon and the backside of the reef. Go north along the rim of the reef for several hundred yards until atop a prominent point. Looking north a quarter of a mile, you will see a round, flat, yellow slickrock area. A red and brown ridge runs into its west end. Make your way to the flat area, then go west toward the red and brown ridge. A line of cairns will lead you down a steep white rib (Class 4+, 30′). The rib is the only way to descend this section of the cliff.

Once on the ridge, follow pieces of an old mining track generally south across the head of Old Woman Wash and behind the reef. The track goes uphill for a while. At its top are terrific views of Temple Mountain to the southwest. Ten minutes after the track starts downhill there is a steep, boulder-filled gully going east through the Navajo cliff. Ascend the gully (Class 3). From the top you are on your own. Wander down. There are many possibilities.

Bibliography

Abbey, Edward and Philip Hyde. *Slickrock—The Canyon Country of Southeast Utah*. San Francisco: Sierra Club Books, 1971.

Aitchison, Stewart. *Utah Wildlands*. Salt Lake City: Utah Geographic Series, Inc., 1987.

Baars, Donald L. *Canyonlands Country*. Lawrence, Kans.: Cañon Publishers Ltd., 1989.

_____. *Red Rock Country: The Geologic History of the Colorado Plateau*. Garden City, N.Y.: Doubleday, 1972.

_____. *The Colorado Plateau: A Geologic History*. Albuquerque: University of New Mexico Press, 1983.

Baker, Pearl. *The Wild Bunch at Robbers Roost*. New York, N.Y.: Abelard-Schuman, 1965.

Barnes, F. A., *Canyon Country*. Salt Lake City: Wasatch Publishers, Inc., 1986.

_____. *Canyon Country Prehistoric Rock Art*. Salt Lake City: Wasatch Publishers Inc., 1978.

Barnes, F. A. and Michaelene Pendleton. *Canyon Country Prehistoric Indians*. Salt Lake City: Wasatch Publishers, Inc., 1979.

Bauman, Joseph. *Stone House Lands*. Salt Lake City: University of Utah Press, 1987.

Bjornstad, Eric. *Desert Rock*. Denver: Chockstone Press, 1988.

Brower, David, ed. *The Meaning of Wilderness to Science*. San Francisco: Sierra Club, 1960.

Castleton, Kenneth Bitner. *Petroglyphs and Pictographs of Utah. Volume One*. Salt Lake City: Utah Museum of Natural History, 1978.

Chronic, Halka. *Pages of Stone—Geology of the Western National Parks*. Seattle: The Mountaineers, 1986.

Crampton, Gregory C. *Standing Up Country—The Canyon Lands of Utah and Arizona*. New York: Alfred A. Knopf, 1964.

Doolittle, Jerome. *Canyons and Mesas*. New York, N.Y.: Time-Life Books, 1974.

Elmore, Francis H. *Shrubs and Trees of the Southwest Up-*

lands. Tucson, Ariz.: Southwest Parks and Monuments Association, 1976.

Forgey, William. *Wilderness Medicine.* Merrillville, Ind.: ICS Books, 1987.

Jennings, Jesse David. *Prehistory of Utah and the Eastern Great Basin.* Salt Lake City: University of Utah Press, 1978.

Kelsey, Michael R. *Hiking Utah's San Rafael Swell.* Springville, Utah: Kelsey Publishing Co., 1986.

Kirk, Ruth. *Desert—The American Southwest.* Boston: Houghton Mifflin Co., 1973.

Lister, Florence C. and Robert H. Lister. *Earl Morris and Southwestern Archaeology.* Albuquerque: University of New Mexico Press, 1968.

McClenahan, Owen. *Utah's Scenic San Rafael.* Castle Dale, Utah: Self-published, 1986.

McKern, Sharon S. *Living Prehistory: An Introduction to Physical Anthropology and Archaeology.* Menlo Park, Calif.: Cummings Publishing Company, 1974.

MacMahon, James A. *Deserts.* New York: Alfred A. Knopf, 1985.

May, Dean L. *Utah—A People's History.* Salt Lake City: University of Utah Press, 1987.

Rigby, J. Keith. *Northern Colorado Plateau.* Dubuque, Iowa: Kendall/Hunt Publishing Co., 1976.

Schaafsma, Polly. *Indian Rock Art of the Southwest.* Santa Fe, N.M.: School of American Research, 1980.

Skinner, Brian J. *Physical Geology.* New York: Wiley, 1987.

Stokes, William Lee. *Geology of Utah.* Salt Lake City: Utah Museum of Natural History, 1986.

————. *Scenes of the Plateau Lands and How They Came to Be.* Salt Lake City: Publishers Press, 1971.

Strong, Emory. *Stone Age in the Great Basin.* Portland, Oreg.: Binford and Mort, 1969.

Welsh, Stanley L. and Bill Ratcliffe. *Flowers of the Canyon Country.* Moab, Utah: Canyonlands Natural History Association, 1971.